D1348810

Fifty Years On

Fifty Years On

*The Troubles and the Struggle
for Change in Northern Ireland*

Malachi O'Doherty

Atlantic Books
London

First published in Great Britain in 2019 by Atlantic Books, an imprint of Atlantic Books Ltd.

1 2 3 4 5 6 7 8 9

A CIP catalogue record for this book is available from the British Library.

All photographs are reproduced by permission of the author.

Hardback ISBN: 978-1-78649-664-5
E-book ISBN: 978-1-78649-665-2
Paperback ISBN: 978-1-78649-666-9

Printed in Great Britain by Bell and Bain Ltd, Glasgow

Atlantic Books
An imprint of Atlantic Books Ltd
Ormond House
26–27 Boswell Street
London
WC1N 3JZ

www.atlantic-books.co.uk

for
Ciaran Carson

CONTENTS

Prologue

I have made it to my bed but I do not feel safe. The shooting continues. Not up close – distant but heavy. I now believe it is real; at first I didn't. When I was walking away from the rioting on Divis Street I was stopped by two American journalists who asked me if there had been any gunfire here yet.

I said, 'Only blanks.'

Why did I say that? What did I know about what people were doing, how bad this would get? I had no insights into the organisation of the riot, no familiarity with the people who led the attacks on the police. But I just assumed that this skirmish would be like others I had seen; and if there was the odd crack or rattle that might have been a gunshot, I had heard these before and no one had suffered bullet wounds or seen holes in walls or windows afterwards. So, pretending to understand the pattern of trouble that had become familiar over the past year, I said no, only blanks.

When I heard machine-gun fire, there was no mistaking it. It was murderous. You wouldn't confuse that with fireworks or something falling over. You could hear the clear intentionality of it in the blunt, abrupt, clean dunts, like rapid hammer blows. I had left Jo to the bus station. We had not been able to go down the Falls Road, so we had detoured to the south of the city and taken a bus along the Lisburn Road and walked across town. We saw a huge water cannon trundle across King Street in front of us, and heard the clatter and banging and shouting further away. She scoffed at the mob. 'If they had jobs to go to tomorrow they wouldn't be at that carry-on.'

She is a protestant and comes at this differently. For one thing, she knows more people in the police, for very few catholics are in the Royal Ulster Constabulary – none at all in the Special Constabulary, those part-timers who were called up tonight for back-up. So she has more sympathy with men in uniform.

Her family probably votes for the Unionist Party, which has been in unbroken control for fifty years and which is challenged by these riots and the demands for civil rights. She doesn't believe that teenagers chucking petrol bombs at the police care a fig about civil rights: they are out enjoying themselves. She's probably right.

I left her to the bus and came back. There were about a dozen of us watching. It was some show. Police in black uniforms with shields confronted young men throwing bricks and petrol bombs at them. The bombs were milk bottles, which arced through the air then smashed on the ground and produced a sliver of flame.

This was all under the view of Divis Tower and there were men on the roof. I watched them throw down a whole crate of bottles, smashing them on the ground. I thought at first they were just discarding them, making a racket, but as the rioters pulled back and the police charged, I saw what they were up to. One of the men on the roof dropped a petrol bomb into the mess and whoosh, it went up in flames.

I saw a young man in a pink cheesecloth shirt and jeans being grabbed by two policemen and led back behind the lines in front of us to the station. The police had their sneaky strategies too. They would pull back, closer to us, and entice the rioters into the range of armoured cars parked in Conway Street and Dover Street. These weren't like the big water cannon. A man near me in the crowd called them whippets. They were small, almost pyramid-like on top. They had mounted machine guns. They whirred and they spun. Two came out from different directions to break up the rioting mob and then the police launched a baton charge after the scattered men and brought one or two down with a strike at the knees and pulled them in.

I saw a delivery van for a sausage factory pull up on our side of the line and special constables with rifles climb out the back and rush along the wall into the police station. A senior officer in ordinary uniform, with a peaked cap, not a helmet, came and spoke to us. 'I urge you to disperse. We cannot guarantee your safety. This is getting much more serious.'

'They should bring in the army,' said the man beside me. 'They'd soon show them. They'd throw their petrol bombs back at them.'

I left the group and went back the way I had come with Jo. The buses were all off now.

That was when I met the Americans and reassured them, and they must have marvelled at my innocence, my ignorance.

*

I walked up the Grosvenor Road, to join the Falls Road on the other side of the riot, anticipating a three-mile walk home. I had turned the corner on to the Falls when I heard the first string of blurts from a machine gun. At first I had no idea where it had come from. There was another.

I was passing the front of the hospital and worked out that there must be a sniper on the roof, for the noise of the gun was so loud it seemed almost beside me. I ran into the front of the hospital for cover and faced the double escalator. Both sides were coming up now. There was no way in. I wondered if my panicked mind was hallucinating. I was fired with urgency – not debilitated by terror, as I would have expected. I was studying everything and reading my reactions. Even as I turned and ran up the road, close to the front of the hospital, I was registering an insight: that if Jo had been with me in those moments I would have been no use to her. Then I walked with my head down, but the shooting started again. Bop-bop-bop-bop-bop. A couple of boys on the other side of the road started running for cover along the stone wall of the convent school, St Dominic's.

I ran. And as I did so a car pulled up ahead of me; a man jumped out and grabbed me by the arm and with his other arm pressed my head down. 'Keep low.' And he ran with me to the car. There was a young fella in the back seat. They drove me home. We passed groups of people at bus stops, apparently still thinking there was some normality there. There was. The man and I did not talk about the gunfire or the politics. He just said, 'Your mother will be worrying about you.'

*

I am eighteen years old. I live in a housing estate called Riverdale on the very edge of Belfast. Beyond our streets when I moved here as a child there were only fields to play in, trees to climb, goats to outrun, the remnants of wartime Nissen huts and coils of barbed wire. When I was smaller I had dreams of war, my imagination fired up by those traces.

Later there were building sites all around me, and I was outrunning the nightwatchman when he caught me and my friends sneaking in after the workmen had gone, on summer evenings, to bounce on planks, climb through window frames.

Eight of us live in a semi-detached house with three bedrooms – or really two bedrooms and a box room. One bedroom at the front is for my parents. The box room is for my two sisters and the rear bedroom is for the four boys.

The house was built for two parents and three children at most, on the understanding (later voiced by the Northern Ireland prime minister) that catholics, if given proper housing, would live like protestants and, by implication, have smaller families.

There are several protestants living in our street, most of them families of policemen. And they are friendly, though their children go to different schools so we don't get to know them as well. Other protestants down at Finaghy are more fearsome and sometimes shout at us when we go to the railway station.

One of the anxieties of British Northern Ireland is that those of us who are Irish – that is, catholic – will outbreed the protestants and take the territory into the Irish nation, where most of us think it rightly belongs.

By that thinking, building new housing estates for catholics is reckless self-harm. The counter-idea is that full citizenship will help us to feel at home.

When I was young, one of the advantages of Britishness was the welfare state. My mother was paid a family allowance for each of her children. The doctor would come out to the house in those days if one of us had a temperature. He would press down my tongue with a flat piece of wood and tell me to say *Aaah*.

And if by some miracle any of my mother's children would get a place at university, or at least at the teacher-training college, the state would pay all the fees and a maintenance grant.

I went to catholic schools, which asserted their distinction from the state while taking most of their funding from the government. My first school in Belfast was the pavilion of a sports ground, Casement Park, which smelled of damp concrete. At Mass every Sunday my parents paid into the School Building Fund to help augment the cost of the new primary school, the Holy Child.

We would be holy children ourselves, the boys going in one door, the girls another, our models being Dominic Savio, who mortified his flesh by sleeping on walnut shells and died young, and Maria Goretti, who resisted the man who would rape her. He stabbed her fourteen times but she forgave him on her deathbed and he went on to become a monk while she went to Heaven.

Discipline in primary school was applied with the cane, three feet of fine bamboo with a curve at the end like the handle of a walking stick, swiped at the tips of the fingers and not just for running in the corridor, scuffling in the yard or failing to do homework but also for bad handwriting and not getting the sums right.

Our house is much more spacious than the redbrick terraces of the back streets where most working-class people live. We have an indoor toilet and a bathroom. In many other houses down the road, children and grandparents make up beds for themselves at night around the fireplace, on the sofa or the floor, and smaller children squeeze in beside their parents. And they wash in a tub brought in from the yard and filled from pots of hot water boiled up on the cooker.

They don't have gardens but open their front doors on to the footpath.

We are on the corner so the waste ground is our garden. It extends like a blade towards a point, and we shout at people who take shortcuts across it. This is a new estate, and some of the best rental residential housing in Belfast for families. I don't know that we are crowded here, that my own adult self will look back and say this was poverty.

I don't know anyone who has central heating in their home, so I don't miss it.

We take heat in the living room from a coal fire, supported on colder nights by a paraffin heater at the other side of the room. Nearly all of us smoke at home. Some of us still maintain a pretence to Mum and Dad that we don't smoke and therefore only light up outside or when we have the house to ourselves.

We watch television together most evenings through a grey-blue haze, from *Teatime with Tommy* through *Crossroads* or *Space Family Robinson* and *Panorama* or *Bonanza*, often arguing over which channel to watch. There are three of them now. The proliferation of choice has only made home life more contentious. Richard Baker and Robert Dougal read the news to us in tones that assure us that everything is under control despite the devaluation of the pound and the grotesque violence in Vietnam.

It's 1969. My mother is fifty-three and my father is fifty-five, their parenting having been delayed by the Second World War. Like a lot of people their age, neither of them has teeth. When the NHS arrived they thought the most sensible thing to do was to have them all taken out and replaced with dentures in order to have no more trouble with them. My father could jut his from his mouth with a flex of his jaw to startle us as children with an impression of an animal struggling to get out of him. This trick might have been the inspiration for the mouth within a mouth of the creature in Ridley Scott's *Alien*.

My schooldays are nearly over. I have been to a catholic secondary school where most of the teachers were Christian Brothers, like half-formed priests in black robes. Each was armed with a coiled strap in a pocket in the robe, which could be curled out ready for swinging as the other hand reached for my wrist to position my palm as a target. The relationship between religion and violence on this scale is familiar to me.

I was raised in religion, to a belief that I had the one true faith. I believed in Hell and damnation; I believed also in Heaven but that was a long way off, for I would still have to endure the fires of Purgatory to cleanse me till I was fit for it.

The Church is changing. After 1964 and the Second Vatican Council our teachers said that protestants might go to Heaven too, though it would be even more of a struggle for them.

It was difficult to be sure of how much of this my parents and teachers really believed. Worries about salvation clearly did not preoccupy them, and they would even scoff at those who took religion seriously. The culture was one in which you fulfilled your religious duties to the satisfaction of your neighbours and gave little thought to how much God noticed or didn't.

By 1969 I have never been more than a hundred miles from my home. My cousins are in Dublin and Donegal, both in the Irish Republic. Day trips to visit them take us over the border to another country that is a bit dilapidated, which has brands of chocolate and soft drinks we never see at home, like Tiffin and Cidona, and cigarettes like Sweet Afton and Major. Sometimes there are armed special constables on the northern side of the border, those men of a force that is all protestant, amateurish and of whom we are taught to be wary. It is always a relief to arrive at the other side, as if that's home.

When I was younger I enjoyed the mischief of wearing a lapel pin of the Irish flag when I was in Donegal, for the flying of that flag was illegal in Northern Ireland – or the Six Counties, as we called it. I wanted a united Ireland. I could sing all the rebel songs, like 'Kevin Barry' and 'Roddy McCorley' and 'Kelly the Boy from Killane'.

Later I had a school friend called John who was a republican. I was a socialist then and argued that the border had become a petty concern. Besides, what chance had you of getting a decent job if you were a rebel, if a police file somewhere said you had flown the Irish flag from your bedroom window?

Very few people I know are republicans. There are occasions when the numbers seem greater, like at the close of a ceili when the Eddie Fegan Ceili Band declares a final end to the night by playing the Irish national anthem – 'The Soldier's Song' – and we all stand and declare our lives to be 'pledged to Ireland'.

I have a weekend job in a bar now, as a waiter in the lounge, where men drink pints of lager and buy Carlsberg Specials or vodka and orange for their girlfriends. I have worked in other bars, where most nights ended with a fight and Bert the barman wading in with the broom to break it up.

There was a lot of fighting then, as there had been at school dances, in the school yard or on the corner of the street. There seems to be a pent-up violence in young men. My brother has read Freud, in summary at least, and says it is sexual frustration, but that can't be right. I'm sexually frustrated myself but I don't want to fight anybody.

Sometimes it surprises me how civil people are. Those who come into the lounge bar are the upper working class, people who behave themselves, who value manners. Class distinction here is between the mannered working class and the unmannered working class. None of us are middle class yet. The disparaging term for the unmannered is 'common'. You don't want it to be said of you that you are 'awful common'. I know immediately whether someone is common or not by their language and attire: the girls who wear bobby socks and chew gum and say 'fuck'; the boys in their winkle-pickers, dressed for a fight.

When the common boys fight they kick and give headbutts. Those of a better class might learn to box or do judo – not so that they will fight better and more cleanly but, they say, so that they will never have to fight at all.

Fighting between boys has always been part of the culture, going back to the school playground. I knew boys who preferred a fight to any other way of amusing themselves, who would stand at a corner, near the chippie, and wait for a likely target to come along, one of the lighter-built nicer boys who annoyed them so much. I was one of those.

I don't seek to understand those who accost me by reference to misfortune in their lives. Why should I? It is just in them to be like that; their fathers and brothers are the same.

They impose themselves on others; they assert that they know better than anyone else what this place is and who belongs here. If they lived in England they would be beating up homos and Pakis but there are no Pakis here and very few homos that anyone knows.

Thankfully, few men of this type came into the public bar, the Star and Garter, which was a 'queer bar' I worked in. Here effete and good-natured older men drank sherry and smoked cigars and, on the occasions I was sent to help out, they spoke very nicely to me, took a great interest in my education, my hopes for myself, detained me at the table to know me better.

The queers came to this bar but there was no particular welcome for them and the staff sneered at them but put up with them. Once, two men who had been drinking in the lounge at the back, the Red Barn, got thrown out after visiting the toilet together. Tommy, the owner, would have none of that carry-on.

I'm still not sure what I want to do when I finish my education. A lot of the boys I went to school with are already working.

Some left at fifteen, into apprenticeships to be plumbers or barmen or electricians. Some that stayed on for O levels left then to get jobs in the civil service or at the City Hall as junior clerks and some went into the post office as telegraph boys. These were considered the luckiest of all because they were issued with little red motorbikes, to deliver telegrams about the city.

Frankie Callaghan from our class has gone into Short Bros to make aircraft. He'll go into the army. Caoimhín de Búrca who sat beside me has gone away to be a Christian Brother. A small few are preparing to tackle A levels, which are considered almost unattainable by my generation, and may go to university. Some among us got redirected for various reasons towards the 'tech' or the College of Commerce to do ONDs or City & Guilds exams. We might end up as accountants or quantity surveyors. I want to be a journalist. Some chance!

I have seen the reporters for the *Daily Mail* and other papers in the Star and Garter using our phone to relay copy to their offices, reports of court cases or civil-rights parades or some of the disturbances in Belfast, Derry and Armagh that came with the political unrest.

I don't know if these are good reporters and I assume that being a reporter is a stage on the way to being a proper writer. I would like to ask them what they think of Hemingway or Steinbeck. I will later meet some of the great reporters, like Simon Winchester and even Christopher Hitchens, when Belfast has become one of the biggest stories in the world, but this seems unlikely now. If I want to cover wars and tumult I will have to go abroad. And I am not sure that I do.

There are big employers in Belfast, managing the heavy industries of shipbuilding, aircraft and missiles, machinery for textiles manufacture. Most of their employees are protestant. Many protestants in working-class areas think they don't need education to get jobs; the way is cleared for them by older brothers and fathers who have jobs in those big industries and can get them in.

The news occasionally includes reports that the Irish Republican Army – the IRA – has been conducting arms training for members on the other side of the border.

Three years ago, 1966, was the fiftieth anniversary of the Easter Rising, which triggered the Irish War of Independence, which led to the creation of an Irish state, though with our six counties in the north locked out of it. That anniversary roused fervour for unity again and paranoia among unionists. The IRA set off a few small bombs. Loyalists shot dead a catholic barman who had gone to a protestant area for a drink, with little or no apprehension that he was taking a risk.

I work in bars near there myself now. There are two of them facing each other on Agnes Street off the protestant Shankill Road, the Enfield Arms and the Cliftonville Hotel. They are owned by a catholic family who have asked my father to manage them. I go there every Saturday and help behind the bar in the Cliftonville. I know all the regulars and they know me. I have learned to pour a decent pint of porter, which costs a shilling. There is an art to it. It might be the cheapest drink in the bar but it is the one that takes most work. You pour the flat body and the high head from different barrels on a shelf and scoop out some of the white with a plastic blade and top up with more black until the balance is right.

Now I am at the College of Commerce, where for the first time in my education I am mixing with girls and protestants and, most illuminating of all, protestant girls.

We are drawn by curiosity to each other. They want to know just how much I am answerable to the Church, what happens in confession when I go every Saturday at noon to kneel in a built-in cupboard in the chapel and unburden myself of my sins, including my sinful thoughts about protestant girls. I want to know if they have casual sex; is it just like being nice to someone for them?

It will be hard for catholics to get promotion in the civil service and big companies. In the expectation of discrimination there, many are seeking employment in small businesses like pubs, law firms, accountants' offices. And they and others are taking to the streets in civil-rights protests now to demand an end to discrimination, better housing, a fairer local-government franchise that isn't weighted in favour of house owners and graduates.

There is a sense among catholics that they have inherited injustice. Ireland was partitioned in 1921. With a strong protestant majority in the North, that is hardly likely to change. People grumble rather than organise. They tell me that with my Irish name I 'would be better off with a number'. Some few organise for a future war against Britain to unite Ireland but I don't know any of them. On occasions there have been big republican parades but I was only ever urged by my parents and teachers to stay away from them. The civil-rights campaigns are different. We think these can focus on rights and entitlements, posing no threat to the state, simply demanding that it meet its commitments to citizens and treat them as well as citizens in other parts of the UK.

I have marched with the students and sat on the street and chanted 'One man, one vote' and sung 'We Shall Overcome'. We have learned from watching other marches on television, in Alabama and Paris. I was bewildered when a protestant cleric called Ian Paisley organised counter-protests and urged the government to ban our parades for we were the puppets of Rome, the pawns in a papal conspiracy against the British monarchy.

He thinks that a 400-year-old war has resumed. And he is eager for it.

One answer to the growing threat of war was that the youth might be rallied to demonstrate their greater interest in pop music. Father Marcellus organised a Pop for Peace concert at Minnowburn, open countryside by the Lagan. Marmalade came. Dave Dee, Dozy, Beaky, Mick and Tich came. John and Yoko sent a telegram and it was awarded to the person who picked up most litter afterwards. We were all such nice people but our manners and enthusiasm made no difference to anything.

The news coming from Derry showed chaos, hundreds of people on the streets for days, chucking stones and petrol bombs at the police, and the police a shambles in their management of it, stumbling about the road, beating the flames off their fallen with their coats, running back uphill with the rocks and bottles bouncing at their feet, regrouping to attack with batons and looking as if they would do less harm by just going away.

Then it spread to other towns.

In the morning we will get the news of the dead and the damage.

My parents are on holiday. I am at home with my two sisters, Ann and Brid, and two of my three brothers. Brid wants me to go with her into town to meet her boyfriend. He is a protestant too. We go by the south of the city, to avoid the mayhem on the Falls Road, and we join Eddie in a pub. I like Eddie. He has a candid smile and he glows when he has a drink in him. He is relieved that Brid is safe. He buys me a beer, though it is only the middle of the day, and it feels good to be drinking it.

'Our Malachi was shot at last night,' says Brid.

'Yes.' I tell him about the sniper with a machine gun on the roof of the hospital.

Eddie says it was probably just one of the police machine guns from further down the road. 'It's really hard to locate gunfire.' I wonder if he has ever been shot at.

Later we walk up Divis Street and the Falls Road and see the scale of the damage. The road is scorched and littered with stones and broken glass. Several shops and pubs are burned-out. One of the old mill buildings is still smoking. Men are stopping and directing traffic and I wonder who they are and who appointed them.

We turn up Northumberland Street, which takes us to the Shankill Road. From here, last night, protestants had come down on to the Falls to join the riot in support of the police. Some of them had been killed, but the Shankill shows no signs of damage or abnormality. We go to the pubs at the top of Agnes Street. My brother Brian is working behind the bar. I know many of the customers from having worked here myself but the atmosphere is different. No one says hello.

Brian alerts me to the mood of the place. 'I think I'll have to close up. This isn't good. People that would be civil to you any other day are just keeping to themselves. They buy a drink and give you the money and then turn their backs on you.'

There is Billy, a trade-union man who would usually be pleased to see me and I think if I catch his eye and give him a nod I can lighten the atmosphere, assure him that it wasn't us who were attacking the police last night; that we had nothing to do with it. He meets my eye for a second and looks away.

Brian will close the bars early. That night both will be burned to the ground by a loyalist mob. My father will keep a copy of *Paris Match* for years with a colour spread showing the flames.

Brid and I walk down Agnes Street and across the Shankill and back to the Falls. The atmosphere is almost carnival. People say the army has arrived. I see a phalanx of soldiers come up Durham Street.

'I wonder where they think they are going,' says Brid. They march with bayonets fixed and helmets on. 'It's not bloody World War Two.'

The Sixties and Me

Nineteen sixty-eight was the year I left secondary school. I had fallen a year behind my peers because I had chosen to repeat some O levels, essentially to take a pause in my education and have an easy year in which to reflect on my options. The school I went to was called CBS Glen Road. Some Christian Brothers schools didn't get saints' names; God knows why. It still stands, but it is nothing like it was then. It was opened in 1962.

Half of the teachers then were members of the Christian Brothers, a religious order founded to educate the catholic urchin poor. The Brothers had a reputation for liberal use of corporal punishment. My father had been to one of their schools in the 1920s and told me that he had sworn he would never send his own children to the Brothers. Forty years later he relaxed his resolve, presuming that they had changed.

The men of the Christian Brothers teaching in Belfast were mostly from the Irish Republic. They were celibate but their strange clerical collars, only the top half of which was white, implied that they were only part way to being real clergy.

The strap each one carried was commonly called the 'leather' and was used for slapping boys on the hands for bad behaviour or poor performance. So, corporal punishment was carried on into secondary school though most of the Brothers preferred the strap to the cane. I would get a wallop for every Latin sentence I got wrong in my homework. The leather wasn't a belt: it was manufactured for its sole purpose, with a sculpted handle and layered to provide the weight that would inflict an appropriate amount of pain.

The Brothers have virtually disappeared now but they retain a reputation for abuse far worse than anything I saw in Belfast, including rape.

The area at the front is now a car park. Fewer people had cars when I went, so there was more space to run around.

I had a basic education there, some of it intended, some not; some of it useful, some merely the play on conundrums. I still don't know what a quadratic equation is for, though I had to learn how to resolve one. I acquired a rebellious spirit through a slow realisation that the authority that I was up against was an unwarranted burden and trivial in most of its concerns.

But in my early years there I was compliant. I made an effort. And I got slapped with the leather all the same.

I went to the Gaeltacht during my first summer, to learn Irish, clustered mostly with other boys from our class: Tony Henderson, who later joined the IRA, and Caoimhín de Búrca, who was Kevin Burke back then and would go on to join the Christian Brothers.

This was an organised educational holiday in an Irish-speaking area of north-west Donegal. We were there in 1963. Tony was homesick and so was I.

We were at a timid age, not ready to understand even the dirty words the big boys used. Because this was a holiday the teacher was not allowed to use his cane on us, so he compensated by shouting a lot.

He taught us rebel songs in Irish. 'Roddy McCorley':

> *Ta faghairt 'na rosc 's feidhm 'na gcos'*
> *Ta id mall, ro mhall, monuar*
> *Mar ta Rodi Mac Corlai ag dul don chroch*
> *Ar Dhroichead Tuam' innui.*

> They come with vengeance in their eyes.
> Too late! Too late are they,
> For Roddy McCorley goes to die
> On the bridge of Toome today.

He also taught us the Irish version of the theme tune to *Z Cars*.

> *Ceol ar maidin, ceol aris trathnona, ceol.*

The house we were sent to was a cottage with a vegetable garden bounded by fuchsia hedges. At the end of the back garden was a little toilet shed. Inside was a bucket under a wooden seat with a hole in it. That was the only toilet for the eight boys staying there and for the women who ran the house, cooked our meals and kept up our spirits.

All eight boys slept in the one bedroom of the cottage, where four double bunk beds had been fitted.

The most amazing thing for me was that the area was so dark and silent. When the lights went out I was in blackness so deep that opening or closing my eyes made no difference and the absence of the slightest sound beyond our room, which perhaps a country person would find reassuring, was unnerving at first.

One of the older boys made ghostly sounds. There was a statue of the Virgin Mary on the mantelpiece. It was luminous green. When he lifted it and moved it around it seemed to float in the air of its own volition.

We were, in theory, conscientious catholic boys sent there to immerse ourselves in spoken Irish. The Christian Brothers who had organised this worked to a theology that, in effect, merged the language with the faith and with the idea of an Irish nation. The revered exponent of this was the martyr Patrick Pearse, who had been executed by a British firing squad in Dublin in 1916 for leading a rebellion while the sons of most of his neighbours were in Flanders.

Pearse's rebellion was linked to the theology of Catholicism through his own writings, connecting his blood sacrifice to that of Jesus. And the Brothers endorsed this, where a more rational reading of scripture and theology might have concluded that he was a heretic.

Sending a concentration of pubescent boys off on holiday together was inevitably going to provide them with a chance to air their own interests. In our house, we organised a farting competition. Each contender had a verifier to follow him through the day and monitor his output. Boys would be seen squatting by their bunks trying to force through their body gases as noisily as they could, as often as they could.

Some of the boys, during those weeks in Donegal, would advance their interest in girls, or claim they had. Word went round that Iggy Jones had got a girl to take her bra off for him. This marvellous information was shared from boy to boy across the whole Gaeltacht region and Iggy came to be seen as one who bore himself with the confidence of having moved on ahead of us.

We learned bawdy songs. At the start of the summer there might have been only one boy who knew the full version of 'Good Ship Venus'. By the end of July thousands could recite it in full, and some were composing new verses to add to it. Though why the 'figurehead, nude in bed' would even want to 'suck on the old man's penis' was beyond my comprehension then.

So, there were people who were devout catholics and ardent Irish-language enthusiasts, but that didn't describe most of us. The Gaeltacht experience was meant to be a chauvinistic reference back to an Ireland that was disappearing.

We didn't imagine that, in decades to come, Falls Road shopfronts and bus stops would be in Irish, let alone that the interest in the language would have come away from the culture of religious devotion. Through the Brothers and the legacy of Pearse, these were seen as organically linked.

The Christian Brothers would organise afternoon ceili dances for us with girls from other catholic schools on condition that we took a lecture in Irish and tried to speak it while there. So I have these celibate chauvinists to thank for helping me meet the first girl I kissed.

And the teaching of Irish was intermixed with a reverence for the republican tradition, the nation building that required Ireland, if a claim for independence was to be justified, to be culturally distinct from Britain. And that meant being catholic and having a native language.

For me, Irish language and dancing became an avenue into fun and love.

But Irish was more a school subject than a cultural definer outside school.

That would change over the period of the Troubles. Now there are Irish-language schools in Belfast, along with Irish-language street signs and shopfronts and bus stops. The casual visitor will likely see these as evidence of a cultural tradition with deep roots rather than of a revival that had yet to happen when Caoimhín de Búrca and Frankie Callaghan and I were trying to impress girls with our vocabulary and dance moves at the ceili.

An early sign of the change after the start of the Troubles was that in 1971 Tony Henderson's comrades in the IRA, many of whom had paid little attention in class, sent out a message from the prisons and internment camps asking the Christian Brothers to send Irish-language teachers to them.

And what became of us boys?

Frankie Callaghan would spend his army career on the Eastern Front anticipating a Russian advance. Tony Henderson would die from gunshots on an IRA training camp at a time when half of the IRA casualties were accidents. Joe McDonnell, a natural prankster like Frankie, would starve himself to death in a prison protest. Caoimhín de Búrca would become a Christian Brother then leave and become the lay headmaster of a Christian Brothers grammar school. I would become a journalist.

Each of us took a journey away from the society we knew back then, but so did everybody.

My first experience of writing to win an argument, the type of writing that would form my career, was there, in school.

Caoimhín de Búrca and Frankie Callaghan and I were members of the Legion of Mary. This was a religious group devoted to prayer and voluntary work. It was structured, in theory at least, on the model of the Roman legion. The school group was a praesidium. The higher administrative group was the curia. Our praesidium was devoted to Our Lady Mediatrix of All Graces. This credits the mother of Jesus with more than any account of her life in the Bible implies, that all of God's graces bestowed on Earth are channelled through her.

We were soldiers devoted to Mary.

To protestants and others who took their religion directly from scripture and admitted of no further embellishment of it, this would all have seemed bizarre and unchristian; but in the catholic tradition, revelation was recognised as having continued even up to recent times through apparitions of the Virgin Mary at Fatima in Portugal, Knock in the west of Ireland and Lourdes in France, and even since then at Medjugorje in Bosnia and Herzegovina.

The Legion had adapted verses from the Song of Solomon into a prayer to Mary, the Catena, that imagined her more like the hindu goddess Kali than the demure carpenter's wife in Nazareth.

> Who is she that cometh forth as the morning
> rising, fair as the moon, bright as the sun, terrible
> as an army set in battle array?

In the hindu Shakti tradition the female aspect of God, usually the consort, Parvati or Durga, is the active agent in His power – what you might call the Mediatrix of His graces, or indeed of His wrath.

Each Friday evening we met in the school and knelt in prayer, then reported how we had carried out our Legion duties during the week and had new duties assigned to us for the following week. My duty, or assignment, might be to go with another boy to visit children in hospital or pensioners in their homes.

We dedicated ourselves more fully at a huge ceremony in St Mary's church in Chapel Lane. We were processed in pairs to stand before the Legion standard. An anthropologist would probably call it a totem; Mary standing on the globe, one bare foot on the head of the serpent, the dove over her own head. The words we had been rehearsed in were: 'I am all thine my Queen and my Mother, and all that I have is thine.'

I said those words with honest devotion, as did hundreds of other Belfast teenagers that night.

It is barely conceivable that such a ceremony could be organised today.

There was a boy in Musgrave Park Hospital who had been there for weeks after a tractor accident. He was always pleased to see us and chatted warmly about the nurses and other patients and even indulged us when we suggested a prayer. After a few visits I thought we could safely waive the praying part and still consider that we had done good work for Mary, Queen of Heaven.

One night Frankie Callaghan went there on his Legion duty and the nurse on the ward asked him if he was going to stay for the concert. A stage had been set up on the ward with microphones and he assumed that some of the staff were going to sing for the children, but as he was leaving the Everly Brothers came in. They had been performing in the city and volunteered a free show for children in hospital.

So Frankie was late getting home.

He told me, 'My mum and dad played the Everlys all the time so I was familiar with the songs, but when I got home I thought I was going to get the dog for lying.'

After a year or two I was made secretary of our praesidium. I had to make notes of all the reports of Legion duties performed, excuses for them being missed and the general trend of the meeting, including a summary of the little inspiring talk from our spiritual director, Brother Quinlan.

One job we might be given was to prepare the newspaper orders in a kiosk in the grounds of St Theresa's church. We would go there on a Saturday evening when we would have bundles of the respectable Irish and catholic newspapers, like the *Universe* and the *Sunday Press*. We would have a list of the names of people and the papers they had ordered and we would roll the papers together, pencil the name of the customer on the front page of the top paper and stack these for collection the next day after Mass.

This could pass a fun few hours on a summer's evening while being more onerous in the dark and in the rain.

At one meeting of the praesidium, I reported on having performed this Legion duty successfully but then the president or chairman said that he had received complaints about the antics of the boys in the kiosk preparing the papers.

I thought it very likely that we had chatted and joked among ourselves as we made up the orders. I didn't offer the defence of being young and hormonally charged but in retrospect it seems a reasonable one. The kiosk was on Church ground but we didn't think of it as a sacred space requiring a sedate and hushed manner; yet apparently we had let ourselves forget the decorum appropriate to that circumstance. Passers-by, coming from confession or from praying before the Real Presence, did not need to be shaken from their inner reflections by the laughter of teenage boys.

I didn't think we had behaved badly. I, and the other boy who was with me, protested that we thought the complaint was unreasonable.

'Well, we'll leave it at that,' said the chairman.

I didn't.

In the minutes of that meeting, I reported the complaint about the behaviour of Brother O'Doherty – myself in the third person – and his partner in the performance of that duty. We were not actual Christian Brothers like Brother Quinlan but on Legion of Mary business we addressed each other and referred to each other by that title.

I took smug pleasure in reading out 'Brother O'Doherty's' defence in great detail and then asking the others if this was an accurate account of the previous week's meeting.

The chairman was disconcerted but all agreed that the account was accurate and the chairman had to sign it.

He said that perhaps I had dwelled 'overlong' on the matter, that he had hoped to put it behind us, and I noted down all his words to recite back to him the following week, for the approval of the others and for him to sign.

I kept this up for three weeks to ensure that my defence was solidly on the record. I had had no previous political or journalistic training, but I'd worked out for myself that the person who writes the record has the last word.

I don't know what happened to the minutes book I kept. I asked the Legion of Mary headquarters in Belfast if they had any ideas where I might find it and they invited me to look through their archives. It wasn't there but I did come across the Legion's record of its experience of the violence of August 1969.

The minutes of the 514th meeting of Legion of Mary Down and Connor Comitium, Sunday 7 December 1969, record that their Immaculata Curia

> reported that St Peter's parish had lost 130 homes
> during the disturbances and in the Relief Centre
> on the nights of the 13th and 14th of August
> over 300 people were attended to, 70 of whom
> had serious gunshot wounds. Medical opinion
> confirmed that 50/60 of those would have died
> had it not been for the efforts of legionaries and
> members of the Knights of Malta. During the
> crisis and after, street cleaning and sanitation was
> organised, and claims for housing were dealt with
> from the Centre.

An earlier meeting had heard that the legionaries had 'helped out in an emergency at a non-Catholic centre at the request of the Minister'.

After leaving school, I was still interested in being part of discussion groups on religious and ethical questions. I wasn't ready to fully break with catholic religious practice and an added attraction of Catholic Information Centre debates was that girls came to them and took part.

These meetings were on Wednesday nights in Belfast near Castle Street, an area distinguished by Smithfield Market, which the IRA had yet to burn down. Kelly's Cellars was nearby, one of the oldest pubs in the city, where the 1798 Revolutionary Henry Joy McCracken was said to have taken refuge. So also was St Mary's church, one of the first catholic churches in Belfast, built with financial support from protestants, and St Mary's Hall, the venue for the routine meetings of the Northern Ireland Civil Rights Association (NICRA).

The Catholic Information Centre meetings were organised by Father Alex Reid.

Father Reid was a stiff and uneasy man of hesitant speech and seemed not to be the type who would have been naturally inclined to running a youth group and trying to rouse us to enthusiasm for devotion. For a time he had a younger trendy sidekick who allowed me to call him Frank, but some of the more conservative young people there took me aside one day and expressed their objection to me not showing sufficient reverence for his collar.

We didn't know that Father Reid would have a central place in the history of the Troubles as a mediator from Gerry Adams and a facilitator of truce talks at Clonard Monastery. In 1986, when political parties travelled to Duisberg in Germany (or West Germany, as it was then) to try to resolve their differences and agree terms on how Northern Ireland might be governed, Sinn Féin was barred from the talks because of its support for the IRA – but Father Reid went along as the eyes and ears of Gerry Adams.

In the middle of the 1960s I was a teenager with little sense of the patterns of change, and certainly no notion that three or four years later my nights would be punctuated with gunfire.

I was interested in Irish history and particularly in the history of what was then called the Troubles, the period between 1916 and 1922, from the Easter Rising through the War of Independence to the Civil War.

One night in the Gaeltacht, at the kitchen table with the *bean a tí* (the woman of the house) and some of the other boys, we had a heated argument about whether Michael Collins should have signed the treaty that created the Irish Free State in 1921 and left the six counties of Northern Ireland inside the United Kingdom with a devolved parliament.

I was repeating an argument I had heard at home, the case made by my mother, that de Valera, who was later the taoiseach and then the president of the Irish Republic, should have participated in the negotiations himself and had no right to turn against Collins if he had not been prepared to face the British across the table.

I was twelve years old and holding forth against the bigger boys, some of them as passionate themselves in insisting that Collins had betrayed his comrades and his people. This was the argument that had divided Irish politics in the Republic ever since; but, while it had split other families and pitched brothers at war with each other, by 1963 the Donegal women looking after us could enjoy the debate and pat me on the head for being eloquent and clever.

I was reading the memoirs and biographies of IRA men and learning the rebel songs.

My mother told me a story about how an aunt of hers had witnessed the Black and Tans drive up the street in a Crossley Tender. A dog was sleeping on the pavement. She saw the vehicle veer on to the footpath to go over the dog.

For me, the Black and Tans were an evil that fascinated.

In the Legion of Mary I was asked with a group of boys to provide some entertainment for a social event with other praesidia in a hall down the Malone Road. I suggested doing a recitation of Patrick Pearse's speech at the grave of O'Donovan Rossa and was scoffed at for coming up with such a stupid idea.

'People are coming here to enjoy themselves.'

Trouble in the Background

I was learning that republicanism and religious belief alike were important but could be made too important. I was similarly belittled for unwarranted seriousness about that same time when I passed through an intensely devotional phase and wanted to be a priest. I had failed to calibrate my relationship with the wider culture and made myself eccentric by reading it literally.

But around the middle of the decade this republican enthusiasm was to grow, for we were approaching the fiftieth anniversary of the Easter Rising.

This was a period of peace in Northern Ireland. I knew about the past periods of violence but I assumed that history was only behind us, that the passions which had produced warfare were expired, not dormant; a toxic residue perhaps, hardly the fresh shoots of a new round of warfare.

I had seen, a few years earlier, a tattered poster on a tree calling for the release of political prisoners. My mother assured me that there were no political prisoners. This was something left over from the IRA campaign that had run from 1956 to

1962 and ended because the IRA itself acknowledged that the people were not interested – were distracted, presumably, by Elvis Presley, *The Black and White Minstrel Show*, *The Lone Ranger* and Sputnik.

Mum would not have viewed the fifties campaign as a legitimate continuation of the War of Independence, though the border dividing the country clearly showed that there was unfinished business for republicans. And this would be precisely the message of the Easter Rising commemorations.

This was also the time of the Second Vatican Council, which would liberalise the idea of authority in the Catholic Church. There was a special relevance in that to Northern Ireland because Unionism saw the Church as a threat. It viewed the Irish Republic as a state that had given an inordinate amount of power to the Church and therefore supposed that if Northern Ireland was absorbed into a united Ireland it would be dominated by catholic bishops.

Since I was a serious young catholic who believed in the Church, I did not see that as a problem at the time, and nor did many other catholics. We saw that perspective as daft – but, looking back on it now, after the increasing secularisation of Ireland and the disclosures about sexual abuse by clergy and the religious orders, it seems more reasonable.

The Ireland that Ulster protestants rejected then is being rejected by young people today. Even back then some protestants saw the beginnings of that liberalising trend.

William Craig, then the commerce minister, saw the Second Vatican Council as a breakthrough, offering freedom of conscience to catholics.

What was more important to him, probably, was that the Republic was interested in trade with Britain and Northern Ireland. Anticipating problems from the evangelical right of Unionism and the emerging evangelical firebrand Ian Paisley, Craig was trying to reassure them that improved trading relations would not expose protestants in the North to perfidious machinations by Rome because even Rome was changing its ways. In 1968, as minister for home affairs, Craig would ban civil-rights parades – and four years after that he would lead Ulster Vanguard rallies at which he'd vow to unleash his forces on the IRA to 'shoot to kill'.

Times changed and people changed with them.

The IRA and the loyalist paramilitaries were small at this time.

That contrasts with the current period. Now the IRA, which led the Troubles from 1970 on, is reduced in size and has cleared the way for Sinn Féin to advance the republican cause through politics. The loyalists in 1966 were as small as the IRA was then but now form extensive organisations among the youth in protestant working-class areas, though they are currently not involved in the traditional pursuits of murder and sabotage to the same degree.

Paramilitary loyalists at that time were organised around Gusty Spence, a former British soldier who had served in Cyprus and come back to organise the Ulster Volunteer Force (UVF), adopting the name of a militia that had been formed in 1912 to resist Home Rule for Ireland and had then merged into a British army regiment that suffered heavy losses in the Battle of the Somme.

Spence believed, in 1966, that the IRA was preparing for another uprising and that working-class protestants should organise to resist it. Essentially the plan was to target key members of the IRA – though, in fact, the UVF devoted most of its energies then to killing random catholics.

Spence and his men killed two catholics in 1966: a barman, Peter Ward, who had felt safe drinking with catholic friends on the Shankill Road, an area populated almost entirely by protestants; and John Scullion, who had been making his way home after a night drinking.

So unlikely did it seem at the time that he had been shot, Scullion was initially diagnosed as having a stab wound. His body was exhumed to confirm the manner of his murder.

The UVF also killed a protestant pensioner, Matilda Gould, by firebombing her house by mistake, demonstrating early that paramilitary organisations would be a danger to the communities they professed to defend.

Remembering Civil Rights

When I arrived at the Junction the first person I met was Dympna McGlade. I kind of knew her, but not well enough to remember the last time we had spoken. She had a funny story for me.

She had been in Madden's Bar in Belfast and had turned to a man she thought was me and said hello.

The man, clearly fed up with this frequent mistake, said, 'I am not Malachi O'Doherty.'

And I understand why the blunder would annoy him. He was Patrick Magee, an IRA man convicted of the bombing of the Grand Hotel in Brighton in 1984, which had killed five and nearly killed Prime Minister Margaret Thatcher.

Magee had been chided about this resemblance before. A satirical website, *Portadown News*, once published pictures of us side by side with the challenge to tell the difference, and in the style of a similar feature in *Private Eye* had given each of us the other's name.

And this would have annoyed Magee because I have often in my writing criticised the IRA and argued that their campaign was brutal and unnecessary. And I have a right to be annoyed with him too, besides his bombing endeavours; for before he was arrested and imprisoned I was getting stopped and searched on the street by police who couldn't tell the difference either. Now that is all behind us.

Dympna McGlade was at the Junction to help organise a commemoration of the civil-rights campaign of fifty years earlier and particularly the protest of 5 October 1968, less than a year before the night the guns came out. Several of the people who had organised or taken part in that protest were in the Junction now. Sixty was young at that event.

The television pictures of the '68 demonstration have often been repeated. You will have seen them, the police officers in their peaked caps moving among cowering protesters, swiping at their heads with batons, one with a blackthorn stick. A man with outstretched arms pleads for sanity and then crumples in agony, apparently having been struck in the groin by a police baton.

None of it makes much sense: not the conviction of the government and the police that they were contending with an IRA uprising; not the hopes of the protesters that they could communicate to such a truculent force that all they wanted was local-government reform and fair housing.

We were here in Derry, fifty years later, to remember the first day of the Troubles, all knowing how different Northern Ireland is today and recalling the decades since then, the routine images of bomb wreckage and bodies with bullet holes. And that riot, which presaged it all, seems so unlike the rest, not just in the bearing and attire of the police but in the stunned expectations of the protesters that they would be taken seriously. No one there was dressed for combat. The only guns were the old Webley .45s that each policeman wore strapped to his side, which none had drawn in years other than to clean or for training.

This was chaos, running to no one's plan, yet in less than a year the police would be firing machine guns in Belfast and the IRA and other paramilitary armies would be recruiting and arming themselves for murder.

The IRA was part of our history but it had been dormant.

Dympna's parents, Rebecca and Frank McGlade, had been republicans, supporters of the IRA who had joined the civil-rights movement. Frank had been interned during the Second World War, as had many other republicans, who were regarded as a danger to the state at that vulnerable time. They included Gerard Adams, the father of the more famous son Gerry; Paddy Devlin, later a Republican Labour then Social Democratic and Labour Party (SDLP) politician; and some Jewish refugees from Germany and Austria, classified as 'enemy aliens'.

I had met Dympna's parents once, in early 1969. They had contacted me because I had written a letter to the *Irish News* in support of the civil-rights movement. They invited me to their home and suggested I join People's Democracy, the student-protest movement, better known then as PD.

I told my father who I had met that day and he frowned; I should be careful who I associated with. The IRA involvement in the civil-rights movement was a slight embarrassment. This was one of the unionist excuses for reading the campaign as the start of an insurgency, a threat to the state. The message civil-righters wanted to project was that they were demanding rights for all: a reform of Northern Ireland, not its overthrow.

At the Junction, Dympna and I would get into an exchange of views on this before the night was over. She said that her mother, as a republican, had joined the civil-rights movement as part of a coming together of radical forces, but that the IRA at that time had no intention to overthrow the state.

I said that, as the history books now show, the IRA at that time was armed and training and seeking to acquire more weapons. Both the Russians and Chinese had turned them down. But now, long into the peace, this seemed an academic argument with little at stake.

The Junction is a freshly painted arts and community centre near the Diamond in Derry, positioned in fact at the point at which the October '68 march was due to end. I had been there before for debates on political issues and literature. The proliferation of centres like this around Northern Ireland seems part of the peace dividend, the funding from the European Union to assist in development and to improve community relations.

The next person I spoke to was Maura Johnston, also of our generation and a poet. I noticed a banner in a corner relating to other events at the centre. This one urged us to fight the patriarchy to save the planet.

'What is this patriarchy?' I asked Maura.

She said that she remembered a time, fifty years ago, when the Church had too much influence in Irish society. That was what the word 'patriarchy' suggested to her.

I said, 'To me it suggests that the oppression of women is something organised from above by a body of male rulers whose ways are imposed by ordinary men.'

'Well,' she said, 'when my husband, Kevin, was going out to march for civil rights he would order me to stay in the house, not to go to the march in case I got hurt. He wouldn't do that now.'

And the civil-rights movement of that time had not concerned itself with women's rights, seemed not to notice that there was a problem there. Its key demand was for 'One man, one vote', content that the male pronoun covered everybody.

Many of the councils were allocating houses on religious discriminatory lines. That was another issue for the civil-rights movement.

We were joined by Paul Arthur, an academic and writer. I hadn't seen Paul for a few years and wondered why he was there. I had met him many times, and others of his generation, without knowing the stories of their earlier lives at the start of the Troubles. We had had many conversations but I had never thought to ask him what he was doing or what role he might have had in the calamitous years.

Paul was there to chair the meeting. He had taken part in the October '68 march and had organised other marches after it.

We were waiting for one of the distinguished leaders of the civil-rights movement, Ivan Cooper. But Cooper was too ill to come.

John Hume would not come either. His wife, Pat, told me that his memory was weak. Hers wasn't.

'On that night,' she said, 'I was eight months' pregnant

but I had bought a new dress, which is a reckless thing to do when you are pregnant, but we were going out that night to a concert and there was no sign of him.'

John had arrived home soaked through from having been sprayed by a water cannon.

'I was furious with him,' said Pat.

Paul Arthur took the podium and introduced the speakers.

Deirdre O'Doherty then came up with her story of the day the police attacked the protesters and outraged the world. Deirdre was a trainee radiographer in 1968, employed at Altnagelvin Hospital in Derry. Her twin brother, Finbar, had been one of the organisers of the planned march. The Belfast West MP Gerry Fitt of the Republican Labour Party had had breakfast in her house before going to Duke Street to take up his place at the front with the banner for NICRA. Deirdre was at the back and told us she grew curious after a time to know why the march was not moving off. She said that she had walked up to the front and seen three lines of police blocking the way. She was walking back to her position when the police charged, swinging their batons at the heads of the protesters.

She was at first frozen with fear, and then her brother grabbed her and took her into a cafe. They were pursued by a police officer but once inside he appeared not to recognise them.

She came out when she thought it was safe.

'The number of people lying injured was unbelievable.'

An ambulance was gathering some of those victims of police baton strikes and she ran after it, asking the driver to take her up to the hospital, where she would be able to help.

He said, 'Get in, love; it's going to be a bloody long night for you.'

In the hospital then, the casualty department was one large room divided by a curtain. People were lying on the floor using coats for pillows.

She said, 'My first patient was Gerry Fitt.' He had an open head wound. He recognised her from breakfast.

The next was the *Derry Journal* reporter Martin Cowley. The police had not spared the media.

Deirdre said that she X-rayed forty-four people who were treated for head injuries that afternoon.

Michael Doherty told the meeting that he had been in Duke Street that day too, not as a protester but working in the family barber shop. He said there were more than forty-four people injured – some did not go to the hospital. 'Our towels helped staunch the blood.'

Deirdre said that on the day after the protest she was scoffed at by colleagues for having got involved in a riot. Some of them sneered when the chief radiologist sent for her to come to his office. She expected more trouble, but her boss thanked her for her work then told her in future not to be jumping on moving ambulances.

'Your first responsibility in a dangerous situation is to look after your own safety.'

The fullest record of that day is in Bob Purdie's *Politics in the Streets: The Origins of the Civil Rights Movement in Northern Ireland.*[1] His book fills out a lot more detail than Deirdre O'Doherty recalled. So also does the Lord Cameron's Report[2] into the disturbances. The official figure for numbers injured is higher than hers, seventy-seven, many of them struck in the head and the groin. There was not one simple attack on the protest but several skirmishes and an attempt by a small number of protesters to march to the Diamond, inside the city walls.

The idea for the parade came from civil-rights activists in Derry rather than from NICRA itself, some members of whose executive had doubts about going ahead. They worried that the initiative was being taken by radical lefties in the Northern Ireland Labour Party and trade-union movement, Young Socialists and republicans. John Cameron says that they organised a meeting in a Derry hotel to debate the wisdom of going ahead, 'and it appears that administrative responsibility for the march devolved largely on Mr Eamonn McCann. He was not in fact a member of the ad hoc committee, but he became prominent in the absence of any other central or local direction.'

Eamonn McCann is famous in Derry and throughout Ireland now as a trade unionist, a socialist, a writer and a stirring orator. He has a long record of experience in journalism and broadcasting. He became so well known that one of his books was simply called *McCann*, on the understanding that it could only be his. Now in his seventies, he remains a socialist and in 2016 briefly served as an MLA for the small left-wing party People Before Profit in the Northern Ireland Assembly.

He has also campaigned on issues that seemed not to concern the Young Socialists of 1968, like a woman's right to choose to have an abortion and same-sex marriage.

Back then he was less well known outside the city.

So Cameron describes, in essence, a division between NICRA and the radical left – the one group wary of trouble, the other eager for it.

But McCann and the socialists would not get the popular blame for the cracked skulls and the chaos. That would go to the police, and the minister for home affairs William Craig himself, and would inspire further protest.

Craig said he banned the parade because he saw it as a republican plot against the state but also because protestant organisations had pledged to organise counter-protests, creating the risk of sectarian clashes. The loyalist Apprentice Boys had made a written complaint arguing that to allow the march to go ahead would be disrespectful to the war memorial at the Diamond, the point at which the parade was planned to end.

Craig might have answered that curtailing civil liberties was more disrespectful of the war dead, who had won us our freedoms, than facilitating them would have been, but he didn't. He might have pointed out that there were no clear grounds for supposing that the dead of two world wars had any particular objection to the reform of local-government franchise or to the building of more houses. If the thought occurred to him, he kept it to himself.

Instead he put an enormous burden on his police force, the onus of stopping a parade through the threat of force, yet without the tools or leadership to apply force neatly and productively. The only circumstance in which the police would come out of this looking competent was one in which the protesters acceded docilely to the request to disperse.

The only weapons the police had were their batons and their pistols. They would not draw their pistols but they would lash about with batons in a manner that might easily have killed people. That none died that day was not a consequence of their measured application of force, but pure fluke.

But they believed they had to do something.

An alternative possibility was that the protesters entering the walled city would be attacked by loyalists and that even greater violence would ensue. And a police force inadequate to barring this parade would have been little use at separating the protesters from another body of people attacking them.

Cameron says that the police had resolved not to let the parade ban be broken for fear that if they did then future bans would not be credible deterrents. This was an important strategic objective for them.

The police in Derry that day, it appears, had no control over the protest and little strategy beyond demonstrating a willingness to use force, in the hopes of intimidating the protesters, and then wading into men, women and children with batons to scatter them. Later there would be technologies and devices for crowd control, but the Royal Ulster Constabulary (RUC) was new to this – though not quite.

In preparation, the force had brought in reserve constables and water cannon. One hundred and thirty men were assembled to deal with the protest, more than double the number normally available in the city. They had no riot shields to protect themselves, nor gas or pepper spray to disable assailants. They were not even wearing helmets, just peaked caps.

These policemen would have watched the evening news

that summer and seen how police in the US turned out to deal with protests against the Vietnam War at the Democratic Party Convention, or how the gendarmes equipped themselves to meet student protesters in Paris; yet they lined up to meet civil-rights protesters in Derry dressed as formally as if they were escorting a royal visit. In the old footage they look ridiculous, inept and arrogant.

For all that their minister for home affairs was warning them that the protest was a sinister front for militant republicans, the police were dressed as if to meet people who posed no threat to them at all.

The first tactical mistake of the police on the ground was their failure to anticipate that the parade might set off in a direction that was not blocked. They had sealed off Distillery Brae, which was on the route the parade organisers had announced the intention of taking; but, since police vehicles were in the way, the protesters moved up Duke Street towards the bridge across the Foyle led by, among others, Gerry Fitt and the Nationalist Party leader, Eddie McAteer.

Then the police rushed to take up positions there.

In their original planned formation their vehicles would have faced the protesters, shielding the police and protesters from each other. Now the police were in front of their own tenders and exposed. Some of them drew batons and lashed out at the front line of the protesters, hitting people on the head. They didn't seem to know any other way of using a baton.

Cameron says:

> We regret to say that we have no doubt that both
> Mr. Fitt and Mr. McAteer were batoned by the

police, at a time when no order to draw batons
had been given and in circumstances in which
the use of batons on these gentlemen was wholly
without justification or excuse. Mr. Fitt was at this
point removed to hospital with a minor head injury
which he ascribed to a blow from a baton, and Mr.
McAteer also sustained a minor injury.

This is perhaps the stage at which Deirdre O'Doherty and her
brother took refuge in a cafe, missing what happened next.
Yet the value of her account is how it illustrates that normal
life was going on even while heads were being cracked.

Fergus Pyle, a reporter for the *Irish Times*, wrote that 'many
of the officers, probably local men, went no further than duty
required'.

He heard one man say 'bastards' as a group of policemen
passed him. 'One of them rounded on him, grabbed him by
the arm, but only asked him for his name and address.' Pyle was
impressed that they were professional enough not to club the
man, which seems a relatively low hurdle for them to clear in
order to prove themselves reasonable and decent.

Máirín de Burca, the secretary of the Sinn Féin Ard Chomhairle, or High Council, had travelled with senior republicans
to the protests. She stood in a doorway and stayed safe.

She told me: 'I found the RUC extremely helpful. Whenever
I would go out on to the street one of them would come over
to me and say, "Look, love, this is not a great place to be."
They really were kind.'

Up in the Brandywell football ground, Derry City was
playing Distillery, a team from Belfast. Probably more people

had come from Belfast to see that match than had to join the
protest. Derry would win 3–2, with Danny Hale scoring the
winning goal.

Some of NICRA's leaders were now arriving late to the protest.
It was just after the first head-cracking session by the police
that Betty Sinclair got there. She was NICRA's chairperson.
She was also a member of the Communist Party of Northern
Ireland with revolutionary credentials. In her early twenties
Betty had attended the International Lenin School in Moscow.

She was a veteran of anti-sectarian protests in the 1930s
and had served a prison sentence for publishing seditious
literature, but on this occasion the police recognised her as
someone who might help them keep order and provided
her with a chair from which she could address the crowd.

She stood up and appealed for a calm and dignified protest.

Others made speeches too, some with a less ameliorative
tone. Eamonn McCann, according to Cameron, 'gave what
could be interpreted as more or less guarded encouragement
to the use of violence to break the police barrier'.

After Betty Sinclair urged the crowd to disperse, some Young
Socialists threw their placards and banners at the police.

Cameron says:

> On the evidence we think that nothing resembling
> a baton charge took place but that the police broke
> ranks and used their batons indiscriminately on
> people in Duke Street. This unfortunate situation
> was made worse by the fact that the other end of
> Duke Street (nearer the Waterside Station) was
> blocked by the party of police which had originally

been stationed at Simpson's Brae but had moved down in rear of the march. This party had not been informed that the march was to disperse and their choice of position had the effect that the marchers felt themselves to be trapped. No specific orders were given to their party to let the marchers through and when a number of marchers hurried towards them some violence was almost inevitable. There is a body of evidence, which we accept, that these police also used their batons indiscriminately, and that the District Inspector in charge used his blackthorn with needless violence. Rapid dispersal of the crowd was also assisted by the use of water wagons which were moved along Duke Street and then along Craigavon Bridge. There is no real doubt that they sprayed the dispersing marchers indiscriminately, especially on the bridge, where there were a good many members of the general public who had taken no part in the march. There was no justification for use of the water wagons on the bridge, while the evidence which we heard and saw on film did not convince us of the necessity of their use in Duke Street. By about 5 p.m. Duke Street was cleared.

The RUC had run amok for want of a clearer idea of how to control a fluid crowd.

Their training in preparation for a future IRA insurgency had consisted largely of square bashing and arms practice. They had faced two major riots five years earlier, in 1964. One of these was when a crowd of protestant football supporters who had passed through the catholic Falls Road to see a match at Windsor Park attacked catholic homes.

The RUC city commissioner Graham Shillington witnessed the eruption of the riot and told his men later that he would not have believed it could have flared up so quickly had he not seen it himself.[3]

The other was a political protest organised by republicans when the police had smashed the window of a republican election office to remove an Irish flag. They had done this to avert a threat by Ian Paisley to lead a crowd up the Falls Road to remove the flag themselves.

A future chief constable, Jack Hermon, who was in charge, ordered his men to pick up rocks from the road, form a phalanx and throw them back at the rioters. So there was no excuse for the police or their boss in Home Affairs not knowing that they were ill-equipped and inadequately trained to control a fractious and frightened crowd.

The most self-defeating strategy in Duke Street was the one they adopted: to attack the protesters.

And that worked out well for some of those who had organised the protest.

Gerry Fitt had brought members of the British Labour Party with him. He would reap huge political advantage from the brutality and incompetence of the police.

The Cameron Report expressed the view that several participants wanted violence.

> [...] we have good reason to believe also that [...] certain left wing activists had decided that their

campaign would benefit from violent conflict with the authorities. The decision to prohibit the march on 5th October from part of its proposed route gave them the opportunity to prove their point.

Television images would go round the world of officers in uniform wading through the crowd, striking out at people who were actually fleeing them and posing no threat.

In his book, Bob Purdie even supposes that this may have been the outcome Fitt desired.

Others in the civil-rights movement clearly wished to avoid confrontation and violence, but they knew by the next day that the police had given them the propaganda advantage.

For William Craig, this was a calamitous failure. A few years later, after further exacerbating things, Craig withdrew from public life into a prolonged depression. For now, though, he would retain his confidence that he was doing right by banning parades. His problem was that, from then on, the parades would be much bigger.

Many more people, appalled by the denial of elementary rights and the force that was being mobilised to assert that denial, would come on to the streets. So also, of course, would those militant groups and frisky young people who relished a riot, confident that the RUC could be easily taunted into overreaching itself.

Revolution in the Air

On October 5 1968, 'Hey Jude' was Number 1, about to
be overtaken by 'Those Were the Days' by Mary Hopkins.
English pop had turned stoical and even nostalgic. The
Beatles urged Jude not to 'carry the world upon your
shoulder', at a time when young revolutionaries were
determined to change everything. Mary Hopkins was looking
back to a past when 'we'd live the life we choose, we'd
fight and never lose' – although in Ireland the living, let
alone the fighting, had hardly begun.

I wasn't in Derry that day. I was seventeen years old and
I still lived with my mother and father, brothers and sisters
on the housing estate in Belfast. I wasn't especially political
in my thinking. A few years earlier I had been an ardent
Irish republican, though not a member of any organisation.
I read the memoirs of the IRA men who had taken part in
the Irish War of Independence fifty years earlier, Tom Barry,
Dan Breen, Sean Treacy and Ernie O'Malley.

By the more mature years, as I thought of them, of my late

teens, I had put behind me any emotional investment in a determination to unite Ireland. The issues that stirred me to argument, if any did, were the Vietnam War and working-class poverty. But these things mattered little beside a sense of excitement at leaving schooldays behind me.

I had started at the College of Commerce to study for an OND in business studies, but I would happily have walked away from that too – for all I wanted was to be out in the world and having experiences beyond the range of those available at home.

When the news came in from Derry that the protesters had been attacked by the police I had a definite sense that the context in which I lived had clarified sharply.

I was not afraid. I had no sense of how a momentum created by that riot would build towards something more like civil war. I did feel that the state I lived in – the Six Counties – had declared itself hostile to the likes of me. And that, at the very moment it had done so, an opportunity had arisen for me to express my objection. There would be more protests and I would be on them.

I talked to my mother about this.

She had not been keen on my earlier republican phase. When I had argued that we should fly the Irish tricolour from our house on the anniversary of the Easter Rising of 1916 she had crushed the idea, probably with added emphasis to make sure that my father got the message too.

'How is that going to help your prospects? Do you want it to go on your file that you are a rebel?'

'What file?'

'What file? The file any employer will open on you – and what chance do you think there will be of promotion if that is on it?'

We had had the same row when she found out that I had written to the Chinese Embassy in London and got a copy of Mao's *Little Red Book*.

'You think life is easy. You think that none of this can come back to bite you.'

But she took a different attitude to the civil-rights protests.

The people she had seen getting their heads cracked on TV were not street hooligans or long-haired ban-the-bombers. They were men in suits and ties, people who wanted an end to the discrimination that would prevent me getting the very jobs and promotion I had jeopardised with my letter to the Chinese.

They were not old chauvinist republicans with pistols in their trench-coat pockets resuming a war that they had already lost.

So we talked politics.

She said, 'It's the old British strategy of divide and conquer. They did it everywhere they went. Look at India and Pakistan.'

She believed – and I was inspired by the insight – that sectarianism in Northern Ireland was a British creation, that sectarianism would be used to put down the civil-rights movement but that it was important to declare that you were not being sectarian in claiming your rights.

I didn't know then that her thinking, as far as it went, was close to the theorising of some of those republicans who reasoned further that the civil-rights movement could be a lever for revolution. While my mother probably believed that we could have a better Six Counties in which catholics were full citizens, republicans believed that that was impossible, that when the government was forced to concede rights to catholics the state would collapse and Ireland would be united.

The protestant workers, having had their privileges removed, would have no interest in separating themselves from the catholics; the two communities would together then recognise their common interest in creating a socialist Ireland free of the imperial yoke.

That was what they believed.

I didn't know that was what they believed. I imagine a lot of other people didn't know either.

Today protestant privilege over catholics has evaporated. Then, there were big industries in Belfast like the shipyard with predominantly protestant workforces. It wasn't republican revolution that crashed those industries but cheaper ships being built elsewhere.

On the Monday, two days after the 5 October riot, I went back to the College of Commerce and found the trouble in Derry animating a lot of discussion there.

I was in a class of about sixteen students, mostly male and mostly protestant. This was OK by me. The thought never occurred to me that the composition of the student population suggested equality concerns every bit as disturbing as the warped local-government franchise and the discrimination that people had got their heads cracked for protesting against.

That there were four girls in the class was exciting enough for me. Before going there I had of course been in my all-male catholic school run by the Christian Brothers. That I was surrounded by protestants now was, in some ways, much better, for when communities are raised apart, distance fosters wariness but it also fosters curiosity. So, unlike a lot of my catholic peers, I was having daily arguments with protestants about politics and learning to see their points of view.

We were in a liberal corner of the education system. Really this was a school but it was called a college and our teachers allowed us to imagine that we were real students and that they were real lecturers, though they stood in front of blackboards, like schoolteachers, and gave us information and we wrote notes.

The differences were that they addressed us as 'Mr O'Doherty' or 'Miss McFarlane'. We smoked in class too. One young man among us always had a can of beer with his lunch sandwiches and this was seen as a perfectly adult thing to do.

Some of the students had cars. They never fought like the pupils at my secondary school but they often played poker at lunchtime, for actual money, those who had some. These were the sons of business owners, sent there to learn the basics of economics, office organisation and accountancy before starting work in their family firms. I had no real notion of being an entrepreneur and had chosen the course thinking it was an easy alternative to A levels and that being in a college would give me more freedom than staying on at school.

But I didn't feel like a proper student there. I saw students on television at protests in Paris or at LSE and we didn't look like them.

We did have one small campaign to assert a demand for a common room. We had no need of a common room. Between classes we could use the classroom itself, since we were all doing the same courses. One of the lecturers encouraged us in this campaign, perhaps to help us feel more like real students and less like oversized school pupils.

I was fascinated by the protestants because I had met so few of them before and because they, in turn, were as curious about me. I assumed that protestants were having more sex than we catholics were. In terms of actual religious belief, I was morphing into an atheist en route to being an agnostic. One of the women in the class, though herself a protestant, expressed genuine shock when she saw me eating a beef sandwich on a Friday.

She might have thought it was a stupid rule that stopped catholics from eating meat on a Friday but she had primed herself in this mixed environment to respect the beliefs of others and was genuinely perplexed at one of the others throwing the rule book away.

Among the discussions in college about the Derry rioting, one view was that the police had been 'bloody stupid'. Another: 'Have people nothing better to do on a Saturday afternoon?'

There was little sense among the students that the issues were serious enough to warrant the risk of getting your head split open by a country copper.

I could have said, 'Look here: I am out of a catholic family with an Irish name and that puts my job prospects behind yours, whatever qualifications we come out of here with. That's what's wrong with this place.'

But the answer would have been: 'Things are changing; they are not like that any more. And anyway, what difference will marching make to anything in the long run?'

But the lecturers were interested in seeing how we would respond to the new mood. The students at Queen's University had planned a protest for the Wednesday afternoon. We were doing exercises looking at media and how different newspapers report the same events in different ways.

One lecturer, Mr Mack, a slightly patronising figure, enjoyed seeing us play at being adults and was happy to encourage this without ever letting up on a tone that betrayed a confidence that he saw through everything. He set us an exercise. We should go to the university protest if we wished, and then he would get us to write conflicting news reports in the styles of different papers.

I joined the parade as it lined up outside the Students' Union on University Road, opposite the ornate old university building. I didn't see anybody there from my class and I did not feel at ease. There was a carnival air that made it more imperative to know some of the people around you if you were to join in and feel part of it. I felt even more of an outsider for not appreciating the wit around me or understanding what they were talking about.

Someone leaned out from a window two storeys up and shouted, 'Rory McShane's funeral.'

Rory McShane is now a solicitor in Newry. The last time I met him we were both judges in a school debating competition. He seemed comfortably middle class and professional. I didn't know him at all at the protest.

Stewards walked up and down the line as we waited to move off, reporting the moves of a counter-protest in the town. Presumably someone was travelling back and forth, perhaps on a bike, to study the positions of the police and the Paisleyites.

That was the term then for the agitators following the Rev. Ian Paisley. Paisley was a powerful orator who lent his gift to evangelical religion and to politics without then making a distinction between them. His philosophy was that the protestant religion was the guarantor of British democracy. The Catholic Church was the Whore of Babylon and the Pope was the Antichrist. Civil-rights protesters were Irish republicans in disguise, taking their instructions from the Pope with a view to absorbing Northern Ireland into a catholic republic.

This all sounds so ridiculous now as to be quaint. But thousands followed Paisley and in time he would become an MP, a member of the European Parliament and then first minister of Northern Ireland. I doubt he would have believed his career would advance so far if I had stepped out of a TARDIS that day and told him.

I doubt anyone would.

On that day in 1968, as we moved slowly off down University Road, past Smokey Joe's and the bookshop, I picked up the chanting of 'Craig out!' and 'One man, one vote'. We sang 'We Shall Overcome', including the line: 'We'll walk hand in hand'. No one held my hand. There wasn't much hand-holding at all.

The stewards moved along the line, advising that if we got arrested we would get free legal support through the Society of Labour Lawyers and telling us how to claim it. I was hoping not to end the day in a cell but I accepted that I was taking steps towards that prospect and I continued.

As we moved down University Road, word came back that we had to avoid Shaftesbury Square and a man at the front relayed this to us with a loudhailer. Ian Paisley had occupied the square. This was close to the working-class protestant areas of the Donegall Road and Sandy Row.

We diverted to approach the City Hall from a different direction.

The Shaftesbury Square route would have taken us right into the commercial centre of the city and the organisers had probably chosen a Wednesday afternoon knowing that most of the shops were closed then and that the march would not disrupt business. Still, it would have looked and felt like a grander affair than diverting east through streets occupied mostly by university offices and into a residential area, ultimately to approach the City Hall from the rear up Linenhall Street, past closed-up small businesses and behind the BBC.

The march leaders had consented to being shunted through streets where few would see us, where we would make least impression and where the pictures for the media would have no key landmarks. No one was going to look at us and think we had occupied Belfast. We had also conceded the point, in effect, that we were sectarian, catholic and intrinsically offensive to our protestant neighbours and that it was reasonable that they should be spared the sight of us.

The Rev. Ian Paisley's assessment of the students lined up around me on that October day was spectacularly off. He said we were the vanguard of a papal invasion, leading another round in a war that most of Europe thought had ended 400 years earlier.

It should have been transparent to him that we were hardly catholic at all. Unionism saw the civil-rights banner as a guise for republican intention. That was a valid reading of what some of them were up to. But catholic? True, most of us had been to catholic schools, had catholic-minded parents and siblings at home; but this was the generation that would lead the secularisation of Ireland, the depletion of Church influence.

Ian Paisley was not such a dull-witted man that he would not have understood this if anyone had taken the time to explain it to him, but no one could.

For this generation of catholic students, this move away from religion was not a light-bulb realisation that changed everything, but a slow adaptation to the new terms they lived under. I knew students who still went home at the weekend with a bag of washing and in expectation of a good Sunday dinner, but who knew that the price of this was going to Mass with their mothers, or at least going out for a walk on a Sunday morning, pretending to go to Mass.

That has changed.

The first generation to break the rules struggled, thinking that they were different from their parents yet fearing that their mothers could never reconcile to their godless ways. With successive generations in the seventies, eighties and nineties, you could assume that children would stop going to Mass at the same age at which they started dating. And through those decades came the progressive collapse of the routine observance of the sacraments and most spectacularly of recruitment to the priesthood and religious orders.

The first domino in that cascading sequence was the

rejection of the Church's rules by the generation of which I was a part, made all the easier by one of those rules being simply as impractical as living without contraception.

So, many of those students lined up to challenge William Craig and the RUC were already engaged privately, and not collectively, in their revolution against Church and family. They had already decided to change the world. And Paisley had stupidly taken them for puppets of the Pope.

But we were changing very little on that march. As we approached the back gate of the City Hall we were stopped by a line of policemen. They were not dressed for trouble. Today they would have flak jackets and helmets, perhaps even flame-retardant clothing. Or the men dressed for combat might be hanging back in side streets so as not to alarm anyone. The science of crowd control and riot management has been refined in Belfast over decades. At this stage, there had been very little rioting; and even those lessons that might have been learned had not been.

The RUC turned out to confront us in dress uniform, with their ties straight, in peaked caps, their only additional cover being their raincoats. They had taken greater care to protect themselves against the weather than against us. Had we had such foresight ourselves we would have brought cushions, for our next move was to sit down on the damp tarmac. 'We shall not be moved.'

And we chanted 'Craig out!' and imagined these country policemen to be vicious fascistic thugs, though they were as hapless as the men who had made a hash of things in Derry. 'SS RUC! SS RUC!'

But I wasn't in the vanguard that day. I was sitting near the back and saw little of what was up ahead.

'We are not a-fraid to di-ay-i-ay-ay.'

I asked a guy beside me: 'Are they singing "We are not afraid to die"?' – which would have overstated my position.

He helped me out. 'It's "We are not afraid *today*."'

We should have been afraid.

Within a year there would be gunfire on the streets, barricades and military patrols. A year after that, the bombings of the commercial centre would have started and the back-street murders. A year after that, internment without trial. A year after that, deaths in the hundreds, the city so dark and bleak none could move through it sure of their safety.

We didn't know that and the policemen in front of us didn't know that either.

Around the front of the City Hall, the apocalyptic preacher Ian Paisley said Ulster was being sold down the river by a spineless government that didn't know how to stand up to papists and republicans.

He was a great speaker. Here's a sample from that period: 'This is not the time for a velvet tongue. It is a day of war and war to the death. The enemy we fear is the enemy within ... If they want to go to Rome then let them go, but they are not taking Ulster with them.'

I left after a couple of hours sitting bored and wet-bottomed on the tarmac. It looked as if it might rain again. There were rumours that workers from the shipyard going home to Sandy Row and the Donegall Road might attack us.

The student leaders made their speeches and went back to

the university to plan further protests and to form a movement, People's Democracy.

On the next day in college Mr Mack asked who among us had been at the protest. Not many. We went through the newspaper accounts and then wrote about the day in different journalistic styles according to the exercise he had set.

I imagined an English journalist sneering at us, drawing on the clichés about students with their dope smoking and free love, flower power and peace, thinking about Monterey and not Woodstock, which hadn't happened yet.

We were nearly a year away from August 1969.

*

I didn't go on future civil-rights marches. I have a twin brother, Roger, and he did join them. But while his education that year was political, mine was sexual. I met Jo in the Astor.

Before then, my experience of dances had been limited to ceilis, mostly in church halls or at the Ard Scoil. I had danced the Haymaker's Jig, the Walls of Limerick, the Waves of Tory, complex set dances with a lot of stepping forward and stepping back then taking your partner for a ceili swing.

The ceili swing might be dainty, each partner holding a hand and an elbow of the other and jogging round with a backward flip of the outer foot. Or it might be much more vigorous, much faster, and sometimes ending with slippery sweaty hands losing their grip on a partner being flung across the floor.

I doubted Jo had ever been swung like that.

She was a protestant from Newtownabbey, just north of Belfast on the lough shore.

For a catholic boy, going to the Astor to meet protestant girls and dance the way they did on *Top of the Pops* was an advance into a more secular modern culture replete with moral danger. That was the attraction.

There were several dance halls in the centre of Belfast then, including the Astor, Romano's, Maxims, the Starlight, the Odyssey. They weren't what you would call nightclubs and didn't have bars serving alcohol. They had bouncers on the door for keeping out those who were drunk or underage or who, for reasons that never needed to be explained, attracted a bouncer's disdain.

The ceilis were not actually segregated, but girls tended to take seats along the wall on one side of the hall, and the boys took seats on the other, and they would look across and assess each other. A compère would call people up for a dance; and often the start-up was slow, as few if any wanted to be first on the floor. There was always a risk of walking across the empty floor to the girls on the other side, asking one for a dance and being refused and everybody in the hall seeing this.

The Ard Scoil ceilis were held on the second Sunday of every month, in the afternoon, and were preceded by a speech in Irish by the presiding Christian Brother, usually Brother Beausang from Cork. One of Beausang's favourite slogans was *Gan teanga, gan tír*: essentially, 'If you don't have a language you don't have a land.'

There seems, looking back, to be a paradox in the fact that the Christian Brothers, who were chauvinistic catholics running single-sex boys schools, were so obliging in bringing us together with girls of our own age. The girls came from schools run by nuns who were apparently as keen that their pupils should meet and dance with catholic boys.

Perhaps they were trying to ensure that we would marry catholics.

The Astor was wholly unlike the parish halls or the Ard Scoil. It was dark inside and the lighting made everything white turn luminous, from the shirts of the boys to the knickers under the miniskirts and the dandruff on the shoulder. When I went in I was charged up by the music. I replay that moment in my memory and the song I hear is Stevie Wonder's 'For Once in My Life'. It took several minutes for my eyes to adjust so that I could see all around me.

Jo was dancing with another girl. I walked over and asked her. She turned round and danced with me, then the DJ put on a slow number and she came in close. There was a platform area at the back of the hall with sofas! The Christian Brothers never thought of providing sofas at their ceilis. We looked out for each other the following week and a relationship was under way.

This was in the year of the first moon landing and Woodstock, of Paisley going to jail and the first-ever firing of Browning machine guns by British police in a British city, but my mind was on other things much of the time, including pregnancy scares and the other guys Jo went out with.

This was before feminism. She modelled herself I think on Jean Shrimpton and Mary Quant. She was a sixties dolly bird. She wore make-up as thick as a mask and I knew her for over a month before I saw her without it, and it was like meeting a different person.

On the very few occasions when we could sleep together overnight she came to bed in a frilly and fine baby-doll nightie, the likes of which I have never seen since.

Of the people of my generation then, I would say that most of them at eighteen were still virgins. Most were at work and a few were at university or college. Those who did go on to third-level education were, nearly all, the first in their families to do so.

Many were observant religious believers. That is to say that they went to Mass every week, less frequently but often to confession to tell their sins to a priest and receive God's forgiveness and a prescribed penance. The Church's teachings about Hell and damnation were giving way to a more gentle instruction, but those of us who were eighteen then were already imbued with fear. So, one of the dread consequences of sex before marriage or masturbation, aside from pregnancy or blindness, was the prospect of eternal fire.

We took these threats seriously, many of us, and outgrew them slowly. The secularisation of Ireland in the interim is largely due to the fact that my generation freed itself from that shadow of a stern God and did not pass it on to the next.

We were not well off. Two parents and six children lived in a semi-detached house with two proper bedrooms and a box room. This was better than what my parents had had before and it was better than the housing that some of my classmates, colleagues and friends had, who lived in the redbrick terraces of the narrow streets of the working-class areas.

Nearly everyone we knew smoked. They would warn children against it on the grounds that it would stunt their growth and be an expensive habit. My mother would die at seventy with emphysema. She would already have lost a leg to amputation at sixty-six after developing a blood clot. Both conditions were caused by smoking.

My father would smoke on for another seventeen years.

As I recall, more of the older people walked with the support of sticks back then. More people were stooped. I may be kidding myself but it seems to me that sixty isn't as old as it was. But perhaps every generation fends off the fear of death with the same fantasy.

When I recall Jo's father I see an older man sunk in an armchair reading his paper and smoking an un-tipped Park Drive cigarette. He didn't talk much. Jo told me that he was an Orangeman, a member of the Orange Order which paraded with banners to commemorate the Victory of William of Orange at the Battle of the Boyne in 1690.

He never discussed politics with me. Perhaps he thought it would have been impolite or pointless to do so, since we would have disagreed.

The Tilt towards War

I wanted to ask Eamonn McCann if he was the man who started the Troubles. The Cameron Report had said he was the one who had urged protesters in Derry to break through the police line on the famous 5 October march in 1968.

No one could have predicted then how bad things would get in the coming years, the thousands who would die, the new prisons that would be built to accommodate the interned and the convicted, the tonnage of weaponry that would be imported and the numbers of young men and women who would train to use it, or the irrationality of some of the targets they would choose.

There had been sectarian murder in recent times and some street rioting with the police over political issues, but the violence of that day registered in our minds as defining the state we lived in with new clarity and demonstrating the urgency of change.

And that was because the protest the police attacked was not ostensibly a sectarian march. This was not people trying to revive the old tribal quarrels or assert that the state was illegitimate. This was entirely different to previous insurrectionary anger. This was a demand for the standard of justice and democracy that British citizens expected for themselves. This was, in essence, Northern Irish catholics doing what had long been asked of them: accepting their British citizenship – but also claiming the rights that were implied by it.

This was too clever for the Ulster establishment to take in. It was such a rational position to advance they assumed it was devious.

Especially with the likes of McCann leading it.

There was no actual threat posed by the parade, other than its participants' determination to carry banners and proclaim their insistence on civil rights.

There were no guns there except those pistols worn as sidearms by the police. There were no paramilitaries; those organisations that would drive the Troubles in the coming decades had not yet even formed. The leader of the IRA, Cathal Goulding, had tried to reach the city to join the march but his car had caught fire on the way. Unionist suspicion that the IRA had an interest in the march was not merely fanciful – it had – but a guerrilla army that couldn't even deliver its chief of staff by car into Derry was not one likely to bring the state to its knees.

Several republicans made it to Derry that day. While Máirín de Burca, a slightly built young woman, stood in a doorway to evade baton charges then followed the action round the city, the men who had accompanied her from Dublin met over drinks in a hotel.

Eamonn McCann was the most ardent revolutionary there. He was also a gifted orator, well able to stir a crowd, something he has done often since.

In 2018, he wasn't hard for me to find.

Since those early days as a Young Socialist, Eamonn has held on to his revolutionary beliefs. He has been active on many campaigns inside the trade-union movement and on behalf of gays and the pro-choice movement but he has sustained himself mostly, as I have done, through journalism.

He was a role model for me. I didn't back his politics but I was impressed by his writing style, his succinctness and logic, his colour, his tactics. Part of the thrill of those times, back in '68, was the eloquence of the public figures representing the civil-rights campaign, notably of McCann and Queen's University student Bernadette Devlin, who was on the 5 October march too. We were not used to hearing trenchant oratory like theirs. Politics had got flaccid. It had long been old, male and grey.

Years later, from the mid-1980s, Eamonn and I shared a slot on the BBC Radio Ulster *Talkback* programme. We were regular commentators for two and a half decades, sounding off once a week on an issue of the day. There was a daily opinion piece. Mine was every Monday; his was on Wednesdays.

One of the complications, of course, was that the issue of the day was often a murder or a bombing. The repetitive pattern of violence made me repetitive in my analyses and outrage. Eamonn was better at changing the tone than I was. He would suddenly turn in a little tribute piece to Ruby Murray or George Best.

Once he did an excoriating talk on a government proposal for varying the salaries of nurses, rewarding the 'super nurses'. Eamonn had an answer: 'they are all super nurses'.

He could be brutally logical and then touchingly sentimental.

He is a genius – perhaps, some would say, a wasted genius – who has spent his energies and his writing talent in the service of unpopular left-wing causes. Eamonn's delivery was ponderous; his voice deep. He introduced dramatic pauses. He made his point with a simplicity that I envied until I worked out how he did it. His trick was to write less and read slower, so where I had to write 600 words he could manage to greater effect on 400.

He was saving his time and energy. And the listener never missed the point, distracted from one paragraph by reflecting on the previous one. McCann kept it simple.

He was seventy-two when he finally won his seat for People Before Profit in the Stormont parliament. This gave the party two MLAs but McCann lost his seat in less than a year, after a political crisis forced an election in 2017.

A further problem for him was that the size of the Assembly had been reduced from 108 to 90 MLAs, cutting into his prospects. It didn't help either that he had come out in favour of Brexit – 'The EU is a capitalist club' – in a city and a region that was opposed to it.

Though I had met Eamonn many times down the years and even interviewed him on other programmes, I had never yet asked him if it was true that he had started the Troubles, as Lord Cameron had implied.

If Eamonn McCann had not urged the crowd forward into the police lines, and if the people had followed the advice of

Betty Sinclair, they would have dispersed and gone home. There had been some scuffles before that point, but from then on the police tore into the crowd, rampaged through Derry, turned water cannons on football supporters coming back from the match – people who had hardly noticed that there was to be a protest march that day.

Had that not happened, the world's media would not have reported that Northern Ireland was a tyrannical little British state where citizens got their skulls cracked when they asked for their rights.

And the shock of that would not have sparked more protests, more reactions and, within less than a year, gun battles on the streets.

Another person in that crowd, though she has said she stood still, was Bernadette Devlin. She was twenty-one years old at the time. Like Eamonn, she had already been on other protests – such as the march from Coalisland to Dungannon, which had been stopped by the police.

In an autobiography, *The Price of My Soul*, written a year after the march,[4] she says that the police knew that Eamonn McCann was the real threat: '… he was turning a mob into a nonviolent force. So they charged.'

Bernadette's background was republican but she saw the logic of a civil-rights campaign that would make no demand for Irish unity.

> So you don't want to be British. But you are British
> whether you like it or not. Let's go and ask for
> British democracy. If they are going to make us
> British by law, we must be British by standard of

living as well. And over the months of 1968, I
moved away from Republicanism to concern for
non-political social justice.

She too could electrify a crowd with her eloquence. She
would do it many times over the years. Now she has several
bullet wounds in her body. Her home was attacked by loyalist
paramilitaries in 1981 when she was campaigning in support
of republican hunger strikers in the Maze Prison.

One day a year before that, I was working on a BBC current-
affairs programme that wanted to interview her. The producer
directed that she be pre-recorded. He thought it would be risky
to put her on live – in case she said something defamatory or
inflammatory, I presume.

McCann, by contrast, played the media game well and
though most of his early journalism had been for underground
papers he broke the surface above ground as a fully formed
professional who knew the rules and knew that he would last
a lot longer as an eloquent irritant if he kept them.

Bernadette, back in 1970, when given a symbolic key to
the city of New York – a stupendous honour – passed it on
to the Black Panthers because, she said, Irish-Americans
who had supported the civil-rights struggle spoke about
black people in the same way that Orangemen spoke about
catholics at home.

She would get elected to Westminster for the Mid Ulster
constituency and there, following Bloody Sunday, a massacre
of civil-rights protesters by British paratroopers in 1972, she
thumped the home secretary, Reginald Maudling, who had
defended the shooting.

A few days after that I met her at a party in Belfast and asked her what precisely she had done to him. She held up her hand, splayed and curled her fingers like a claw and snarled at me.

*

Eamonn arranged to meet me in Derry in a pub named after a Nicaraguan revolutionary called Augusto César Sandino. Sandino's is a revolution-themed pub. It is a dark wee bar opposite the bus station; more long than deep, so that no part is more than a few feet from the bar counter itself. Upstairs is a more spacious nightclub. There are images of Che on the walls and a large silver rocket – presumably a replica – hanging from the ceiling.

It would be easy to suppose that this decor treats revolutionary socialism as a joke. On the day I met Eamonn there, the men in the bar sat either in pairs at small tables or on benches against the wall, some of them drinking tea, none of them drinking pints of stout and one of them drinking hot whiskey, perhaps because that is a standard cold remedy and there was snow on the ground outside. The snow didn't deter half the customers from sitting at tables in the shaded street, shivering for the sake of a smoke. The marvel was that seasoned street fighters obeyed the law when it told them to smoke outside.

Eamonn arrived in a leather jacket and woolly hat and ordered tea for us.

Fifty years ago, or a little later, when I had mingled with revolutionaries in bars in Belfast, nobody drank tea. If you had ordered tea in a pub they would have thought you were a queer. That's the word they would have used.

Eamonn pointed out some of the people around us, like Joe who was in PD. These were people who had been revolutionary socialists in their youth. Some of them had gone straight, taken professional jobs, raised families and cleared their mortgages and were retired now. So they could afford to be revolutionaries again without raising the suspicion of an employer – who might be the government. This was the real thing, then. These were old comrades. They had not given up on the revolution, though they were too old now to lead it themselves.

Eamonn was a revolutionary in 1968 and he is still a revolutionary, although he told me that reflecting on the past is embarrassing because he did some stupid things. But go back to that day in October 1968 when the police attacked the protesters and he is clear that that is what he had hoped would happen.

William Craig banned the parade because he did not believe that it was solely concerned with civil rights but rather with overthrowing the state – and in effect he was right. At least, he was right about some of those leading it. He was right about McCann. But McCann wasn't interested in forcing a million unionists into a united Ireland. He was a socialist.

McCann had been living in England and had a job planting trees for a London council, work he enjoyed. He had been active in protest movements there too, particularly in opposition to the Vietnam War, which was radicalising young people across Europe and the US.

'In London in 1967 I spoke at a huge demonstration in Hyde Park. I was at Grosvenor Square. All that was going on.'

He had intended to come back on just a short visit in the spring of 1968 to meet a sister who was coming home from Canada.

One day he was walking through Derry when he met a group of people pulling a caravan out on to the road. The caravan was the home of a catholic family, with four children, who needed a proper house and could not persuade the council to give them one. This was part of the bigger story of the council's gerrymandering of the council boundaries to preserve a unionist majority, perhaps out of fear that if the catholic majority was properly represented it would make an irresistible case for the border to be redrawn around them, which in fact it would never do.

Eamonn helped pull the caravan out on to the road to protest the family's need for a home. He got arrested and bailed and had to stay on in Derry until the case was completed.

'And things began to develop and I stayed and stayed and never went back to London which was … I'm not sure if that was a good thing or not.'

Because hopes of catholics and protestants coming together to advance the cause of Labour and democratic socialism were proven futile during the years of the Troubles to follow. The sectarian division through Northern Irish society would prove much deeper and more intractable than any other political dispute and would make every other dispute subservient to it.

Eamonn had been a member of the Northern Irish Labour Party and its youth wing, the Young Socialists.

'If you look at the 1967 local-government election,' he told me. 'The Derry Labour Party got about 30 per cent of the vote and ran in every constituency and canvassed everywhere and so forth. It was a significant achievement. There were four Northern Ireland Labour MPs in Stormont. So the idea that we were seeing a coming together, a realignment of politics in the North, particularly in Derry, this wasn't a crazy idea.'

That 'coming together' seemed a wonderful prospect in a region that had previously been in dispute over whether it was Irish or British. This was nearly fifty years after Ireland had been partitioned, granting gradually unfolding independence to the twenty-six-county region that is now the Republic, retaining six northern counties as Northern Ireland inside the UK.

Eamonn, and many others in the left, thought that the old argument about the legitimacy of partition was expiring and giving way to a new politics around class and social and economic issues – and that this was a very good thing. He did not foresee that the national question was about to bounce back with horrific vigour or that his own political activism might trigger that calamity.

'I thought that the leadership of the official civil-rights movement was very tired, unambitious. They had no audacity about them at all. I thought they could go much further much faster than they were imagining.'

One who did have a sense of what was to happen was the poet Seamus Heaney, still decades away from receiving his Nobel Prize.

Writing in the *Listener* after the 5 October riot, Heaney said:

> We were all afraid, and still are, of returning to the
> old polarisation of public life … but it seems now
> that the catholic minority in Northern Ireland at

> large, if it is to retain any self-respect, will have to
> risk the charge of wrecking the new moderation
> and seek justice more vociferously.

Heaney was recognising that there had been, for a time, a
new mood in Northern Ireland, a suspension of the 'old
polarisation', but he foresaw what others did not: that persisting
in the legitimate claim for civil rights would reinvigorate
sectarian tension, and that catholics would have to take some
responsibility for that.

McCann agrees that the 'old polarisation' was waning for
a time. 'Looking back on it now, you'd think it was fucking
stupid; you're imagining all that. I can remember the meetings
in the early spring of 1968 up at the Fountain and in protestant
areas got a lot of protestants in the Labour Party, who were
the traditional Northern Ireland Labour people.

'Labour was attacking the Nationalist Party for advancing
a Green [Irish nationalist] agenda while people were living
in horrible housing conditions. And we made the point all
the time that there were thousands of protestants living in
desperate situations in Derry as well.

'So we were preaching against the Orange/Green divide,
which was inadequate to the needs of working-class people.
It certainly was not crazy to see – and indeed in retrospect I
don't think it is crazy to say that things did not have to develop
in the way that they did.'

How they developed was towards sectarian civil war. It wasn't
what the protesters wanted.

'Look at the placards and banners we used from 5 October.
You will not see a single placard on Orange versus Green. Not

one. Eamonn Melaugh [another march organiser] and myself
made eighteen placards the night before the march. There
were three slogans. "Tories Out – North and South", "Terence
O'Neill – Two-Faced Tory Trickster" – we really liked that one –
and the third one was "'Tories are Vermin' – Aneurin Bevan".
Bevan had said that during the debate in 1947 instituting the
National Health Service. The slogans all came from a British
Labour tradition, not from Irish Republicanism.'

William Craig believed that the civil-rights campaign was an
IRA front. He had intelligence from the police about prime
movers behind it. Former members still express themselves
as appalled with this allegation. The playwright Anne Devlin,
daughter of Paddy Devlin, said on a radio discussion about
the origins of the movement that this charge was 'like calling
a woman a witch'; it invalidated the movement's right to have
an independent position.

And when Declan Kearney of Sinn Féin wrote a blog
article in 2018 claiming that Sinn Féin had contributed to
the formation of the civil-rights movement he was mocked
in much of the media. And rightly so, for the Sinn Féin that
did help to form the movement is the one that modern Sinn
Féin broke away from.

Still, there were leading members of the breakaway faction
who had sat at the tables at which the management of the
civil-rights movement was discussed.

Gerry Adams, a former president of Sinn Féin, has a slightly
more legitimate claim than some to have been there at the
start, in that he was a member of the Sinn Féin movement in
1968 before it split in 1970.

In his autobiography, *Before the Dawn*,[5] he claims that he was at a meeting before the 5 October march to discuss tactics. Those there agreed that when they were confronted by the police they would push the front line of notable personalities forward, because they being injured by the batons would be more newsworthy and better publicity.

But the plan that Adams shares with us contradicted the aims of the Sinn Féin leadership at the time. The leadership initially wanted to set a large protest movement in action but did not want violence on the streets. It was aware that it had 'another branch', the IRA, the militarists, but it believed it had the assent of the IRA leadership to this plan.

The logic was simply that they had to create a movement that would attract support from the protestant working classes. By a theory of agitating for a united Ireland in stages, they believed that the first stage was for Northern catholics to accept their British citizenship and with the moral force of that position demand full British rights.

The main thinker behind this strategy in Sinn Féin was Roy Johnston. He had been elevated within the movement under the tutelage of the IRA chief of staff, Cathal Goulding, one of the key brains behind Sinn Féin's strategy of fostering the civil-rights agenda. Members of the IRA had been ordered to join and instructed on who to vote on to the executive of NICRA at its first election. Gerry Adams was a teller counting votes.

But the republicans were not very energetic in their strategising. In his book *Century of Endeavour*,[6] Johnston has left a record of internal discussion about the plan inside Sinn Féin and the IRA's endorsement of it.

The Sinn Féin Ard Chomhairle meeting of 26 October 1968 concerned itself mostly with considering a draft constitution. According to Johnston: 'It paid no attention to the opening up of the NI situation arising from the Derry civil-rights events.'

A month after the 5 October riot a Sinn Féin standing committee met to discuss a response.

An immediate priority for Sinn Féin at that time was to defend the positions of communists on the executive, primarily because it viewed them as protestants. This is not strictly as daft as it sounds in that the communists were from protestant areas of the city and represented workers in industries that were predominantly protestant. You can be called a protestant or a catholic in Belfast without any interpretation of your actual religious beliefs being implied.

Yet, when the violence increased, some of these 'protestant' communists – like executive member Terry Bruton – moved into catholic west Belfast to be safer.

Johnston writes:

> It was agreed that MMcG [Malachy McGurran]
> would instruct the clubs not to support in NICRA
> any move to dislodge Betty Sinclair [a communist]
> from the chair. The link with the Belfast Trades
> Council, and protestant radical activism, as
> expressed through the CP, was to be maintained.
> The NICRA must not be allowed to become simply
> a protest organisation of the catholic ghettoes.

Betty Sinclair had annoyed some in Derry on the day of the march with her efforts to keep the protest peaceful, but Sinn Féin saw her as a possible bridge to the protestant working classes who, by Johnston's theory of stages, would have to be won over before the revolution could proceed.

Eamonn McCann was not impressed by this theory of how the civil-rights agitation might be the first step in a revolution. He told me, 'I remember Roy Johnston debating this up in the Bogside Inn; quite a formidable debater, Roy. The theory was the stages theory of revolution. Any Trotskyist could trace that back to Stalin's attitude to revolution outside the Soviet Union from the mid-1930s. The theory was that you had to do things in stages. So first of all you win civil rights in the North. And while you were doing that you should seek and welcome the support of anyone who would go that far with you. Once that was established you would then go on to a united Ireland and you would move on with whatever support you could get. And at that stage, after you got a united Ireland then somebody would wave the red flag to start the fight for socialism.

'Now, I thought at the time – and still think – it's fucking ridiculous. Ridiculous!'

But McCann acknowledges now that he too had underestimated the effect the civil-rights campaign was having on the protestant community. He thought that sectarianism could be overtaken by a politics that focused on the shared interests of working-class people from both communities.

'I don't think it was clear that it was going to be a sectarian war and I don't think it necessarily had to be a sectarian war, if you mean that naturally, inevitably ...'

But people who remembered the stresses of a previous generation warned him then that the protestant community would throw up a violent reaction.

'All my people came from the New Lodge Road in Belfast. When I was growing up I used to stay there with all my uncles and cousins. I remember in the early days staying up in my aunt Cissie's and she said, "You know, son, if you keep on with this, we're going to be burned out."

'What! Now, we were never burned out of that house but a lot of the houses just down the road above the corner of Lepper Street … It may feel foolish in retrospect but the feeling was that the way to break down the sectarian barrier was not to be moderate; it was not to say, "OK, you do your thing and we won't object, we'll do ours." It was to go all out – not just to get over the problems of sectarianism but to get over sectarianism itself, to get over the whole fucking thing.'

So, instead of ignoring the rankled protestants, Eamonn went out to talk to them.

'We tried to avoid [sectarian strife] by campaigning as best we could in the protestant community. I spent a lot of time in Bishop Street and in the Fountain [protestant parts of Derry]. I knocked on every fucking door in the Fountain and talked to people. And nobody hit me or anything. A few people of an unfriendly disposition surrounded us and we had a loud speaker with us and somebody brought out a chair in the middle of the Fountain and I stood on the chair and spoke to a good-sized crowd. The significance of that is that I could do it.'

But he told me that he had seriously underestimated the strength of communal politics. 'We had seriously underestimated the grip of nationalism on the catholic community too.'

Like Eamonn McCann, the students of People's Democracy believed that they could assert their socialism and the rights of the working classes and blithely ignore the sectarian context in which they lived. When they went out to protest they were confronted by Paisleyite mobs but they demanded that the police protect them.

In Derry the police response to the 5 October march produced a huge popular reaction, a massive turnout of support for the civil-rights campaign at another event, registering the anger of a huge catholic population in the city asserting the rights to a fairer franchise and distribution of houses and jobs.

Faced with the scale of protest, and in a tenuous position, the prime minister of Northern Ireland Terence O'Neill promised reform and asked for a period of calm. In a television address to the whole population he asked, 'What kind of Ulster do you want?'

In her book, Bernadette Devlin described this speech as 'hilarious'. It promised reforms in the future. That wasn't good enough.

NICRA meanwhile decided to suspend its plans for further marches.

This was apparently supported by Sinn Féin. Máirín de Burca told me she was at all the civil-rights marches but opposed the idea of a march by PD going ahead after O'Neill's speech. Sinn Féin was content to ease up the pressure on O'Neill and give him a chance to prove himself.

Delegates from People's Democracy had raised the idea of a long march to Derry at a NICRA meeting in St Mary's Hall in Belfast and had been advised against it. It had taken a vote on the idea at the university and the majority had rejected it, some arguing that the logical response to O'Neill's speech was to relax the pressure, now that he was trying to concede their demands, if slowly.

Another vote – some say the third – taken after most students had gone off on their Christmas holidays, was carried. The long march was to go ahead.

Eamonn McCann was on that march, though he has said he was never a member of PD.

Bernadette Devlin was one of those who supported the idea and took part.

From the start, the march was opposed by loyalist protesters, led by a Major Ronnie Bunting.

McCann told me: 'The difficulty with PD was that it was impossible to say you weren't in it. On 1 January 1969 we were all outside the City Hall in Belfast, setting off to Derry. There was about eighty of us I suppose. Cyril Toman [one of the prominent members of PD] was standing on a little box. A lot of loyalists had gathered on the fringe, shouting at us. By later standards it was very mild. We had to conduct a vote because we had to vote in PD every day on what to do, so Cyril said that they could vote too – come on! – because they were citizens too.

'This sort of fucking shite was going on all the time. I thought, *Holy fuck!* Later, at the bottom of Glenshane Pass, after staying in Gulladuff Hall, somebody suggested as we were pressing up against the cops that we should ask the cops to discuss this with us. We should all have a meeting and vote on what to do next.'

The march was frustrated at several stages by the police and as it passed through a little river valley outside Derry it was ambushed by a protestant mob with clubs and stones.

The students were scattered. Bernadette Devlin writes that she had thought it tactically wiser to stand still than to run. Then someone took a swipe at her with a lump of wood with two nails in it. She raised her arm to protect her face and the nails went into the back of her hand. She was brought to the ground from behind and a group of men beat and kicked her as she curled up to protect her face and head.

There was huge sympathy for the students and a massive reception for them when they arrived in Derry through further stoning attacks that the police did little to protect them from.

The ambush at Burntollet changed the whole mood and created a renewed momentum towards sectarian conflict. O'Neill had said Ulster was at the crossroads. He was right. And it had chosen to take the high road to Hell.

Roy Johnston was not impressed:

> This coat-trailing exercise was disastrously counter-
> productive. It certainly exposed the true face
> of Orange thuggery, but were we not already
> aware of this? It helped reduce civil rights to a
> Catholic ghetto movement and made it difficult
> for Protestant trade unionists to rally in support of
> local-government electoral rights ('one man one
> vote'). After Burntollet, civil rights became a crypto
> Nationalist issue.

What was not clear on the surface was that Sinn Féin, which had been seeking to direct the campaign through NICRA, was also dividing on how to respond.

Máirín de Burca has told me that the whole point of the civil-rights campaign for republicans was to move the IRA away from militarism and towards political activism. But some in the IRA looked hopefully on the evolving violence in Northern Ireland and saw it as an opportunity.

Johnston was aware that there were some among the militarists who wanted trouble. These were in the main the people who would become the Provisional IRA after a split. They saw a prospect of building disturbances on the streets to a level at which the government at Stormont would not be able to cope. Then Stormont would fall and the British army would come in to restore order. That would present a perfect reminder to the Irish people that Britain was a colonial power, ultimately responsible for denying civil rights in the North.

So, two contradictory ideas were being entertained by republicans inside the one movement at the one time.

According to Máirín de Burca, 'It was certainly the longer programme that they had in mind. Breaking the northern state would hardly prove to be a unifying cause and that is what was sought – a genuine cause that would unite at least some of the people on both sides. That is what I supported but I wasn't a part of the discussions, which, I think, were largely conducted by the military people.'

In his book, Johnston says that the republicans were distracted by discussion of internal reform at a crucial time. He quotes from the diary of another republican thinker, Desmond

Greaves, who suggests that even Cathal Goulding, who had been following Johnston's advice, was now interested in disruption.

On 4 March 1969, Greaves arrived back at Cathal MacLiam's to find

> ... C(athal) G(oulding), S(eamus) C(ostello) and another republican drinking with Tony ... there was a great argument. I find them personally very modest but politically very arrogant. I was trying to head them off this move that is being planned for creating a breakdown of law and order that will compel England to abolish Stormont. "But that would be no harm," says CG, "it would show it is Britain's responsibility." I had great difficulty in persuading him that this was now admitted (and) we must move on to the next stage – working out a policy. I don't know whether much was agreed, but they will think over what has been said, and, what I forgot to say at the start, they had come up so as to find out my views on matters in general ...

Having started out supporting the civil-rights movement with a view to working through it to unite the protestant and catholic working classes, and as part of a broader effort to politicise republicans, the leadership was now considering that an opportunity had arisen to bring Stormont down, and that this was more worth pursuing.

Around that same time, republicans started discussing direct rule as a possibility: Britain standing down the Stormont government and running Northern Ireland from Westminster.

Ruairi Ó Brádaigh, who was on the army council of the IRA at the time, told me some years ago that republicans had come to regard Stormont as 'a rotten door' that might be easily kicked in, bringing back direct British rule and then giving the IRA a clearer opportunity to present the British as an invader.

Clearly, within the republican movement there were diverse opinions on how the civil-rights movement might fit with their strategy – and bringing Northern Ireland to the brink, making it ungovernable, was one of the ideas under discussion.

But, much as Sinn Féin then wanted to control the civil-rights movement, that movement had become too big and diverse after Derry and the subsequent formation of PD.

Revolutionary and Moderate

Máirín and her friend Hughie went to all the civil-rights marches in Hughie's little Morris Minor – Máirín in her role as secretary of the Sinn Féin Ard Chomhairle believed that the civil-rights movement was its own project, part of a grand strategy to attract the protestant working classes into a radical movement that would take them ultimately into a united Ireland.

Máirín and her allies on the Ard Chomhairle saw themselves as both revolutionary and moderate. They wanted the civil-rights movement to thrive peacefully. Their political analysis said that if the protesters clashed with the police the protestant working classes would sympathise with the police and the plan to weave them into the grand strategy would fail. But by the start of 1969 the plan was unravelling and marches were turning into riots against the police or sectarian clashes with protestant mobs led by Rev. Ian Paisley.

Máirín blamed People's Democracy.

'It was part of the new strategy for republicans when they abandoned the gun. Get an issue that could unite some unionists and nationalists and which was vital to the wellbeing of the citizens and build on that. It is my belief that this strategy could have produced serious benefits if the civil-rights movement hadn't been hijacked by what became the People's Democracy with their march, which was guaranteed to arouse sectarianism.'

But the ambush at Burntollet really scuppered her plan. From then on, it was impossible to view the civil-rights movement as anything but a struggle for the rights of an oppressed minority in a sectarian state.

According to Máirín: 'Sinn Féin was not interested in disruption. That was People's Democracy. That's what they were at. The last thing we saw coming out of the civil-rights movement was civil unrest.

'You did get unionists who had – I'm not saying there was a huge mass of them, but there were enough of them there to give us some sort of a … to cheer us up a wee bit. There were enough of unionists there who had no other way of expressing their kind of disagreement with gerrymandering and what was going on and the civil-rights movement gave them that, and then of course …'

The tension now was between viewing the claim for civil rights as something that would benefit the whole working class or a claim for the particularly disadvantaged catholics. But discrimination was not always intelligently managed. In the 1960s, a district council like Lisnaskea in Fermanagh would allocate houses on a vote in the council chamber, and a unionist majority would favour protestants, who were likely to vote unionist.

There were incidental protestant victims of this system. Billy Ferguson, an RUC constable from County Down, had been posted to Lisnaskea and shared sleeping accommodation with three other policemen, all called Billy. After he got married he applied to the council for a house and thought he had a good chance.

I had lunch with Billy in Lisnaskea years later. He told me: 'I did canvass them and was promised that I would probably get a house all right. Not too many were available. I heard later that on the night of the meeting there was a catholic curate in the town called Father Ferguson, who lived next door to the police station. And somebody raised the point: would that man be related to the curate down here? Anyway, the upshot of it was that I didn't get the house. They weren't sure that I wasn't a catholic.'

By 1969 Billy was the district inspector confronting the People's Democracy parade through Newry, just ten days after the rout at Burntollet.

Máirín de Burca and Hughie had travelled up from Dublin in the Morris Minor. The PD members had travelled down in rented Ulsterbus buses. The journalist Fyffe Robertson travelled with them and interviewed Michael Farrell, one of the organisers, on the bus. In the old footage the students look incongruously respectable, in their duffle coats and with hair that was longish but combed. They didn't look like a rabble.

Robertson tried to get Farrell to concede that most of them were catholics and Farrell was determined that they were representative of the broad spectrum of society in which catholics were a third of the population.

As the bus trundled along the country roads the students sang a parody of the Beatles' 'Yellow Submarine': 'We all live in a Fascist regime!'

Billy Ferguson's men stopped the students as they marched towards the police lines chanting, '*Sieg Heil! Sieg Heil!*'

In one of the news reports from the scene you can hear someone shouting for the stewards of the march to keep order; but the crowd, enraged by the attack on the students at Burntollet, charged through the barrier.

The police tenders were lined along the side of the canal. The rioters managed to tip several of these into the water.

When I spoke with Billy he remembered the riot with amusement in his retirement, scary as it had been on the day.

He said, 'One of the big things that came out of the big civil-rights march in Newry from the policing point of view was that an awful lot of old police vehicles were pushed into the canal by the protesters – and it really did us a favour, because we got a fleet of new vehicles in consequence of the loss.'

Máirín de Burca told me: 'What I always remember about that was they were so politically inept – the PD. They offered to replace the vehicles they had thrown into the canal. They said they would make a collection and everybody said, "Get real; nobody is going to contribute to that."'

Ferguson was there with the RUC confronting the marchers: not as a protestant bigot but as a policeman who already had had more experience of violence in Northern Ireland than any of those in front of him had.

When most of these students were still in primary school, Ferguson had been ambushed twice by the IRA – the people

Máirín de Burca thought she was helping towards unarmed political activism.

Ferguson recalled: 'On 12 December '56, the IRA launched the border campaign and blew up bridges and on the fourteenth blew up Lisnaskea station with the four Billys in the room upstairs. They put a boiler-box bomb at the front door. When it blew up the meter box was just inside the front door so all the lights went out.'

He said that police training had anticipated an IRA campaign by teaching the men how to fire rifles. The IRA men had taken over a building across the street and opened fire from there.

'We were prepared in that everybody had a weapon. But the bomb blew my wardrobe over on its face and the rifle was in there and it was dark, and by the time I got it out most of the shooting was over.'

Ferguson recounted the whole story as a joke.

'The most serious injury was to the station sergeant, Billy Scott. He was one of the few people who had a car, and for safety he put it in the back yard. We had a constable back there called Charlie Holden, a County Antrim man. Once the shooting started he let fly into the back yard with all that he had and when daylight came the sergeant's Morris Minor was sitting like a colander and Billy was not best pleased. He said, "Holden, fuck! What were you doing?"

'He said, "I didn't want to let them get into the back yard, sergeant." He had succeeded honourably in that.'

That IRA campaign of the 1950s informed the expectations of many about the civil-rights campaign.

Máirín de Burca routinely sat down with senior members of the IRA who had managed that campaign, Cathal Goulding, Seán Mac Stíofáin, Tomás Mac Giolla and Ruairi Ó Brádaigh.

She was not a member of the IRA herself and therefore did not sit in on meetings of the army council, but these were army-council members who sat with her and Roy Johnston and others in their political deliberations. And she and Johnston and others were very keen to urge the IRA away from militarism.

According to de Burca, 'Somebody like Cathal Goulding was first and foremost an IRA man rather than a Sinn Féiner. There were people like that, more on one side than on the other, and Cathal would have been more on the gun side, so maybe he would have seen [the growing violence on the streets] as an opportunity. I think Cathal came late to total disarmament, if you like, where some came to it a lot earlier. I was pushing all the time; that was my purpose.'

The police knew that senior members of the IRA were involving themselves in the civil-rights campaign and presumed, naturally enough, that they were doing so in order to create opportunities for a renewed armed campaign. Sinn Féin, meanwhile, at least up to the early months of 1969, was still working to keep parades peaceful in the hopes of retaining some small protestant working-class support. It would try to manage the election of the executive of NICRA by ordering members of the IRA to join and to vote for the communist Betty Sinclair again.

At the same time, People's Democracy had its own plan for managing the campaign. It also urged members to join

NICRA and to vote for its leaders, Michael Farrell and others. The outworking of that was that PD had more influence on the shaping of NICRA than Sinn Féin had, and Betty Sinclair was out. Roy Johnston believed that an IRA order to vote for Betty Sinclair was disobeyed.

Máirín de Burca continued to travel with Hughie to the civil-rights marches in different parts of the North, witnessing the decline into further disruption and violence as the prospect of a purely peaceful movement slipped away.

She told me, 'I was at one parade where Paisley and his mob were going round with sticks with six-inch nails in them.'

She and Hughie would arrive in town as strangers, inevitably wary of the sectarian division that characterises all towns in Northern Ireland even still. But they had to ask for directions – and that involved the risk that they would offend.

'It could have been Armagh, but anyway, we were coming in to the town and we knew there was going to be a Paisley counter-demonstration but my friend said to me, "There's a woman coming down there; roll down your window and ask her if she's a catholic." I said, "There is no way I am going to ask anyone what their religion is!" And he rolled down the window and he said to the woman, "Are you a catholic?"'

The woman said she wasn't but gave them advice on where to park.

'She said, "I'll tell you what you'll do: there's a little cul-de-sac there and it's dead safe up there."'

From there Máirín and Hughie walked to the police barrier separating the Paisleyites from the civil-rights protesters, unsure which side they were actually on.

'And we said to the RUC man who was standing behind it, "Are we in the right place for the civil-rights march?" And he came up close to us and he said, "I'm going to open this gate. Now, you two, get yourselves across that square as quickly as you can." We were obviously at the wrong place. We were at the Paisleyite side. And again, he was so kind. He could have left us there. And he just said it very quietly. And we went to the civil-rights march.'

Later Máirín decided she wanted to mingle with the Paisleyites on the other side and gather some sense of what they thought and intended.

'So we headed for the Paisley march. I was kind of pushing myself to the front because Paisley was speaking. After about a minute or two I began to be aware that people were moving away from me. There was a gap forming. I heard someone saying, "Fenian bitch." I hadn't spoken – nobody had heard my accent – and I went over to Hughie and I said, "What are we going to do, Hughie?" And he said, "One step at a time, let's get out of here. Don't look as if you are running."

'So that's what we did and we got away. And I said, "How the hell? What was that about? How did they know?" And Hughie said, "Next time you go to a Paisley march take off your James Connolly badge." It was hairy.'

The Troubles Tour

Fifty years after the night the guns came out, I was standing in front of Divis Tower trying to describe the cascade of petrol bombs, the snatch quads and the Shorland armoured cars zipping out of the side streets. I had been asked to stand in as a tour guide. My audience was a group of people about my own age from Australia, Scotland and England. The organiser was a retired British army officer called Patrick.

I had to shout to make myself heard over other tour guides who had brought groups to the same spot.

I said, 'This was the scene of a gun battle. Of course, the whole layout was different then. Where that major junction is now was the site of Hastings Street police station.'

I walked them – slowly, for some were a bit frail – to the ruins of the old St Comgall's school with its dark redbrick frontage with concrete trimmings.

'See the bullet holes. This was a three-sided battle. The police were firing up here from Hastings Street. The IRA had a light machine gun on the roof of the school. And a protestant crowd had come across from the Shankill Road, which runs almost parallel. The IRA commander ordered his men to shoot over their heads, but they killed one man.

'That green fence you see across the street is the Peace Line. In its first incarnation it was a coil of barbed wire supported by wooden Xs.'

'Who put that there?' asked one of the women.

'The army. And now few people want it removed, though you can walk through any time.'

I showed them the plaque on the wall of Divis Tower remembering the death of nine-year-old Patrick Rooney, killed by police fire that night.

'Had he been looking out the window?' said the woman.

'No. He was taking cover but the bullet came through the wall.'

I said, 'The thing you have to understand about that night is that it traumatised Belfast. It exposed the reality of a society that was so divided that it might erupt into civil war over issues like voting rights and marching rights. This trouble had started in Derry three days earlier when nationalists had opposed an Apprentice Boys parade.'

And I thought, *Dear God, am I now going to have to tell them who the Apprentice Boys are?*

They are a marching order, related to the Orange Order, wholly protestant, committed to remembering the siege of Derry in 1690, when apprentices closed the city gates to prevent invasion by the catholic King James II.

I said, 'Different people remember that night in different ways.'

They were picking up a sense of that from snatches overheard from other tour guides who spoke of the catholics being attacked in a pogrom – keeping it simple.

I said, 'In the folk memory of this area, the locals were simply attacked by the massed ranks of the police force, Special Constabulary and loyalist paramilitaries. But a fundamental had impressed itself on everybody: that this city could erupt in chaos and the police could not control it or even be trusted to treat both sides equally. Therefore the British army had to come in to keep order.

'They marched up Durham Street there, in tin hats with bayonets fixed, so God knows what kind of battle they thought they were going into.'

I told them how many on the catholic side argued that they had to arm themselves for their own defence.

'The IRA split in two, leaving the old leadership in charge of a socialist and secular movement and creating a new wing, the Provisionals, which at first was chauvinistic and catholic and has evolved considerably since.'

This wasn't easy, making the past fifty years intelligible to a mixed group of people.

I took them up to Sevastopol Street and the mural of Bobby Sands, the lead hunger striker in the 1981 prison protest in which ten men died demanding political status.

Patrick, the ex-soldier, was keen to direct everyone's attention to the name of the street.

'Sinn Féin now operates out of a street that commemorates British Imperial achievement,' he said. 'Such irony.'

We stood before a gable wall painted with the portrait of

Sands, and with smaller portraits around him of the other hunger strikers who died.

A tour guide beside me said, 'This is Bobby Sands MP.'

He had indeed won a parliamentary seat in Fermanagh and South Tyrone while starving to death in prison.

I said, 'Whatever you think of the IRA, Sands knew he was going to die. A previous hunger strike had failed because the leadership couldn't allow a prisoner to die while they waited for formal word from the British that a compromise was available. Sands took over. He was the officer commanding the IRA prisoners, serving a sentence for bombing a furniture shop. He organised the strike on a rota, not all men starting at the same time. And his plan depended on him dying and another being ready to take his place.

'The sequence of deaths followed because the other men coming behind felt they owed it to Sands to keep their resolve.'

And I told them how there are different accounts of whether the British had wanted to make a deal to end the hunger strike and that there was now considerable evidence that they did.

I pointed out a little portrait in the Celtic patterned garland round Sands's head.

'That's Joe McDonnell. He was in the same class as me at school. I liked Joe. Everybody liked Joe. He was cheeky. None of us ever thought he would end up like this.'

I took them to the front of the building, Sinn Féin offices and a shop specialising in republican memorabilia. You can now buy a Bobby Sands mug, though in fairness to his memory you should probably only drink water from it.

Above the shop was a plaque in tribute to Máire Drumm, who was murdered in hospital by loyalists.

'One of Máire's sons was in my class at school. I danced with one of her daughters at a school ceili. Her children were soft-spoken, gentle people like her husband, Jimmy, but she was scathing. Another friend of mine set up a peace group in Andersonstown and Máire damned her from a platform at a meeting. She went to Derry after Bloody Sunday, when Paras killed fourteen people, and said the people deserved to be killed by the army if they didn't support the IRA. That's what Máire was like. She knew what she stood for.'

I said, 'I last saw her in a black taxi coming up the Falls Road at Christmas 1972. She was with Jimmy. Jimmy himself was a very senior republican, but he didn't have that scary demeanour. They were both in good form. There was a Christmas ceasefire on. We chatted all the way about how we were getting on and stayed off politics. I suspect she had had a wee drink after her shopping trip. You'd have liked her.'

My group then went into the Sinn Féin shop to buy souvenirs. One bought a book of photographs. I bought a Henry Joy McCracken badge. Some bought T-shirts. The women running the shop thanked me for bringing them in and then we got back on the bus and went round the corner to Clonard Monastery.

I stood outside with them in the car park and told them the story of how Gerry Adams had negotiated various truces over the years here, accompanied by Father Alex Reid. I explained that this church was run by the Redemptorist fathers who were not under the control of the bishop and therefore were free to talk to the IRA, and even mediate for the leadership, without compromising the Church.

'What's that word?' said a woman.

'Redemptorist – from redemption. Commonly shortened to the Reds now that they have a liberal reputation, but when I was a boy they ran the parish mission during Lent and were famous for their scalding depictions of Hell as they summoned us all back to decency and grace.'

Even then, times were changing. One afternoon I was sitting in the Cafe Florida with my brother chatting and joking. A Redemptorist priest came in and told us we should go home and not be hanging about like this. We ignored him and he left, though the poor girl at the counter turned pale.

Of course, I knew Father Reid myself a little after that, through the discussion group in town at the Catholic Information Centre.

All of this fascinated my group, though I wondered if it was a lot to take in.

'But remember his name: Alex Reid. He comes back into the story.'

We went into the huge beautiful church. A priest was saying Mass on the altar for a group of young people in red sweatshirts. I couldn't work out who they were but I thought we should leave them in peace.

Patrick observed that there were no war memorials in the church at all.

'That's normal. You won't see regimental flags or anything of that kind in a catholic church, though you will in other denominations.'

That bothered him.

'Far more Irish people fought and died in the wars than in the Troubles.'

'True. We haven't really got our heads round that yet.'

I told him I had had two uncles in the British army, though one deserted in '43 and was never caught but died peacefully at home in Belfast in his nineties.

'Can you imagine,' I whispered, 'that all of this grandeur was paid for by the people who lived around here in slum housing and worked in the mills. And there is another cathedral a mile away, just as grand.'

'Why do all the big churches have two spires?' asked a woman. 'Is it true they are giving two fingers to the protestants?'

'I think catholic pride comes into it. This was a people treated as second class so they wanted to outshine others in something. Who knows?'

From there we went to Milltown Cemetery.

It was a beautiful day, in the heatwave of July 2018. This middle section of the Falls Road is the part that has changed least since the 1960s, though it has changed a great deal. Many of the shopfronts are the old buildings. The housing developments that have transformed the area are behind them.

When I was fourteen I had a part-time job with a milkman, delivering to prefabricated bungalows here that had been erected after the Second World War as temporary accommodation.

In our group we passed the Royal Victoria Hospital on one side and the huge convent school, St Dominic's, on the other, where not a single nun teaches now.

I stopped to show them a plaque in memory of Angela Gallagher, shot dead by the IRA in 1971 at the age of seventeen months, not deliberately but carelessly, the bullet ricocheting off a wall.

The plaque reads: 'May you stop here to remember the innocents amid the tragedy of conflict.' As if only impersonal history was to blame. The plaque was erected thirty-six years after wee Angela's death, after the IRA admitted that it had fired the fatal shot, but no mention of that appears on the memorial.

'On our right is the City Cemetery and the Falls Park, where I did some of my courting. On our left – there it is – Milltown Cemetery.'

I told them first the story of how the different organisations that called themselves the IRA would parade here in turn on Easter Sunday to honour their dead and ritually connect them back to the dead of 1916 and the Easter Rising in Dublin. Once, the Official IRA parade had been bombed as it lined up in Beechmount. The Provisionals had been blamed and a feud was on. By the time the Officials reached the cemetery gates, someone had closed them with a bicycle lock. There were scuffles. Pistols were drawn.

And yet that huge space, more densely populated with the dead than the city beyond is with the living, must surely have had a calming effect on the paramilitary armies that paraded here. The cemetery tilts down into Bog Meadows, bounded at the lower end by the M1 motorway but far enough from it to be virtually silent.

And once you are at the heart of the cemetery, halfway down that slope, the view of the Belfast Hills is almost uninterrupted by the intervening urban landscape.

It is a space that puts life in the city into a diminished perspective in which political concerns should really evaporate.

The old killers and their supporters with their flags and banners coming in here would immediately see illustrated for them the relative scale of their importance, for among the tens of thousands of graves the small clusters or plots in tribute to the dead of different republican factions seem very small.

Over 3,000 people died in the Troubles. A lot of them were buried here. But many more people died of old age, bad hearts, cancer, road-traffic accidents and in other, bigger wars.

Down the years I saw many grandiose funerals head for this place: Patrick Rooney's in August 1969, led by a lone piper; the funeral of three IRA members of a bomb team shot by the SAS in Gibraltar; and that funeral attacked by a lone loyalist gunman, Michael Stone. But there have been thousands of smaller funerals representing the ordinary lives of people, many of whom shared to a lesser extent in the passions of the paramilitaries or just tried to focus on making a living, raising a family, finding love or pursuing a hobby, supporting a team or crumbling away unnoticed through loneliness or some other form of physical or mental distress.

What is appalling about the paramilitaries and their related parties, I tell my group, is how they simplify life, reduce it to political concerns, and you might expect that when they stand here and see the diverse dead of Belfast spread out around them they would find some correction of their simplifications in this terrain.

Tours like this are easy because the whole Falls Road has been adorned with tributes to the IRA and its campaign.

It has been turned into a republican propaganda theme park, a tribute to the resilience of a noble but oppressed people. But while the road itself conveys the message, as a monument to struggle, the graveyard is a more representative sampling of life in that area and there the republican dead and their victims are lost in the vast array of monuments to the common dead.

I took them to the republican plots.

We stopped on the way to notice that some IRA volunteers are buried in separate graves and speculated on why they were not with their comrades. Perhaps the families didn't want an IRA funeral; they didn't all support the IRA.

We stopped first at a white stone cross, a monument to various dead republicans, including men who had served as officers in the US army and Tom Williams, executed at Crumlin Road Gaol in Belfast for participating in an ambush that killed a policeman in the 1940s.

The people in the tour group were amazed by this. I wanted to move them on to see much grander memorials.

There was the huge black marble monument to the republican dead of County Antrim.

I pointed out the name of my classmate Tony Henderson, who, according to the tribute, died on active service – though the word at the time was he had died in an accident in a training camp.

I once made an awful joke at Tony's expense and regretted it immediately for it went down far better than I expected and I made a fool of him in front of the whole class. We were in the school gym and had to swing on ropes from one beam to another. Tony was in front of me and he was hesitating. I said, 'Come on, Hen, or are you too chicken?'

Tony came back from the school holidays the next year transformed into a wee tough guy who wore winkle-pickers and swore.

After he died, one other boy from the class formed part of the colour party for his IRA funeral, in a black beret.

There was the grey stone spread of graves of the Official IRA from which the Provisionals broke away in 1970, accusing them of having failed to defend the catholic people from the pogroms of August 1969.

Billy McMillen was there.

From this position on the hill we could spot other graves some distance away with Irish tricolours erected beside them, or the Starry Plough flag of republican socialism.

'That one down there is the grave of Tommy Crossan, shot dead in 2014. So the traditions of killing and of honouring the dead as martyrs is still with us.'

And then, enfolded by a sandstone wall, inclining back and front in parallel from one end to rise like the prow of a ship, was the memorial to the Provisional IRA dead.

'This is astonishing,' said one of the women. 'I had no idea.'

I gathered them round me at the slab marking the dead of the failed Gibraltar plot to bomb a British army band. Mairéad Farrell, Sean Savage and Daniel McCann had been spotted and gunned down by the SAS. The defence for the ambush was that the IRA members might have had a remote trigger switch for detonating the bomb and would have to be finished off to be sure no movement was possible.

'As the crowd gathered for the lowering of the coffins,' I said, 'a lone loyalist gunman opened fire from over there, between here and the motorway. I am sure you have seen the pictures on television. You can find them on YouTube. He threw several grenades and fired shots at the mourners, and some of them chased him down to the road. A white van had been parked there, which many assumed was his getaway vehicle, but it took off before he reached it. They caught up with him at the same time as the police coming from the other direction. They got a few kicks in and took his gun before the police took him away. His name was Michael Stone.'

Stone killed three men that day: Thomas McErlean, John Murray and Caoimhín Mac Brádaigh, who was a member of the IRA.

As we left the cemetery, Patrick the former soldier asked me to show him the war memorial. 'There must be something here for the catholic soldiers who died in the wars.'

Indeed there was. He had parked the minibus beside it and not noticed it. It was a large stone structure like a crescent on which the names were barely legible. There were streaks of dried liquid on it. Part of the stonework had been broken away at one side. The floor was broken and scorched, perhaps by a small bomb. How else?

And a single wreath lay propped against it.

Then I took them through the rest of the story about the attack on the funeral of the Gibraltar conspirators.

Later that week, mourners following the cortege of Caoimhín Mac Brádaigh thought they faced another attack. Two men approached the front of the funeral in their car then tried to reverse rapidly away. A crowd gathered round the car and one of the men produced a gun. They were apparently undercover soldiers attached to a Signals regiment responsible for maintaining secret communications equipment and they should not have been there.

I brought the tour group then to the scene beside Casement Park football ground where the two men, taken from the car, were stripped and beaten.

I showed them the wall from which they had been dropped several feet and then I took them to the waste ground – now a car park – where an IRA executioner finished them off.

I handed them out copies of a photograph of one of the near-naked soldiers lying spread-eagled and dead on the rough ground, a priest kneeling beside him.

'That priest is Father Alex Reid.'

The Past in the Present

I could have fun bringing my eighteen-year-old self forward in time to see how this country has changed. Of course, even back then he had a naive sense of what it was really like. He did not know, as we know now, that many of the priests and religious brothers were sexually abusing children. He had little idea that anyone took sexual pleasure from those who hadn't even reached puberty themselves. He may have read articles about paedophiles in some shock exposé in a Sunday newspaper. He may even have read of discussions among European lefties that the sexual rights of children should be protected by law, allowing them to have sex with adults if they wanted to.

But he didn't have the modern sense that this was a huge social problem. The media that he was familiar with was not showing as much interest as it would later.

And he would be appalled to find out that the Troubles in Northern Ireland, whose start he had witnessed in Divis Street on the night the guns came out, would last for decades and are not yet really properly over, since some paramilitaries still plant bombs and shoot people.

He thought, in the autumn of '69, that the Troubles were over, now that the army had come to suppress street violence and the British government was committing itself to reform.

The build-up to the horrendous violence of the early 1970s was slow.

I have been thinking about where I would take him, how much I would tell him if I could get him into a TARDIS and bring him here today.

There was a weekend in May of 2018 that combined two events that would have amazed him.

On the Saturday night I was at a wedding party for two women friends.

On the Sunday morning, having been careful not to land myself with a hangover, I went to my nephew's First Holy Communion ceremony.

The party celebrated a marriage that was still, then, unrecognised by law in Northern Ireland, where same-sex marriage had not yet been legislated for. So Phyllis and Laura had been married in the Irish Republic, but this was treated simply as a civil partnership back home. Young Malachi would have difficulty with that. More surprising than lesbians being able to marry each other at all would be that they could make their vows to each other in catholic Ireland but not in the North.

The Republic that he knows does not ban lesbianism – because it inherited its law from Britain and Victoria, who did not believe such a way of relating was even possible.

But that Republic of his time is a morally conservative country. It does not allow women to own property or to sit on juries. Homosexuality between men is illegal, as it is in the North, having just been legalised in Britain. Marriage is so tightly protected by the state that it makes no provision for divorce.

Contraception is banned. So is abortion.

Indeed, the laws against abortion will get even stronger in the Republic before they relax.

So how come this catholic state has more liberal laws in my time than my own British Northern Ireland has?

'Well,' I'd have to tell him, 'it is not as catholic as it was.'

Nor indeed is Northern Ireland, for here it is not the catholics who are blocking legislation permitting same-sex marriage but the protestants. The Church is opposed, of course, but the political parties representing the catholic community—

'You mean the Nationalist Party?'

'We'll get to that in a minute.'

The political parties that represent catholics are Sinn Féin and the SDLP.

In his day, Sinn Féin was negligible, didn't win seats and wouldn't have taken them if it had – and the Social Democratic and Labour Party did not yet exist. Since his day, the SDLP was formed out of a cluster of radical small parties, grew to represent the majority of that community and then sank into decline.

'And both would legislate to allow lesbians to marry?'

'Yes. But the Democratic Unionist Party blocks that law.'

He's never heard of it.

'It was formed by the Rev. Ian Paisley. You've heard of him?'

'He's a header; a rabble-rouser.'

'He was our first minister but he's dead now.'

It would be a lot for the poor boy to take in.

The wedding party is in an upstairs bar in the Errigle Inn on the Ormeau Road in Belfast. I know a lot of the people there and can introduce him.

'Are they not bothered that this wedding is illegal here? It counts for nothing. They are not actually married at all unless they live in the Republic.'

'Or in England, or America or most of Europe or Australia.'

'Wow.'

He'd be using that word a lot.

'See at that long table – those women are all teachers from the school Phyllis works in.'

'What do the nuns think?'

As a young teenager, Malachi had known some of the girls who went to that school. They were the smarter young catholics who passed the eleven-plus. He had been to school debates there. Most of their teachers were nuns then. The girls were much talked about among boys for their legendary sexual conservatism.

It was said then that the nuns advised girls to take telephone directories to dances so that if a boy invited one to sit on his knee she could put the phone book on his lap to shield her from any stirrings in his pants that her proximity might arouse.

Not that the nun would have framed the problem so precisely.

Girls were also (it was said) warned against wearing patent-leather shoes whose reflective properties might let a boy she was dancing with see her underclothes.

But now one of the teachers is a married lesbian.

'We don't really use the word "lesbian".'

'What do you use?'

'"Gay", or "LGB" or "LGBT" or "LGBTQI". "Gay" is best.'

'What about "dyke"?'

I'd have to explain that if he used the word "dyke" he would probably not get thrown out into the street but nobody would talk to him.

'That's Dawn Purvis over there with her husband.'

'Who's she?'

'She was an elected representative of the Progressive Unionist Party.'

'Never heard of them.'

'Heard of the UVF?'

'The gang that murdered the barman?'

'That's them. She was the leader of a political party that advised them.'

They are better known now for having spawned the Shankill Butchers, who terrorised the streets in the 1970s, capturing catholics, torturing them and killing them with knives.

For him none of this has happened yet. It is hard enough for some people who have lived decades beyond that trauma to concede that there is decency in the tradition. It would surely be harder still to foresee such a change when there is blood in the gutter. Dawn Purvis was a socially liberal leader of her party. She left it rather than ignore murder. A man had been shot dead on the Shankill Road one afternoon when the organisation was supposed to be observing a ceasefire. Dawn was having no part of excusing that. She then became a campaigner for abortion rights in Northern Ireland.

'Abortion?'

'Yes, one of the major liberal causes of our time.'

'I don't think I could ever agree with abortion,' young Malachi would say.

I'd tell him they are having a referendum in the Republic in a couple of weeks on whether to remove a bar to abortion from the Irish constitution.

'I didn't know there was one.'

'There wasn't in your day. It came later.'

The referendum result will surprise even me and most people with its huge endorsement, allowing the government to legislate for a right to end a pregnancy in the first three months.

I danced with my wife at that party but most of the people on the floor were women. It seemed almost as though everyone wanted to be a lesbian for a night. They were celebrating the love of two women for each other, dancing in a circle round them, cheering Phyllis and Laura when they hugged and kissed.

Young Malachi would find this weird. He had never knowingly met a lesbian. He had only heard the word used in contempt, often for women who had simply refused a dance or a date.

I would buy him a drink. I would not tell him yet that it cost about three times what he earned in a night's work in a bar.

And I wouldn't want him to get drunk, since we'd be going to Mass in the morning.

I don't often go to Mass. I am not in any sense a practising catholic and do not want a Church funeral. I am a bit of an exception in that; not in that I don't go to Mass – that's normal enough. What is not yet normal in Northern Ireland is for people not to have christian burials.

'Why do they want catholic funerals if they don't believe?'

'It's tradition. Or maybe death comes and the families don't know how to shop around for a humanist or civil ceremony; they just do what the neighbours expect or the undertaker recommends. Look at Seamus Heaney.'

'What! Seamus Heaney is dead?'

'I'm afraid so. And though he had declared himself a non-believer he had a catholic funeral. It's what people do.'

'Did he make it big?'

'Oh yes, he got the Nobel Prize for literature.'

'Wow!'

In this fantasy exercise in time travel, we arrive at the church, as I did in reality, forty minutes before the Mass begins. It is about a quarter full with family groups, glamorously attired. The little boys are in smart suits, some wearing trainers. The girls wear white bridal-type dresses. The fathers are in suits, mostly, though I see some in jeans and open-neck shirts, one in a multicoloured jacket a singer might wear on stage. There are mothers more variously turned out. They are wearing the clothes they would wear to a formal dinner, say to a wedding. There are floral trouser suits, cleavages, new hair-dos. Some of the women have tattoos; one has hair dyed pink.

Young Malachi goes to Mass even less than I do – for, being younger, fewer of his friends and colleagues die. But he has recent memories of weekly attendance and knows what to expect. It is not what he sees.

None of these women is wearing any kind of head covering. In 1969 all women going to a catholic church covered their heads, often with a black veil, a mantilla.

The buzz in the church is as it would be in a marketplace or lounge bar. No one feels compelled to whisper or just stay silent in this holy space. When people come and take their seats they do not genuflect at the pew in homage to the Living Presence in the tabernacle on the altar.

This surprises young Malachi. This is not the norm as he knows it.

Nearly everyone is white. That does not strike him as odd either, but then he hears other languages being spoken.

'Polish,' I explain.

But Poland, as he knows it, is behind the Iron Curtain. He has never met anyone from Poland and is immediately fascinated.

'Aren't they all communists?'

And there are Filipinos, Lithuanians, some Chinese and Koreans.

We go through the order-of-service booklet, which seems very strange to him. He doesn't know any of the hymns. And we study the lists of names of the children who are making their first communion today.

There is a Kwiatkowski, a De La Paz, a Dangcal, a Tanguanco. Out of sixty-nine kids receiving communion in this church today, twenty-seven are, judging by their names, migrants. Just over a third.

He would say, 'This is not the Belfast I know.'

I would say, 'We had thirty years of trouble, routine killings and bombing. It seemed to be our normality. It became axiomatic to say that nothing ever changes here. Yet this society is transformed. There has been a revolution but it is not the one the paramilitary armies fought for.'

This fantasy that I could bring my younger self forward in time to see how Northern Ireland has been transformed can take me wider than just surprising him with the things that he would never have predicted, like a popular demand for gays to be allowed to marry or Polish children making their First Holy Communion on the Newtownards Road.

If I could walk him through these events I would also, of course, have to consider helping him through the years between us, when he would at times be in extreme danger, or heartbroken, short of money or wasting years in unemployment and foolish notions.

I love that man and I pity him. The more I identify with him the more I am inclined to feel ashamed of myself for how badly I – he – managed the Troubles when they broke, for he hadn't the maturity to cope.

I might say, 'One day you will be drunk and you will blow a whistle out your bedroom window to alarm soldiers crawling through your back garden. They will kick in your back door, take you out and drag you off by the hair. Best not to have a whistle near you.'

And: 'The closest you will come to being killed will be on the Donegall Road when loyalists will surround you. Obviously you don't get killed because I am here to tell you this, but you can spare yourself the stress.'

But we have both seen a lot of *Dr Who* and read enough about time travel to know the dangers.

If I tell him not to bother any more with Jo but that in future years he will wonder why he didn't ask Clare out, then he might go back and do that and marry Clare – and then where would I be now?

And I would want to keep him out of trouble. At least he would know from seeing me approaching seventy that I survived the violence. I wouldn't want to tell him about the other times I came close to being killed or the stress and fretfulness of staying alive and sane.

He has heard gunfire in the night, but not yet right close to the house. He doesn't yet know anyone who has been killed – they haven't yet been killed on his timeline.

I could say, 'You know Denis, the guy you sit beside in college? His brother Terry will go out with a protestant girl one summer, while working in a factory, and he will be caught by loyalists and shot dead. The boss will offer his protestant workmates time off to go to the funeral and they will decline to take it. That is the sort of place your Northern Ireland is turning into. Danny Rouse, round the corner: strangers will pull him into a car and take him away and shoot him.'

I might be tempted to tell him to urge his own father – my father – not to go to work in a north-Belfast bar on a night he will have to flee and actually jump over a bomb to get through the door and across the street before it goes off. He will have to drive home with the shakes in a car with no windows.

Young Malachi will go back to 1969 and then work as a journalist through the decades in which every book about the

Northern Ireland Troubles will conclude with the depressing observation that our society is so irrevocably divided that no political solution is possible. But he will know now that, while foreign correspondents and trainee war reporters are obsessed with violence and political conundrums, real change is happening elsewhere, in the transformation of religious attitudes and sexual culture, in the status of women; and that these together will make up the real revolution.

If he was later to announce to colleagues in the BBC canteen that Sinn Féin, the party of the IRA, will be campaigning for abortion and gay rights in years to come they might be so dismissive of his crazy predictions that they would be wary of giving him serious stories to cover.

He will go back to a time in which some few others will also be predicting that the concept of a catholic minority in Northern Ireland will have expired by about 2020 – but in which no one is preparing for that.

There has been a revolution in Northern Ireland but it is not the one recorded in the history books.

Women's Rights Movement

The biggest obvious change in the character of Northern Irish society is in the status of women. I am sitting with my friend Anne in the Hope Cafe under the library of Queen's University. She is making that very point. 'Look around you. Do you think it was like this in 1969?'

The people at the other tables are students and lecturers. Most of them are young-ish. Most are white, though there are a few Asians, and most are women. The contrast is evidence of a social revolution that occurred in the period that coincided with the Northern Ireland Troubles. This was a time in which men and women too were killing for ideals.

Indeed, some women complain that they have not been given enough credit for their contribution to the 'war' – that sexism taints the record. The wall murals of men with Kalashnikovs depict the struggle as male-led. There were women with guns. There was one that my mother nicknamed Machine-gun Kate because she had seen her from her kitchen window in 1972 firing at a passing army vehicle.

But the image of the guerrilla fighter as depicted on the walls is a lie whether the person with the gun is male or female. It really wasn't that kind of war, one fought across urban battlegrounds or open countryside. Very little if any of it was combat at all.

There were women activists, like the two who left a bomb under their seat in the Abercorn Bar in 1972, killing and maiming other women. If they want the credit for that act, they are welcome to it.

Women often served as 'honey traps', luring off-duty soldiers into ambush at the prospect of a party and a ride.

There were the Price sisters, Marian and Dolours, who led the bomb team to London in 1973. Dolours later disclosed that she had been part of the team that had interrogated and executed Jean McConville, a mother of ten, on the grounds – disputed – that she was an informer.

There were the nine women and girls who tortured and beat to death their neighbour Ann Ogilvy in a UDA club in 1974.

The IRA at the start of the Troubles was an all-male organisation, supported by a woman's organisation called Cumann na mBan. The basic idea was that the men did the fighting and the women bandaged them up if they got hurt; but a modern terrorist organisation could take great advantage from using women in surreptitious roles, especially in a world in which they did not think women were fighters. And that easy sexist assumption of the innocuous female enabled the IRA and others to use women to smuggle guns. One, Mary McArdle delivered two pistols to male killers, carrying them stuffed down the front of a pair of surgical tights and further concealed by a tweed skirt.

The victim in that attack, in 1983, was Mary Travers, a primary-school teacher and the daughter of a magistrate. She actually taught in the Holy Child School in Andersonstown, the school I had gone to myself.

The Palestinians had set an example in the deployment of women with Leila Khaled's part in the hijacking of planes to Jordan in 1969. So, perhaps it can be argued that some of the paramilitary groups were indeed in the vanguard of according equality to women in allowing them to be just as deadly as the men.

Niall Gilmartin in a recent essay, 'From the Frontlines of War to the Sidelines of Peace',[7] explores the failure of the IRA to give due credit to the contribution of women, citing earlier research.

> An analysis of over 500 republican and nationalist
> murals in 1996 revealed that just six made
> reference to armed republican women [...]
> Lorraine Dowler's extensive research in west Belfast
> in 1998 found vast levels of frustration among
> republican women at the male dominance and
> bias within songs and ballads. Of the seventy-four
> republican songs analysed by Dowler, she found
> just four made reference to women's roles in
> armed struggle.

These conclusions are undermined by the fact that at the time of writing the president and vice president of Sinn Féin are both women, as was the party's candidate in the Irish presidential election, though none of these women are regarded as having been active terrorists themselves.

But there were also women who preferred to campaign primarily for women's rights than to take sides in a sectarian war. They too can argue that they have been written out of history.

Lynda Walker was a communist from Yorkshire. She came to Northern Ireland in the late sixties and married Terry Bruton, a communist member of the NICRA executive. When the sectarian violence heated up, they felt safer living in a catholic area, Twinbrook, because some protestant neighbours of the Brutons in east Belfast saw them as traitors to the loyalist cause.

Coming from Sheffield, Lynda saw immediate differences between the profiles of women here and there.

'I could compare what there was for women in England to what there was here, in terms of the abortion laws, in terms of women at work; postwomen, traffic wardens, bus conductresses – you didn't have any of them here. In Sheffield we had a couple that cleaned our windows. You never saw women cleaning windows here. So, little things like that.'

She and her sister involved themselves in the Communist Party in Belfast.

'We used to sell the Communist Party paper round the Markets every Friday night and we always finished up in the Black Bull with people like Joe McCann.'

Joe McCann was a leading member of the Official IRA, the Stickies. He was shot dead by British soldiers in Joy Street in April 1972 at a time when he is thought to have been working to steer his movement away from a planned ceasefire.

According to Lynda: 'He used to come up to our house and we used to have good discussions on the whys and wherefores of the military campaign, and we were opposed to it. Joe was a bit of an adventurist. I think he used to see himself in this kind of Che Guevara light. He was a very likeable fella. I saw him in his coffin. He never came across as religious but he had the rosary beads entwined in his fingers and I thought, *That's how naive I were.* I didn't expect to see that, you know.'

While Joe McCann was fighting for an Irish socialist republic, Lynda and her colleagues in the women's movement were fighting for free school milk, just then scrapped by education secretary Margaret Thatcher.

'In 1971 we were protesting against the milk being took off the schoolchildren. We actually addressed the education committee twice and we addressed the full council once. I phoned the Farmer's Union and they brought two cows and we walked them from McClure Street down to the City Hall and it were pouring it down.'

She believed then that giving the milk back to the children was an attainable goal, partly because farmers were going to lose money and therefore supported them.

'Then we walked to Stormont and back and that were quite a united campaign but there were some people in City Hall saying, "Oh, catholics have got more children so they take more milk." It weren't a major thing but nevertheless there was some school-meals women from Newtownards Road and they were told not to be involved. And I have still got petitions from that period. Belfast City Council voted unanimously to condemn the decision to take the milk away.'

Lynda said that the Stormont government could have chosen to provide the milk out of their education budget so they focused the campaign there.

But Belfast was consuming itself with political energy directed elsewhere.

For Lynda, as for many of the women who worked for women's rights, late education opened up new possibilities. There were problems in the way of uniting women in a broad movement, not only because of sectarian divisions in society but also because of divisions within the separate communities. Local political activists in republican areas might be at odds with each other through rival paramilitary organisations, the Provisional IRA and the Officials or Stickies.

'You wouldn't have got the Sticks and the Provies working together in an organisation at that time because there had been internal strife. By 1979 we had been organising International Woman's Day since 1975. The first one was on childcare.

'By 1980 we had affiliated to the International Women's Democratic Federation based in the German Democratic Republic. They would organise conferences and have people from South Africa, Turkey, a lot of women who were in exile but also England and America, and we made a lot of good contacts. We had people over from Angola, from Iraq, from Finland. I can't remember them all.

'That was anti-imperialist but we never said we were going out as an anti-imperialist thing because people don't even relate to the term itself. What we were doing was basically trying to lay a basis to unite on progressive issues.'

Another campaigner for women's rights was Angela Courtney. Like Lynda Walker, she had come from England, accompanying her husband who had got a job in Northern Ireland. He was a civil servant and worked alongside a woman called Barbara Harvey, who had come back from doing a PhD in Canada with a plan to help women seeking refuge from violent partners. A previous refuge in Camden Street had burned down and a new house had been procured in north Belfast.

Angela helped out at first by sewing curtains as part of an effort to get the new house ready for women who needed shelter.

She told me: 'What I witnessed there I could not walk away from. That was 1967. I saw the first battered women in the house. We called them "battered women" in those days because that was the name that was given to them. We changed it to "abused women". They were actually called "battered wives", on the assumption that they were married.'

While she and others were working on getting the house ready a man arrived at the door with his daughter and her children.

'Her face was beaten black and blue and she had four children under five, including twins and a baby. I had three children under five at the time myself but I had been married quite a long time before we decided to have a family.

'She wasn't married. She had been raped by somebody called Tommy who had just come out of prison. The baby was in her arms clinging to her. The twins were playing around the floor and the older boy was just standing there, looking shattered. The house hadn't opened. That opened it. Nobody turned them out. I just carried on making the curtains.

'There was a certain amount of joy in seeing that woman because I had found my purpose in life,' Angela recalled. 'The words I heard were: "Jesus is stripped of her garments." And that held me in that place. And being in that place, going back and forwards, just listening to women and talking to them and bringing them optimism and brightness, this transformed my life.'

She added: 'It was always a religious mission for me but it was a secular movement and that suited me to a T.'

The refuge was a big house; they didn't have to make women double up in rooms. And they gave help to women who needed it.

'She went back a lot of times to the guy who had raped and beaten her. It was 1969 and the place was falling apart. We were offering refuge. We didn't make rules as to when people could come and not come. They could come when they needed to. But we sat down with them and said, "What's this back and forwards doing to the kids?" They had to change schools. Local social services were brilliant because you got people in there who knew the problem. And they didn't have a solution and saw us as a solution.'

Angela once gave a talk to the police on the needs of women suffering domestic violence and found little sympathy among some of them.

'"Sure they bring it on themselves." A policeman said that. I just stood my ground. His mates were all sitting around. They isolated him; I didn't. I didn't have to. That's the way it works.'

Another woman I spoke to for this book, Lisa, told me her own experience of being an abused woman. Lisa had decided to seek an education in her thirties, having left school with no qualifications. Her husband wasn't happy about this at all.

'He was just becoming more violent and more addicted to drugs. Every time I threw him out I brought him back. I think I felt that I needed him.'

She still sympathises with the difficulty he had in adjusting to change.

'I have to be honest for him. Part of me knew that this was a journey and he didn't. I had a dependency on him, but as I was getting stronger he was getting weaker and I suppose more frightened. And I was getting this life. I was having a social life, going to the theatre and places, and trying to bring him with me, but he couldn't do that and he knew that so he was becoming more and more violent and frustrated.

'I had black eyes and bruises. He split my head open one time. It came to – I can't even remember what year it was – I just got to the end of my tether and it used to always be worse at Christmas because of the drink. We were just all very damaged.'

Lisa told me: 'There were two families, us and a family at the top of the street – he was an alcoholic as well – and the police were never out of our street. If they weren't at our door they were at theirs. I called the police when he hit me or somebody else did. I remember the police woman saying, you need to get help. You need to get help.

'The university was an escape. I used to drive over and you see when I got to the embankment, I felt a weight lifting off me. I remember one night, the first Christmas, the tutor had a wee party for us and I wanted to go. I said to him and he says, "Don't you fucking go." I went and when I came home he had wrecked the house.'

Finally she threw him out of the house and kept him out.

Women like Lisa and Lynda Walker and Angela Courtney, and the women who came to the refuge and picked up the threads of their lives and remade them, were part of a revolution expressed through individual experiences and nurtured in support groups. And they changed Northern Ireland more than the bombers did.

The town centres were rebuilt and the men came home from prison and the activists became community workers and politicians, but the routines of civic and family life had changed in fundamental ways because of the new freedoms that women had achieved. And this had had nothing to do with the armed campaigns. The paramilitaries and the political parties had focused on other objectives and failed in the pursuit of them but the country was different anyway – and better – despite them.

Angela Courtney told me that the refuge for abused women was located between protestant and catholic areas, though the services were used more by catholics. She was given assurances by the IRA that the house would be protected.

Her curtains didn't last long, she said, because little boys would swing on them. A volunteer from Germany then solved that problem by painting the windows. Angela gave secretarial help and went on to become a coordinator for the Northern Ireland Women's Aid Federation.

'We went out and talked to women's groups and to start local support groups. There was a lot of resistance to talking about battered women because you could be sure you had some sitting in front of you, because it was too close to home and nobody could speak about it. So there was a silence around it. It's nothing to be ashamed about. It's the men who should be ashamed. We were just breaking down prejudice. There was that feeling that if he had hit you he had good reason. I had heard people say that.'

My personal hero from that time is Eileen Calder.

Eileen is a little younger than me. She grew up in a working-class part of north Belfast, in a street from which you can see the massive cranes of the now defunct shipyard. The view is clear, not because she is close to the docks but because she is high over them, in streets that are icier in winter than the nice parts of Belfast lower down. She has had seven children but she is not a docile housewife; indeed, she is not someone you would be wise to get into an argument with, as bigger and stronger people than me have found out.

Eileen worked for the Rape Crisis Centre in Belfast through the nineties and noughties. When political energies were being directed towards ending the bombings and the shootings she was saying, 'You people have no idea how common rape is in our society and you have no plan to end it.'

I had seen her rage in interviews she gave but she was right to be angry. She had heard the presumption that women bring rape upon themselves, seen how raped women had to prove their own innocence as well as their attackers' guilt and how cases failed. She scowled when she made the most reasonable case – unlike the polished performers in parties that spoke for gunmen, who kept their poise and affected reason while saying the most appalling things, such as that there had to be a few more killings yet because conditions for negotiation were still not right.

She wasn't the only strong woman fighting for change. It's embarrassing when I count them and realise myself, as a journalist who covered the Troubles, how I overlooked them.

Because if you think the IRA was more interesting than the social revolution that happened in the same time period you are simply being sexist; you are taking an option for men in hoods with guns over women who took similar risks for change. Of course, the easy refutation of that is that women were in the IRA too, and that's true. And even feminist groups in Belfast at the time were divided on the relevance of the 'anti-imperial struggle'. But these women changed our society in more radical and more healthy ways than the paramilitaries did.

Northern Ireland's first Rape Crisis Centre opened in 1982. Eileen Calder started work there in 1984 after a close family member was raped. That attack had been what she calls 'the standard nightmare', a man taking hold of a woman on the street on a dark night. What she learned in the Rape Crisis Centre is that this is the rare type of rape; most of it happens in the family.

Her new job exposed her not just to clients of the centre coming for support and counselling but to people she met socially now wanting to open up their past secrets to someone they could be trusted with.

'People that I had known for years and who never came to the centre as clients … once I was working in that field, relatives of my husband, friends of friends, would say, "This is what happened to me." To be honest, we couldn't go into the Duke of York or the John Hewitt [Belfast pubs] but some strange woman would come up and say, "I saw you on TV. This is what happened to me but I never reported it."'

Clearly the scale of rape in our society was much greater than was suggested by the numbers convicted of the crime.

'It's like a pyramid. The convictions are the wee tiny bit at the top. The ones that get to court are below that. The ones that get reported, below that. And then there's this big giant part of the bottom of it. The vast majority of incidents of rape and sexual abuse just aren't reported and sometimes never told to anyone. There are women who go to their graves without telling anyone.'

Eileen became a familiar face on the local media, speaking on behalf of rape victims she had accompanied to court and participating in campaigns. The Rape Crisis Centre had been established to provide counselling and legal advice to people who had been raped. She and her colleagues understood that help has to come as early as possible, so that evidence can be preserved and so that survivors can be given emotional support at the time of their deepest trauma.

She believes that one of her achievements in those years was getting the media and the police to use that word 'survivor' instead of 'victim'.

'I saw it as a war against sexual violence against women. And winning the war was about changing the laws and changing society. And the people who had been raped and sexually abused, they were the wounded in the war and they had to be looked after. But we were more than just the Red Cross; we had to be the army too.'

Her militancy was attractive to the media. When I was with her in her house and she was laughing more than scowling, I asked her why we had never seen that part of her. According to Eileen, the media always asked her not to smile; they liked to preserve the severity in her manner.

And she knew how to use the media to advance her cause. She did once go to jail for contempt of court and told me that others should have the courage to do it too. She had gone to court in August 1997 to support a man charged with harassing a convicted paedophile he had seen loitering near a school. The accused had made a complaint that he had been beaten by the police. The case had ended – with a conviction – and Eileen called out from the public gallery that the magistrate should ask the accused to lift his shirt and show his bruises.

'And that's when the magistrate said, "Who is this woman and what has she got to say?" I said, "I am Eileen Calder from the Rape Crisis Centre. These are the reasons why this man was there; the police did not do their job of trying to protect children and he was seriously assaulted." He was black and blue. I got three days for contempt.'

When she protested the magistrate, John Edwards, raised the sentence to seven days in jail.

'And then this big peeler stood on my foot. I screamed and he then said, "Fourteen days." And by the time they had got me to the door he said, "Twenty-one days." If the courtroom had been longer I would have got three years. And I'm going: "I want – I want to speak to my solicitor. I'm entitled to a phone call." And this wee screw just laughed and said, "No, love; you're not. You've been convicted."'

This was on a Friday afternoon. Eileen had planned to spend the weekend with her children in a caravan but went to Maghaberry Prison instead. With journalist friends she was able to draw publicity to her case.

She told me, 'It was funny, like. I was taken first to the cells in the court. Then they came to pick me up – a couple of hours later. Or it seemed like hours. I remember writing something with lipstick on the wall, because it was the only thing I had. They eventually did let me have a phone call but I think that wasn't until I got to the prison.'

At prison she was stripped naked and searched.

'To be honest, they made an effort to make it as non-humiliating as possible. There wasn't an intimate body search. I had to have a bath. They put me in a red tracksuit and a big nightdress. And jeans; they weren't that bad. And a pair of trainers; they weren't Adidas but they weren't Primark either.'

She was in jail for three days then brought back to court for an appeal. She instructed her solicitor to appeal only the conviction and not the sentence.

'And if the conviction wasn't squashed I would just go back to prison. I didn't want their fucking mercy.'

In prison she had insisted that she was a political prisoner. The Provisional IRA helped her settle in. Ailish Carroll, who was serving a fifteen-year sentence for possession of rifles and who knew Eileen was a protestant from north Belfast, arranged for her to have a phone card with money on it and sweets for her kids when they came to visit.

'And they agreed that when I came back – if I did come back – that they would take me into the republican wing, because the wee girls that were in for prostitution and the shoplifters didn't like me. They said, "You're a stupid bitch for getting yourself into here; it's your own fault."'

At the appeal hearing the magistrate refused to quash the conviction but sent her home.

'On another occasion I was threatened with prison if I did not hand over the case notes relating to a rape trial. This victim herself did not want them handed over. The case did not go ahead, because of "abuse of process". So your man got off. But I did what I thought was the right thing morally. The victim lived in Australia. The next day her sister gave an interview to the *Irish News* saying that it was my fault that the case had failed, that I ought to have handed over the notes. These were the confidential counselling notes. But the defence will often call for those.'

She thinks she wouldn't fit into the women's movement of today, or the #MeToo phenomenon.

'I don't like the title of it for a start. That's what a three-year-old shouts: "Me too, me too!"'

She aired her scepticism of the movement in scathing terms.

'Very famous, rich, privileged, Hollywood actresses creating a fuss about things that they were quite happy to be quiet about in order to get where they are. I think Angelina Jolie was one who stood up in the Weinstein thing, but very few others did. And it has just become a bit of a trend really.'

Citing the example of Martha Kearney having her bottom touched as a young journalist, she said: 'It is absolutely horrendous and it shouldn't have happened. Of course it shouldn't have happened. But the whole idea that you destroy someone's life, someone who is perhaps a great-grandfather now, because he once touched your knee inappropriately, does seem a bit …' And at this point she grabbed my knee to make her point.

'I hope that wasn't too traumatising for you. but that kind of thing, there is some stuff that has gone too far and we need to concentrate on important issues like rape, like the right to control your own body, choose whether you want to be pregnant or not, rather than whether a workman is allowed to whistle at you on the street or some other nonsense.'

Boys Will Be Boys

We don't know her name.

We do know that she hadn't shaved her legs that night and we have seen her knickers, have had them described in newspapers. They were held up in court.

We know that the knickers were bloodstained and that there was blood on the bed.

We have her story that she was raped by two rugby players. We have their names, Paddy Jackson and Stuart Olding. They said that they didn't have intercourse with her but oral sex, initiated willingly by her. I'm not sure how oral sex would have drawn blood from her vagina but that puzzle did not detain the court for long. Conflicting medical evidence said that she had a contusion in her vagina or that the shading that suggested as much may have been an optical illusion.

Four men stood accused at the trial: Jackson (rape and sexual assault), Olding (rape), Blane McIlroy (exposure) and Rory Harrison (perverting the course of justice and withholding information).

In their WhatsApp messages to friends the day after the incident, these men talked of 'spit-roasting' (Olding) and 'sluts get[ting] fucked' (team mate Craig Gilroy). Paddy Jackson said, 'there was a lot of spit'. Harrison, who was more sympathetic to the girl, said he walked upstairs and 'there were more flutes than on the twelfth of July' – flutes presumably meaning erect penises.

The young woman had met them in a Belfast nightclub, where she had gone to celebrate passing her exams. There was a VIP area in Ollie's. There was nothing like Ollie's in Belfast when I was young; not that I knew of anyway.

I worked for a time as the guard on the door from the dressing rooms in Tito's in Cromac Street. I wasn't expected to use force to restrain any drunks wanting to go backstage to meet Candy Devine or Jake the Peg; I was too small and light for that kind of work. They made me a waiter for a time and then dropped me.

Candy Devine was terrific, a big woman in voluminous dresses who sang and compèred and chatted at the tables. But some of the other waiters were men who had the same attitude to women as that expressed in the rugby players' WhatsApp messages.

One night, at the bar, one waiter in a tux and bow tie was bragging that he had had sex nine times the night before. Since none of the rest of us had ever put that challenge to the test, we were not well placed to call him a liar and a braggart. I thought it, though. The manager was impressed.

Back then, the pubs closed at ten and you might have had a fish supper on the walk home, having missed the last bus.

In the VIP area of Ollie's, the girl joined the rugby players and other girls in their company and they all spilled out into taxis and went back to Jackson's house to party.

During the trial, one of those other girls said she looked into Jackson's bedroom and saw her having sex with him, apparently enjoying it. Jackson, she said, asked if she would like to join in. Group sex was what these boys enjoyed. She declined.

Her evidence helped the defence, though it contradicted the men's assertion that they hadn't had intercourse with the girl.

Olding and McIlroy made similar claims of how she had generously offered them both oral sex.

Another of the defendants, Harrison, had brought her home that night, distressed. She said herself that she didn't think he should have been charged with an offence; he had been so helpful.

All four men were acquitted.

And a shockwave went through the country, like the one that had followed the police attack on civil-rights protesters in Derry in 1968. Protests followed.

Lynda Walker and I discussed it in her living room. She hadn't really been up to protesting at the time because she had just had knee-replacement surgery. She still speaks in a northern-English accent. She told me: 'They were condemned for what they did do. If they didn't rape her, what they did do was certainly not commendable, not in people who are role models to young children. They are not above social mores.'

Kellie Turtle of the Belfast Feminist Network was among the organisers of the protest on the day after the case closed. The first impulse of local feminists was to rally at Belfast courthouse to proclaim their sense that the woman had been wronged; the second was to exercise caution. People, mostly women, came to voice their anger in their hundreds, some carrying signs and placards reading #IBelieveHer. But this first protest was strangely muted.

From where I was, I could not hear the speeches.

The police were being civil. At one point I climbed on to a ledge of the court building perimeter to get a better photograph. Two constables came over. I thought they were going to tell me to get down.

'Are you OK?' said one of them. 'We don't want you falling.'

So solicitous. Back in the days of PD they might have dragged me down and whacked me with a baton. I have to admit that, unfairly, I still anticipate that reaction in some situations. There must be a lot of people in Belfast who, like victims of abuse, live anticipating a slap that doesn't come.

I looked around at the faces of the protesters. For some this was a festive event on a bright morning in early spring. Some were in apparent emotional pain. Other photographers and reporters mingled, trying to get a shot of the speakers, trying to hear what the speakers were saying, trying to get someone to speak to them.

I put some of my pictures on Facebook and commented there about the lousy sound system.

There was a second protest in Belfast on the Saturday, outside the City Hall, this time organised by a socialist-feminist group called ROSA Northern Ireland. There were the same problems with the sound system. Nor was there much clarity about the demands this new movement would assert. A young woman spoke of the faith-based sex education she had received in school and suggested a campaign to have better education for children about sex and consent.

I had received a sharp reaction on Facebook from Kellie Turtle for criticising the sound system at the first protest, and I asked her if we could meet.

Kellie is interesting. Like a lot of people in activism in Belfast she has family connections back to the Communist Party. She looks like the sort of person you would want on your side. She is tall, fit and elegant and has grey hair, short, nicely styled.

I visited her at her office in the university area, where she works with a charity supporting women. She led me upstairs and gave me a glass of water and we talked. First she wanted to apologise for having been so sharp with me on Facebook but she took my point. Next time they would have a better sound system: somebody was donating one.

She said that even before the acquittal of the rugby players was announced, women in different groups were contacting each other about organising a response.

'What happened outside the courts was very much an outpouring of anger, so we were having conversations in the week running up to that saying this verdict is coming. We had a strong sense of what way the verdict was going to go and we felt that there was so much anger that people would want to take to the streets.

'I hadn't spoken to a single woman who didn't feel like her heart was being ripped out every time she turned on the news by what we were having to listen to.'

People could see the weaknesses in the case as it unfolded. They knew the legal test of guilt beyond reasonable doubt was a hard one. But, as Lynda Walker said, there were things those men had done that they were not being tried for, having spoken of women as expendable.

Kellie said, 'Even some of the things that were being employed by the prosecution were problematic, like the idea that she couldn't possibly have been consenting to sex because she hadn't shaved her legs that day. The idea that you consent to sex four hours before you've even left the house.

'No matter what you looked at in this case it was just completely saturated in every possible harmful stereotype that we have been talking about for years.'

So there was a sense in the country that a moment had arrived, that feminist arguments that had not previously been taken to the centre of political activism were now affirmed and obvious. This was similar to what happened with civil rights in October 1968. Events put an old problem into sharp focus. People were shocked that the cross-examination of a woman about her complaint of rape would take so little care to avoid exhausting and humiliating her.

Like 1968, it wasn't so much the rights and wrongs of the legal judgment that mattered as what the whole process disclosed about how much justice a woman may feel entitled to expect.

But why had the protest been so quiet? Why had activists not come out and spoken to the media? They had all sent reporters and news crews.

Kellie said that journalist friends had told them that they

had all been warned to be careful how they discussed the verdict. They could not question it without being in contempt of court. The protesters wanted to make plain that they were not challenging the verdict, only saying that the messages of the men showed they hated women and that the conduct of trials like these still puts the onus on the woman to prove her innocence, still humiliates her.

Kellie said, 'We are quite safe. What is that about? Is it the fact that we have been lulled into thinking that if we do it in the right way and do it by the book they will listen to us?'

She was taking the approach that Betty Sinclair had recommended to the protesters in 1968, and which they rejected. Had they followed it, there would have been no big riot and no global story that day.

There had been an even bigger protest against the conduct of the rugby players in Dublin than there had been in Belfast. But Kellie was planning another.

The Belfast Feminist Network placed a full-page ad in the *Belfast Telegraph* calling on Ulster Rugby to drop Paddy Jackson and Stuart Olding from the team. There was pressure on the club from its sponsors. The Bank of Ireland, the main sponsor, whose logo the players wore on their shirts, said that the behaviour of the men, as disclosed in court, conflicted with their company values.

For some years, since the financial crash of 2008, banks that had been stripping people of their homes had not really been associated with 'values' but nobody pointed out this incidental satire. The company was afraid that it would become a target of protest and that women would take their accounts to banks that didn't fund players who bragged of spit-roasting and slut-fucking.

The *Irish News* reported that the #IBelieveHer protesters planned to picket the rugby ground in Belfast on the following Friday before a big game.

Kellie Turtle told me she knew nothing about this plan. She had asked her friends in other organisations and they didn't know about it either. They concluded that the story was wrong, but since an expectation of a protest had been created they should fulfill it.

And they did.

I went up to the rugby ground to see the protest there.

The entrance to the Kingspan Stadium is in a residential area on a narrow road divided by a little grassy island with trees. The houses are mostly two-storey terraced and semi-detached redbricks. This is where George Best grew up. Traditionally the families here would have been upper working class, people employed in the heavy industries of east Belfast, the shops and small businesses on the Newtownards Road and perhaps in the civil service, parliament buildings being just a ten-minute bus ride away.

On the night of a big game, thousands come from all over, clogging the neighbouring streets with their cars, some of them having to walk the last mile, unable to park closer. Some come on coaches, which as they near the ground have to negotiate the sluggish traffic and the fans on foot.

The protest was an additional concern for the police, who are always there to guide the traffic. They had agreed with the feminists that they would confine themselves to the grassy island, with trees at each end marking the boundaries they would keep to. They would not disrupt the traffic flow.

When I arrived the little green island was full with perhaps a couple of hundred women and children with their banners, some with drums and musical instruments. Photographers moved around them trying to find the telling picture that would connect the protest to the gates and the fans, but that was a hard picture to get.

A policewoman told me to get to the other side of a tree and not to stray on to the road. The police appeared nervous. They presumably thought there was some danger that someone would raise the temperature to a level that would be more difficult to manage.

Fans arriving on foot paused to look across at the protest and then moved quickly through the gate, making no comment or objection.

The band beat their drums and chanted their slogans. Kellie was on form, at one point scoffing at the media in her speech and eyeballing me as she did so. It made for a nice picture. She demanded change to the way rape trials are conducted and reported.

There were two main groups there, Belfast Feminist Network and Reclaim the Agenda. They held up the banner of the old Northern Ireland Women's Rights Movement – Lynda Walker, who couldn't be there, had dug it out and washed and ironed it for them.

Some of those there were children of the original civil-rights activists. Breedagh Hughes held a banner; her father was Fred

Heatley, a member of the NICRA executive. Clare Bailey of the Green Party stood beside her.

There was a huge media turnout and this time the organisers gave interviews calling for a reform of the criminal-justice system and changes within the media in how they report rape cases.

I was left wondering how Northern Irish history might have followed a different course if, fifty years ago, the police had managed protest as well as they do now.

Kellie and the feminists were determined to show that they were law-abiding people. That's arguably the best way to manage a protest and there were many in the old civil-rights movement who had wanted to conduct their protests in the same way. But they would not have got as much publicity and support if they hadn't clashed with the police. Kellie, though, was not going to do that.

'At the rugby event they were nervous about the numbers and the police were nervous about the locals. We had a big debate in our own private organising space around whether we would have the drums. I live around the corner from the ground and I don't like the noise – and these are largely elderly people who live in these houses that front on to it. We really debated that and felt like ten minutes of drums was worth it and hopefully people would understand.'

So if this was to be a revolution it was to be a nice revolution in which protesters cooperate with the police and keep the noise down for the neighbours. In this, it might be the first of its kind.

I asked Kellie whether she thought that being more of a nuisance would have had greater impact.

She said: 'This isn't very radical but we have got very good relations with the police. And the police were extremely supportive. It made me suspect they might have been a wee bit pissed off with the whole rape case and how much their investigating was dragged through the mud.'

Indeed, the police, while declaring their respect for the verdict that the men had not been proven guilty, made clear that they did not believe that the young woman had made a gratuitous complaint. According to a report in the *Irish News* on 28 March, after the verdict Detective Chief Inspector Zoe McKee, senior investigating officer in the case, said that the complainant was 'upset and disappointed' at the verdict. DCS Paula Hilman, meanwhile, said the woman 'had the resolve and confidence to come forward and put her faith in police and the criminal justice process'.

And the protest, while well behaved, did get results.

Jackson and Olding were dropped by the team.

A retired appeal court judge, John Gillen, was appointed to review the ways in which sex offences were handled in court. He would recommend that, with the exception of family members of the accused and accuser, the public be excluded from rape and sexual-crime trials.

The concerns around this trial, however, were wider than those voiced by the Belfast Feminist Network, ROSA NI and the other groups involved in the protests. They included fears that social media would compromise impartial consideration by juries, that anonymity of complainants could not be preserved and that contempt of court was now easy and routine with thousands of people sneering at the judgment.

When Paddy Jackson announced that he would sue those who questioned the verdict, a torrent of slanders trended on Twitter for three days with the hashtag #SueMePaddy.

A year later, Jackson was signed up to play for London Irish by former Ulster Director of Rugby, Les Kiss.

Whose Body Is It Anyway?

I was in Donegal on the day of the referendum count, a beautiful sunny day. Maureen, my wife, and I had driven to the beach at Culdaff for a walk but then she got so immersed in listening to the coverage of the count on the radio that she stayed in the car while I strolled around.

A group of kids in wetsuits gathered on the pier and took turns at jumping into the water. That was another change from the Donegal of my youth – wetsuits. I still swim in the sea without one, almost as a matter of purist principle.

My parents brought the family here every year and the ability to brave the chilly North Atlantic – next stop Iceland – was proof of what we were most proud of: that we were native to this place. But Donegal had now voted against repeal and was the only county of the twenty-six in the Republic to do so.

We called into the pub to see our friend Maria McGuinness. She was still wearing three Yes badges. She had been canvassing in Galway and we joked that she might have done better staying at home and working on her neighbours.

Frankie Callaghan, my old classmate.

Caoimhin de Burca – used to be Kevin Burke.

Deirdre O'Doherty treated the injured on 5 October 1968.

Paul Arthur, reviving interest in the civil-rights movement.

Eamonn McCann, socialist activist.

airin de Burca was on the Sinn Fein committee that tried to shape the civil-rights movement.

Protesters against rape at Belfast City Hall.

Kellie Turtle of the Feminist Network.

*'There are people who really feel
that it is virtually impossible to get
a prosecution for rape where the issue is
a dispute over whether consent
was given or not.'*

Kellie Turtle, Belfast Feminist Network

Claire Bailey leads the Green Party.

Protesters after the Rugby Rape trial.

Protesters calling for reform of rape trial

Breda Highes – her father was a member of the NICRA executive.

Lynda Walker, a communist and campaigner for women's rights.

Grainne Teggart, Amnesty International.

Sara and Jane Ewart – Sara was refused a abortion in Northern Ireland though he foetus had no chance of surviving.

Angela Courtney, one of the early members of Women's Aid.

Bernie Smyth of Precious Life opposes abortion in all circumstances.

A pro-choice campaigner dressed as a Handmaid.

The robot that prescribed abortion pills to protesters in Belfast.

A policeman is cut off and surrounded by protesters and the media.

'I saw it as a war against sexual violence against women. And winning the war was about changing the laws and changing society.'

Eileen Calder, formerly of the Rape Crisis Centre

Pro-life protest at a Sinn Fein rally in Derry.

She was shocked by the result. She had spent weeks on the doorsteps and was convinced, as had been the pollsters, that the margin would be narrow, that they might even lose. 'We were afraid that there were shy No voters who would nod nicely and take your leaflet but go into the polling station and be good catholics there.'

The evidence of the scale of the victory suggested that there had, in fact, been shy Yes voters who had not owned up to their secret support for abortion-law reform, even when talking to a pro-Yes canvasser like herself.

A couple of weeks before this, I had been in Derry where the radical left-wing party People Before Profit was organising canvassers to go into Donegal and I heard some of the stories they told.

One said he had talked to an older man. The man had said he didn't think there was any need to change the law. The canvasser said, 'But what if it was your daughter?' And the man had conceded that he would rather she had an abortion at home than have to bring a child by a rapist into the world or to travel to England to be rid of it.

There were clues to a change in thinking among some of the most instinctively conservative people in the country, of the type that had even voted against legalising divorce in 1986 and given way by a small margin to allow it in 1995.

Ireland had been transformed in the intervening years.

The old argument of unionists against a united Ireland was that it was a country that was effectively run by the Catholic Church.

In the 1980s the Fine Gael taoiseach Garret Fitzgerald had believed that social reform in the Republic would make it easier to improve relations with unionists and get them to contemplate a united Ireland. That logic was now reversed. Unionists of the Democratic Unionist Party (DUP) saw the Republic as excessively liberal – an affront to their evangelical Christianity, which inspired their defence of the unborn child. There's no pleasing some people.

The grandchildren of Eamon de Valera's generation, who would have wanted a united Ireland in which they could participate in a catholic culture, were now arguing that a united Ireland would be secular and liberal and a refuge from the protestant dogmatism that blocked social reform north of the border.

I think my own father would have been giddy at the sight of this change.

The debate over the legalisation of abortion has been complicated by the availability online of two pills used in medical abortions and ruled safe for use at home in some countries during the first twelve weeks of pregnancy. Women can now exercise the choice of a termination with greater ease than before, yet anyone assisting a woman to take these pills is in the same legal position as someone running a back-street-abortion service.

It seemed only common sense that the law should change to allow people to get these drugs through the family doctor or at least to seek medical aftercare without incriminating themselves.

*

Of the feminist groups that organised protests in Belfast after the rugby rape trial, ROSA NI was the smaller but was also much more experienced in challenging the law and staging dramatic protests.

They demonstrated their skills at a pro-choice gathering outside the Belfast courthouse on 31 May 2018. There were hardly any actual protesters there apart from those with roles in the drama, yet the event attracted a counter-protest – always good for publicity – and drew in the police and the media too.

I went down on my bike with a camera and a digital sound recorder.

In the courthouse square about a dozen young women were helping each other into robes modelled on those worn by handmaids in the television remake of Margaret Atwood's *The Handmaid's Tale*.

I asked a policeman where I might chain up my bike and he pointed to a lamp post.

'You won't be causing an obstruction.'

I asked him if he expected to be making arrests today.

He said, 'I hope not.'

The plan was that the handmaids would form a circle, as the handmaids in the drama did, and would be given Mifepristone. This is an abortion pill, the first of two that can be used to end a pregnancy within the first three months. In Northern Ireland, as in the rest of the UK, it is illegal to take these unless under medical prescription and supervision. And since abortion is illegal in Northern Ireland other than when the woman's life is in danger, women who procure this pill on the internet for use at home have been prosecuted.

The organiser Stephen Boyd was explaining to the media that no law was being broken here. The pills were being prescribed legally under European law by a doctor in the Netherlands. The handmaids would each be examined by a robot linked to the Dutch doctor and he would prescribe the pills and the women would take them.

It was brilliant. TV was going to love this. It was so cheeky.

Boyd said, 'We are not breaking the law. It is only illegal to take this pill if you are pregnant and none of these women are pregnant.'

Members of ROSA had gone on the Stephen Nolan radio show that morning to explain the plan for the protest. It was that appearance that prompted the staging of a counter-protest, by the anti-abortion pro-life group Precious Life.

While Boyd was talking to the media, a senior policeman approached and spoke to Rebecca Gomperts, a doctor 'from Holland and Austria' who was there to help organise the protest and to advise the media on the medical aspects of the story. The policeman was very civil but insisted that he had a responsibility to stop the illegal distribution of drugs and asked for the drugs to be handed over. The exchange was polite and Gomperts agreed to his request. The police then took away some packets of Mifepristone and a little white plastic robot, like a child's toy.

The handmaids then lined up along the courthouse railings and chanted their protest slogans.

One, two, three, four! We won't take it anymore!

The woman leading the chants said they had a new slogan and rehearsed it with them, a little clumsily at first.

No more buses, trains or flights! We demand abortion rights!

By now, Bernadette Smyth of Precious Life and a group of supporters, including the DUP MLA Jim Wells had gathered in the square to make their case. The reporters, photographers and camera crews moved back and forth between the two.

Wells had been health minister at the time of a major story in the local media about a woman called Sarah Ewart who had had to travel to England to abort a foetus that had no brain. He had opposed a change to the legal guidelines that might have allowed her to terminate that pregnancy in Belfast under the supervision of her own consultant, holding the hand of her own midwife.

Wells considered that such changes would open the door to full abortion on demand. He had been on radio with Sarah Ewart since the referendum in the Republic and claimed that 6,000 people were alive in Northern Ireland today who would not be alive if abortion had been made legal.

The main speaker for the protesters was Ruth Coppinger, a member of the Irish parliament for Dublin West, representing People Before Profit. She said that the campaign would continue after the referendum for the complete separation of Church and state. She sneered at the declaration by the taoiseach Leo Varadkar that the next stage was to get more women on to boards. As far as she was concerned, that amounted to integrating them into the capitalist system, when the point was to bring that system down.

I asked Stephen Boyd if his plan to have the women prescribed pills through the robot had now been scuppered by the police.

He said, 'No, Malachi. You are not to tell anyone this but we have other pills and another robot.'

However, the police interference did curtail the drama of the protest a little. The handmaids now had to get into a huddle to keep the police out. The media gathered round them to try to get the pictures and the police stood behind the media and tried to film proceedings with a small camcorder. I walked round the outside and got a picture of the robot through the legs of the handmaids, camera crews and police. It looked bewildered, a little white vehicle with its own camera looking up.

I got on to a bollard to try for a better view then gave my place to another photographer and walked round the mass of people focused on the robot.

Then just at my feet the wee robot came out from the circle and I was pushed aside as about six policemen lunged towards it.

'We've got it,' said one of them.

Stephen and his team seemed entirely indifferent to this. They were enjoying themselves even though most of the media had failed to see what had just happened.

Now the handmaids prepared for the next stage of the protest: their march across the road to the bus station to take a bus on a tour of Northern Ireland to stage demonstrations in other towns. As they were lining up a police officer approached one of the women who had taken a pill and led her away.

I was beside her and asked her if she was being arrested, but she didn't speak. She was clearly frightened.

Other protesters quickly followed after them, chanting their slogans. The media was on to this now. There were almost as many photographers and reporters as there were protesters and they were just as much of a nuisance to the police. They walked backwards in front of the policeman and the woman, turning their cameras and microphones on them. Ostensibly they were just watching events and recording them, not obstructing the policeman, but he had to stop.

Other police officers stood watching from a few yards away and several police vehicles had drawn up, but this one cop was surrounded. He was a stocky man who was dressed in the standard dark flameproof uniform of the units that deal with serious security challenges, unlike the police in their white shirts monitoring the Precious Life protesters, though they wore flak jackets too. They wore the standard peaked caps. These were older men, armed but more equipped for routine policing without the security dimension. The cop caught in the middle of the crowd was a trained fighter, the type brought out for counter-terrorism operations and other occasions when policing is likely to get physical. And many others in the same kit were at hand to help him. A couple of them were women.

I have been a reporter at tense and violent protests and I don't like to be the journalist who might make things more difficult for the police, so I stood apart, on one of those handy bollards, and watched. The policeman had a hand up to his ear to help him follow radioed instructions.

He didn't look frightened. None of those close to him, who might easily have reached for his gun, would even have thought of doing so, I'm sure. But they were there to make life awkward for him. They demanded that a lawyer come and stand with the girl before he would be allowed to ask her any questions.

Indeed, most of the protesters and even some of the journalists and photographers were so young that they would not have known a time when a policeman cut off from his colleagues would have had to fight his way back to them.

During the Troubles, had he been in a situation like this, he might have drawn his pistol; the other police officers might have waded into the crowd with batons and shields to retrieve him. The change in the country is so great since then that everyone in that melee felt safe, including the policeman himself.

But he released the girl and the crowd dispersed to line up for the march to the bus station.

The handmaids formed two columns and led the way. The police stopped the traffic on the main road to let them across.

I went back for my bike and as I was leaving saw the policeman who had been surrounded. He was chatting and laughing with two others from the Tactical Support Group. I caught his eye and he said hello.

I said, 'That looked a bit hairy there for a time. I'm sure it wasn't comfortable.'

'Nothing compared to having to stamp out the flames of petrol bombs,' he said.

I said, 'I'll not ask for an opinion, since you wouldn't be allowed to give one.'

He said, 'I honestly don't have one.'

And I wished him well, got on my bike and left.

*

For modern feminists in Northern Ireland abortion is not a serious moral problem. It provides a simple test question of authentic commitment: do you support a woman's right to choose to terminate a pregnancy?

It was not always so clear. Many of the great feminists of the past, like Eileen Calder and Angela Courtney, still have difficulty with it. To be fair to Angela, she would probably say she has no difficulty at all – she simply disagrees with it completely, in all circumstances. She has a vote in the Irish Republic and used it in May 2018 to vote against a reform of the constitution that would enable the legalisation of abortion there for the first time.

The legislation following from it sets far more rigid timelines than the British law provides for. But it also formally makes the decision easier, without the British need for the consent of two doctors.

In Women's Aid, when it was set up, there had been little discussion on the law on abortion because it would have been divisive.

Angela told me, 'There was a couple of girls in one refuge and they were free to go to England themselves. I was on the rota that weekend when I was working in the federation. And I got a phone call. They couldn't get to the airport. I said I would drive them. And I knew why they were going. And there was a sort of giggling about it. And I left them at the airport and I don't know whether they got on the plane or not. That was not my responsibility and I rather suspect they didn't.'

Eileen Calder told me that when a raped woman came to her for help and found that she was pregnant, there was little that she could do under the law in Northern Ireland. So she would call round the other organisations, including Women's Aid, who supported women in crisis and raised money for their fares to London or Liverpool and their treatment in clinics there.

Eileen said that now she has serious doubts about late-term abortion.

'I am a wee bit conservative. I think in the past I pretended to be less conservative than I was. I don't think I could agree to abortion up to twenty-eight weeks; there's very few women who do. I mean, I have seven children and I have had four miscarriages – a careless protestant, I might add, not a good catholic – but my daughter had a baby that was born dead at twenty-one weeks; this was a few years ago. My husband was actually worse than me. He held the wee thing in his hands and cried his eyes out. I'm looking at it from the other side of the bed; he's standing holding it like this [hands together, palms up]. And I was thinking to myself, *You've actually helped a few women have abortions at that stage.*

'The two cases that I am thinking of … one was pregnant to an old man in his seventies. She actually regretted the abortion years later and believed she was forced into it by her mother and her aunt, and we colluded with them in that. We thought we were doing the right thing at the time. We thought it was what she wanted. People out there who don't have experience of it – it's so cut and dried for them. It's not.'

Angela is a catholic and wouldn't even use contraception.

'Safe-period sex, because I was a catholic and Alan found it conducive too. He didn't want to mess with bits of rubber, and I certainly wouldn't want anyone to have a vasectomy.'

She has had three children and one miscarriage. For her, abortion is simply killing a little person who has a right to life.

'I went to see Pope John Paul in Dublin, on the bus in 1979. That was great crack. I dreamed about it afterwards. I had big dreams about Ireland changing, but it didn't include people cheering because they had passed abortion. It wasn't on anybody's agenda and then to see all those women cheering [the referendum result] … God save us. That's about as angry as I get these days.'

Younger feminists like Kellie Turtle and Grainne Teggart don't feel conflicted about abortion.

Grainne works with Amnesty International to campaign for the legalisation of abortion in Northern Ireland. She told me, 'There was never a time when I agonised over the big issues like abortion. I have always grown up in a family that was liberal. For me it was always about a rights-based society and that is what I was passionate about from a young age.'

She was appalled by the response of the nuns at her school to a girl getting pregnant.

'I have a little religion. I went to catholic schools. In my catholic secondary school was probably the first time I thought about the issue of abortion because a girl in my GCSE history class was pulled into the nun's office and told to buy a bigger jumper and not to talk about her pregnancy in school. I remember thinking at that time that that was a really wrong response to something like this. This was someone who was going to have a hard road ahead of her and this was just not what she needed, and that made me think about the catholic ethos of the school, and I had more conversations with my mum.'

Her mum steered her towards a more liberal and compassionate approach than the nuns had been capable of, though their crassness on that occasion was a gentler answer to the problem of a teenage pregnancy than might have been offered previously. In the past, girls who got pregnant were incarcerated and used as slave labour in Magdalene Laundries.

Grainne turned away from formal religion but described herself to me as 'spiritual' in that she does not believe that death is the end of our existence, though she has no idea what comes after. And she argued that the churches cling to old mores for the sake of exercising power, but that if they eased up on people more would return to them.

She married a protestant and had both a priest and a presbyterian clergyman officiate at her wedding, and she has become an ardent campaigner for integrated education. Now she has relations in both communities and both churches. She also had relations killed during the Troubles, one by the IRA and one by the British army.

She campaigns on issues that leave other feminists behind, like the legalisation of prostitution and the scrapping of a law in Northern Ireland that makes the purchase of sexual services a criminal offence.

'What we said is, this issue is complex but when we listen to sex workers, what they are saying is that criminalising the purchase of sex poses dangers to them. It drives it underground. It damages relations that they might have with the police. And the police have said: "We're not going to have time to police consensual paid sex; we are too busy going after the traffickers and where the sex isn't consensual." So that was, for me, much more like a moral crusade.

'But I also think some feminists were on the wrong side of this argument. Belfast Feminist Network gave us support on that position but few others did and there were a lot of organisations who were on the wrong side of that debate as well, in my opinion.'

One of those feminists on the 'wrong side' of the argument is Eileen Calder, the champion of countless raped women.

Eileen told me, 'Now we have people who claim to be feminists saying that women like me who say that prostitution should not be fully legalised are excluding sex workers from society. It is utter and complete nonsense and it makes me angry.

'We are not going to get rid of prostitution but we don't legalise housebreaking just because we are not going to stop it. Some say there are top-class hookers doing well and happy with their lives. My response to that would be that there were house slaves – domestics – who on the face of it were happier and freer than really poor white people. Did that make it OK? No, it didn't make it OK.'

Currently abortion in Northern Ireland is medically available only when the woman's life is in danger; and doctors have seen recent tightening of their guidelines that makes them much more cautious exercising what little discretion they have.

The most shocking example of this was the case of Sarah Ewart, the woman who was refused a termination despite the foetus she carried not having a brain and having no prospect of surviving after birth.

Sarah had been told by a sonographer in a private clinic that there was a problem but that she would have to see her consultant. She would have to go home knowing that something was wrong with her pregnancy but not knowing what. This was the beginning of weeks of appalling stress.

She went through more tests at the Ulster Hospital and was told that the foetus in this condition would normally survive to the thirty-second week of pregnancy but that if it went to full term it might be an organ donor.

She was told that she would not go through normal labour but would have to be induced. And she was refused an abortion on the grounds that her life was not in danger.

I met her at her mother's home, in an impeccable living room with a large photograph of her wedding on the wall over the sofa.

She said, 'We left the hospital and came home and got out the Yellow Pages, didn't really know what we were looking for but found Family Planning. We phoned them and made an appointment.'

But in Belfast, if you go to Family Planning or to the Marie Curie clinic for advice on abortion, your path may be barred by ardent christians.

'On the way in, we met the protesters. I had a noticeable bump at this stage because I was halfway through the pregnancy. They tried to offer us leaflets. I said, "No thank you."

'In Family Planning you walk through one glass door that is open to another glass door that is locked. There is a buzzer system on the wall and you press which floor you are going to. The ones standing outside were watching to see where we were going.

'So we went up and spoke to Family Planning. And in the end, they don't make any arrangements for you but they will sit in and prompt you with questions you need to ask when you book on the phone. I explained why I wanted to have a termination and she gave me the number to call.'

Even this stage was complicated – because the person taking the call at a clinic in Liverpool was assuring Sarah that she could have a termination there at twenty-one weeks, while the staff at the FPA knew this wasn't true. Yet the staff could not intervene without legal risk and simply urged Sarah to ask the question again and again until it was clarified for her that she would have to go to London.

'On the way out of FPA we met the protesters again. This time they knew where we had been. I was being called a murderer. They said I didn't know what I was doing. I was going to regret this for the rest of my life. They were shoving these horrible pictures in my face. The protesters were coming at us. I was walking back on to the traffic warden's feet, who was standing in shock at all this shouting. I was so embarrassed and upset. Everybody around us was watching what was going on and this woman had got to the car and was still shouting at me through the car door. We couldn't close the car door. My granny and granda were picking us up and it was really awful for them too.'

Sarah's mother e-mailed all of the Northern Ireland MLAs to make the case that the law in Northern Ireland should provide for a woman with Sarah's problem. The PA for Nigel Dodds MP wrote back to give her the phone number for Edwin Poots, who was health minister at that time and had previously tightened the guidelines for doctors. Naomi Long of the Alliance Party wrote to say that Sarah should go back to her consultant to see if some help might still be possible within the terms of the guidelines.

Grainne Teggart explained: 'After guidelines went out for consultation, a lot of medical professionals pushed back and said no. The whole document was just reinforcing the threat of prosecution and said nothing about the care of women. Even though that guidance didn't become policy it was enough for everyone to back off.'

But Sarah went back to the hospital to plead again with a consultant for a termination.

'Mum showed her the letter [from Naomi Long] and asked, "Can my daughter have the procedure here?" At that point she spun round on the chair, banged my folder on the desk and said, "I am not going to prison for anybody." And Mum said, "I am not asking you to go to prison but I am asking you for some help." She said, "I am sorry; I am not willing to do that."'

The trip to the London clinic was embarrassing. Sarah was the only client there who was conspicuously pregnant and even some of the staff were unsettled by that. The waiting area was crowded and some of the women there had a more relaxed attitude to abortion than Sarah had ever encountered at home in Northern Ireland.

'We were breaking our hearts that we were there losing a baby that we very much wanted and yet the people in front of us were laughing and tee-heeing, trying to work out when they had last had sex, to work out how far along they were. It was just a horrendous situation to be in.'

The Northern Irish media was now interested in her story and she met with broadcaster Stephen Nolan to give him a full interview about her experience. This raised sympathy for her and fired up a media debate on the abortion law. It also meant that when Sarah returned to her consultant she was recognised by other patients.

'People were getting out of their cars to come and say, "We're behind you; keep going." That was nice.

'The night I came home from having the procedure there was a bit of a war on Facebook. Precious Life had tagged me on a blow-by-blow account of how an abortion is carried out. And then my friends were jumping in defending what I had done. It was just horrible, something I didn't need to see at that time. So hearing that support at the hospital was really good.'

But the law had not changed and other pregnant women with no hope of delivering a living baby were still travelling to London for terminations.

The then justice minister and Alliance Party leader David Ford opened up consultation on whether abortion might be legalised in limited circumstances, for women who were pregnant as a consequence of rape and in the case of 'fatal foetal abnormalities'.

Eileen Calder spoke to me in scathing terms about the proposed rape clause.

'What they are talking about is having restrictive abortion laws that may allow women who have been raped to have an abortion. Women have been accused of lying about rape for centuries and if you legalise abortion because of rape, what you are actually doing is encouraging women to lie and there will be young vulnerable women who will say they have been raped when they haven't. I think that it would be a terrible mistake. And you know it takes three years to get a rape trial to court so how will they prove it in time?'

But the Northern Ireland Assembly voted down any change in the law.

In February 2016, following David Ford's consultation, the Assembly debated on whether to include a provision in the Justice Bill that would at least legalise abortion in cases of fatal foetal abnormality. This was defeated by fifty-nine votes to forty. The Executive had agreed to initiate a fuller consultation on the question and had asked members to wait. Some may have voted against the change in the hope of coming back after an election and changing the law at a time less likely to jeopardise their re-election prospects.

One female member of the SDLP, Dolores Kelly, even argued that her party had received medical advice that there was no such condition as 'fatal foetal abnormality'.

Before the Assembly could get to debate this again, it collapsed. Negotiations to restore it were deadlocked over what some people saw as a more pressing civil right, an Irish Language Act.

Fighting for Life

Fifty years and one day after the civil-rights march in Derry that inflamed passions and, essentially, started the Troubles, another gathering of civil-rights campaigners assembled in Duke Street. This demonstration was organised by Sinn Féin, claiming the legacy of the original protest movement, which had demanded an end to discrimination in housing, a reform of the local-government franchise and, after the violent policing of parades, reform of the RUC.

Sinn Féin had participated in that movement. Indeed, Máirín de Burca told me she believes they initiated and directed it.

The Sinn Féin of today is a breakaway movement from the Sinn Féin of then. Its claim to represent the legacy of the civil-rights movements is mocked as deceitful by Eamonn McCann and others but a thread of a connection is there, through the republicans who broke away in 1970 to form the Provisional IRA and Provisional Sinn Féin. But these were the militarists and old guard, who had resented the strategy of supporting a civil-rights movement as a distraction from the key goal of uniting Ireland as a nation independent from Britain.

And the issues now were different.

Hundreds of people stood in the car park in front of the railway station, chatting to each other and waiting for instructions to line up and move off. It was a beautiful sunny day and there were other events in Derry to mark the anniversary of the march that had been attacked by the police. Irish president Michael D. Higgins would deliver a lecture in the Guildhall. I would sit on a panel in a discussion hosted by the SDLP in the Bogside to discuss how Brexit was being turned back on us as a sectarian issue, the way civil rights had – I'll get to that point later.

And there were readings in the Playhouse that night, More Female Lines: Reflections on '68. The event was led by Anne Devlin. Her father, Paddy Devlin, had been a founder member of the SDLP and Anne had been beaten by loyalist thugs at Burntollet. My wife, Maureen, took part.

So the riot of fifty years earlier was now cause for a carnival – and Sinn Féin was determined to be a big part of it.

Outside the station, I stood at the edge of the line-up and talked to people. I had a chat with Mitchel McLaughlin, a leading party member and former MLA, now an academic at Queen's University on a fellowship. I asked him if he thought power sharing would ever come back.

'Ach,' he said. 'It's not really power if you have to share it.'

Around us stood dozens of protesters against the party's changed policy on abortion. These were mostly women and some men in their fifties or older, holding up pink placards

with photographs of a foetus, and they harangued the Sinn
Féin stewards, who were placidly trying to ignore them.

Then the campaign bus arrived with the Sinn Féin presidential
candidate Liadh Ní Riada and the party president Mary Lou
McDonald, giant colour photographs of whom were printed
on the sides and back. Now the procession could move off,
with the prominent women of the party at the front.

The parade set out with banners demanding justice for
victims of the McGurk's Bar bombing of 1971, an Irish Language
Act, condemning Brexit, calling for the legalisation of same-
sex marriage. The main banner proclaimed that the struggle
continues for equality and freedom, being about as unspecific
as it could be.

The stewards had not been able to get rid of the anti-
abortion campaigners so they kept them at the back. After
the abortion-reform referendum in the Republic, Sinn Féin
party leaders had joined the celebrations and held up an
improvised card saying 'The North is Next'. This had alerted
Precious Life to the need to turn its ire on the republicans.
Since the rights being demanded here were loosely defined
and no one was marching to actually demand change in the
law on abortion, they felt entitled to present themselves as
civil-rights campaigners too.

Their placards read: 'Civil Rights Begin in the Womb'.

At the start, they had formed a counter-protest in the tradition
of the original struggle, when parades were challenged by Ian
Paisley and his followers and often banned or rerouted as a
consequence. This time, though, the protesters were ready to
join the parade itself.

The parade had an almost festive atmosphere. Other groups organising protests would benefit from watching how Sinn Féin does it.

Stewards walked ahead and passed directions back to the women at the front. They and the leaders laughed and joked with each other, familiarly, having done this so often before. When the stewards needed to direct the parade into the left lane of Duke Street to enable a right turn on to the upper deck of the bridge, one of them, noticing the clumsiness of the manoeuvre, joshed the party president, 'Use your indicator.'

As the parade filled the bridge and photographers climbed on a monument for a high shot, the lead steward ordered all the other stewards off the road so that they wouldn't disrupt the line of sight.

But no one could do anything about the anti-abortion protesters who had tagged themselves on to the parade with similar tactical brilliance and pure gall.

The parade marched up Carlisle Road to the Diamond and the war memorial that fifty years earlier loyalists had feared would be tainted by the proximity of civil-rights campaigners. The march turned down Shipquay Street. At the bottom of the hill a platform had been arranged on a flat-back lorry.

I got a place close to the lorry.

When Mary Lou McDonald looked out from the platform, she saw the whole crowd raised up in front of her on the hill like the audience in a theatre. She saw the Sinn Féin banners and the other marks of several protests. But she also saw at the very back and towering over everything, the dozens of pink placards held up in support of Precious Life. These surely reminded her that abortion-law reform will be contested and will cost her party votes. And that she will have to survive censure from the leader of the Precious Life movement, Bernadette Smyth.

Smyth is a strident and caustic speaker. She organised the pickets at the Brook Clinic and the Family Planning Association, intercepting women seeking advice and urging them not to abort – and, on occasion, abusing and taunting them regardless of their reasons for being there. I went to visit Mrs Smyth in the office of a company that she is connected with near Shaftesbury Square in Belfast. I was expecting her to be civil and amenable, since I had spoken to her at a street protest and she had been happy to record a brief interview with me. She is, in fact, glamorous and genial when she is not shrieking about the slaughter of innocent babies and accusing pregnant women of plotting murder. She is a gifted professional campaigner and knows the value of being accessible to journalists, who can often be expected not to agree with her.

I had appeared on radio programmes and written articles arguing for a woman's right to choose. I had made the case that the availability of abortion pills online effectively grants choice to women, enables them to make their own decision and act on it without the law even knowing. I had said that the law needs to change now to allow women who use those pills to consult their own doctors for follow-up care without fear of prosecution.

So she knew that I was unlikely to be persuaded by her argument that abortion is murder at any time after conception.

She was fifty-six years old when we met and had been campaigning for twenty years.

There is a way of reading her commitment as arising from her early life experience. Her mother had conceived a child by an American GI when her husband, a prisoner of war in Japan, was presumed dead. The GI went home and her husband came back and accepted the child as his own.

The parents were both deeply religious. The family said the rosary together every night and in the mornings her mother said a prayer in honour of St Joseph, another working man who had fathered a child not of his own loins.

They grew up in a protestant town, Ballymena, where her father worked for the army and would have known that he was regarded by the IRA as a legitimate target. He might reasonably have expected to be shot or kidnapped and used as a human bomb, as others had who worked for the army.

Bernie left school at sixteen. In her teenage years she partied and drank and went to discos and met boys but she still then regarded it as a 'mortal sin' to have sex while not married.

'I had two friends who as teenagers had abortions and I always remembered the state that they were in. I always remember one girl telling me one week that she was pregnant and then, the following week, it was like the light went out of her eyes. So when we socialised, she always drank too much; and she cried more and you were always embracing her and comforting her. It always came out when she was drunk and then she put this face on every day.'

Bernie was shaken out of her religious faith after her mother died of cancer when Bernie was nineteen.

She married a protestant man. In her married life she used contraception for a time but now regrets not having the children she might have had then. She has four. She returned to Catholicism but told me that she stopped using contraception for practical reasons – because the pill is unhealthy, not because of Church rules against it. 'The Church says nothing about it,' she said. Which is generally true, although officially artificial contraception has been banned to catholics since 1968.

'I know many of my friends use natural family planning and can space their children out well and it's good for them, it's good for their marriage. I don't believe women should be sex objects in marriage; I believe that there are spaces in natural family planning that are good for everybody. I would have liked to have been told that.'

One of her daughters got pregnant at the age of nineteen.

'So – what do you do about that? You say, "Welcome to the family, little one."'

But by her values, her daughter had committed a mortal sin.

'And what? What do you want me to do about it? What difference would it make to scold her when the child is already there? What would that achieve? I'm not God; I am a mother.'

She added, 'Abortion was not even going to be considered because that is the most important thing for me, to protect life. She is married to the guy now.'

Pride

Du Barry's in Belfast was the bar best known for prostitution in the 1960s. It was in the lower end of High Street, in Princes Street, near the Albert Clock and closer to the river than respectable people would venture back then. This was where sailors coming off the boats would go to spend their money on drink and sex. I was only ever in the bar once, with friends when we went for a dare, and a woman in charge took control of us immediately we were in the door, ordered us to sit down and behave. I have never been received like that in a pub before or since and I have no idea what she feared we might do.

She seemed to be saying, 'This is a respectable bar and don't you forget it.'

Today Du Barry's is part of McHugh's, a classy restaurant. There you can savour dishes unheard of in Belfast in the 1960s, like pale Belfast smoked haddock and poached egg with Granny Smith vinaigrette. Back then we were content with ordinary fish and chips, for we still didn't even have our first Chinese restaurant.

The river, at that point, now has a footbridge. There is a ceramic sculpture, *The Big Fish* by John Kindness, that tourists like to pose beside and this is where, on a Saturday afternoon in August, tens of thousands of people gather for the annual Pride parade.

It used to be called Gay Pride. The change has come with the extension of the label LG to LGBT to LGBTQI or LGBTQI+.

Everybody was there – well, nearly everybody; not just those who could locate themselves in that growing string of labels. In fact, most of the people there would probably identify as heterosexual and cis, bearing contentedly the gender designation implied by their genitalia, while acknowledging the right of others not to.

The police were stewarding the parade lightly and had officers actually marching. Trade unions were there, including Unison and the Irish National Teachers Organisation. Ulster Television had more people marching under their banner than actually reporting the event. I spotted Frank Mitchell and Barbara McCann; the weatherman and one of the reporters and several other personalities from the station. Action for Mental Health, the Ambulance Service, American computer companies and political parties were all gay for a day.

Pride is a huge event in Belfast and, clearly, you don't have to be gay or queer to participate; you just have to be proud that the city has LGBTQI+XYZ people in it.

The Sinn Féin banner was held up by party front-runners Michelle O'Neill, the vice president, and Alex Maskey, a former boxer who was shot by loyalists who understood him to be prominent in the IRA. The police were once so concerned about Mr Maskey that they stopped my car and questioned me after I had waved a greeting to him, which seemed to be only the civil thing to do since I had interviewed him a few days earlier.

Michelle had the rainbow colours painted on her cheeks. Alex hadn't. That wouldn't be his style. Even Gerry Kelly, the former bomber of London, had the rainbow on his cheeks. But not Alex.

They were chanting: 'What do we want? Same-sex marriage. When do we want it? Now!'

So, for them, Pride was a protest march that was well suited to their political project, for at that stage Sinn Féin was boycotting the Northern Ireland Executive and thereby making it impossible for the Assembly to meet. In fact at that stage it had not met in eighteen months.

The core Sinn Féin demand was for a stand-alone Irish Language Act.

If it had waived that demand, it could have entered Stormont and held a vote on same-sex marriage. There was little demand that they should do so, though, since few people really believed that these parties wouldn't soon find something else to fall out over.

The last vote on same-sex marriage was carried by a majority but vetoed by the DUP through a device called a Petition of Concern, which allowed either the nationalist or unionist blocs to bar any legislation that they considered would disproportionately affect them.

The DUP was not challenged to explain how same-sex marriage disadvantaged unionists more than nationalists, protestants more than catholics. It was the only political party that was not marching with Pride.

The only banner in the Orange style, held on a frame, with trimmings and catching the breeze, belonged to the Fire Brigades Union.

The Alliance Party was accompanied by Gerry Lynch, a gay man with a big grey beard who was now at Oxford preparing to take holy orders in the Church of England.

Even the Northern Ireland Civil Service was out, and it was, in effect, the government while Stormont wasn't sitting and while the Westminster government was declining to legislate in its place.

But one of the banner carriers, the head of the civil service, the de facto proconsul of Northern Ireland, would later have to issue a statement to the press insisting that his presence at Pride did not imply support for same-sex marriage, an issue on which he had to be neutral until the Assembly decided on it.

So, while for Sinn Féin and others Pride was protest, for still others it was not.

Alliance for Choice had a banner pledging support for LGBT rights while urging abortion-law reform. The Belfast Feminist Network marched with their banner too. The Dog's Trust was there, with members in yellow sweatshirts that read 'LGBT – Labrador, Greyhound, Beagle, Terrier'.

Pride has become a general-purpose march that others can bring their issues to.

But where do you go if you are gay and anti-abortion, or a supporter of Sinn Féin and the demand for an Irish Language Act but opposed to same-sex marriage?

When the parade reached the City Hall it was met by two other protests. One of these was for the right to fly the Union Flag in public buildings throughout the year. This practice had been routine until Belfast City Council voted to follow the regimen adhered to in England, whereby the flag is flown only on eighteen designated days.

The other protest was an evangelical-christian challenge to Pride. This one was small and confined behind a barrier. A protester had a little girl on his shoulders – a common sight through the Pride parade too. One placard read: 'But as the days of Noah were, so also shall the coming of the Son of Man be.'

An elderly grey-haired man with a microphone poured out a tirade of abuse about the evil sin of homosexuality and the unlikelihood of many on the parade being saved from the fires of Hell.

A younger man in a white shirt wore a red baseball cap with the slogan 'Make America Great Again'. He had badges pinned on it representing the flags of England, Scotland, Northern Ireland and the UK and one that read 'I Love Jesus', with a red heart symbol filling in for the 'o' in 'love'.

Some of those on the Pride parade seemed amused and went forward to engage the christians in conversation.

The Robinson and Cleaver building, which in the 1960s was the classiest department store in Belfast, now houses a cafe behind the old balustraded balcony. From there, diners watched the parade and the protests from under sun umbrellas.

It was a wonderful day; a day to be gay.

*

I hadn't noticed back in 1968, when I was a waiter in the Star and Garter, that a slow-burning revolution was under way among the 'queers'. That was the disparaging term for gay men then. I thought some of the gay men I encountered were quaint and a bit creepy. There was one little fat man who would sit in this rough public bar, with its black-and-white tiled floor that was impervious to spills and spitting, and order a Bristol Milk; this among working men who had come in to watch the racing and who drank pints of Guinness and Bass.

Jim behind the bar would raise his eyes to Heaven, appalled.

The man would dip his cigar in the sherry. Or sometimes a Drambuie.

I saw that the gays lived with an indulgence among others that tipped over into contempt sometimes, or bemusement; that they lived and moved among people who stood away from them, commented on them with – usually – mild derision.

I never saw anyone express hatred for them. Perhaps there was even a degree of affection, at least a bemused acknowledgement that they were interesting and harmless.

The more popular bar among gay people was the Royal Avenue, across the street, a part of the hotel of the same name. Jeff Dudgeon had found out about it through a coy newspaper advertisement. As a young homosexual with no links to any gay community, he was already campaigning for gay rights.

He had written to Roy Bradford, a minister in the Stormont parliament, urging him to work for the legalisation of homosexuality, following the decriminalisation in England and Wales of sexual activity in private between consenting adult men aged twenty-one and over. Bradford had written back to say that there was no hope of such a change in the law in Northern Ireland but urging Jeff to join the Unionist Party, which he has since done.

Bradford clearly didn't think that Jeff was an unsuitable member of his party by virtue of his sexuality but neither did he think that a majority in the party would regard him as anything other than a criminal.

One day, Jeff saw an ad for a book offering guidance on 'the male world'. He sent off his £2 and received a cyclostyled document recommending, among other meeting places, the bar at the Royal Avenue Hotel.

'I went to the Royal Avenue with a copy of the *Belfast Telegraph* and ten cigarettes, which was a bit of a mistake because that started me smoking. It was a little invisible public bar. You wouldn't know it was connected to the hotel except by the name. Plastic yellow seats, bright lights…

'Pubs closed at ten then. The first seats at the front of the bar were very quiet because the deaf and dumb people gathered there, so it was all swishing hands and silence. And then the back end was the gays, which was like nineteen men and one lesbian – on a good night.'

Jeff was twenty-one at the time and had known that he was gay for five years and yet had had no contact with other gay men in that time.

'My guides were novels – James Baldwin *Giovanni's Room*; particularly that one I think – because there was very little published that could help, and there was no internet and no cataloguing. It was just chance.'

Occasionally he risked declaring an interest in another boy.

'I had a couple of passing episodes at school, one of which was a bit dicey, but I knew what I was. I could detect if something untoward was going to happen to me. I think there was only a couple of times I was interfered with along the way, but I escaped rapidly.'

I had a small insight of my own into the miserable prospects gay men had in Belfast in those days. Often when I'd leave Jo at the Smithfield bus station I would go to the small public convenience on the street, and I was occasionally propositioned there. A man I once spurned when he followed me into the cubicle wasn't bothersome, just disappointed.

Some nights I would hitchhike up the Lisburn Road and grew to rely on older men who drove slowly, looking for company, to get me home. Sometimes they would give me a little pat on the knee when I got out.

The Royal Avenue and the Star and Garter were not gay bars, as such. The gay men who frequented them could not show affection for each other there.

Jeff told me that the Royal Avenue was staffed by two men who had formerly been in the armed services and 'stood for no nonsense'. So if gay men gathered in places in which they would be supervised with suspicion, they can't have had any refuge in which they could fully relax.

Seán McGouran when I met him painted a similarly bleak picture of life for a young gay man in Belfast at that time. He was a member of the IRA and of NICRA. He was later a founder member of the Northern Ireland Gay Rights Association

(NIGRA) and a friend and ally of Jeff Dudgeon's despite their differing politics.

He discovered the various 'cottages' around Belfast, most of them public toilets, and now remembers those days with a wry humour.

'You weren't going to bring people home. Bringing strange people, sometimes very strange people, into your bedsitter could be noticed and you might be chucked out. Nowadays people are happy to have gays in their bedsitters because they keep the place tidy.'

Like Jeff, he went to England in the early seventies and even participated in the first Gay Pride parade in London, then served a prison sentence for his militant republican activity. He returned to Belfast in 1979 to find that gays were more confident now. A lot of that was down to Jeff Dudgeon.

I told Jeff that I still wince at the sound of the word 'queer', a response informed perhaps by recollections of having used it disparagingly myself in the years before homosexuality was respected. It has now been reclaimed from those who used it as a term of abuse and in the inclusive spectrum of identity politics does not simply mean 'gay'.

Jeff told me: 'The word "fruit" annoyed me more. I didn't get it at school but I heard it. There was always something very pejorative about the way it was said. "Queer" was more of a slightly descriptive term. "Fruit" was aggressive.'

Jeff did not march with Pride this year, though some senior members of the Ulster Unionist Party did.

But he has a right to be proud of his own contribution to bringing radical change.

In Northern Ireland, as in Scotland, the change in the law that would spare gay men the threat of going to jail came later than it did in England and Wales. Jeff did not stay in Northern Ireland through the year of tumult around civil-rights agitation to point out that if people wanted British rights, these should include the rights to abortion and same-sex relationships. His decision to leave was partly triggered by a major prosecution of homosexuals in Bangor, County Down, which gave him a sense of the danger he was in: not just that he might be imprisoned but also that he could be sectioned and confined to a mental hospital.

'Two of the guys [who were prosecuted], Ernie and Jim, I knew from the Royal Avenue Bar. They used to have parties in Belfast, which I would have once or twice attended.'

But Ernie and Jim survived arrest and incarceration with their spirits intact. When they came out of jail they opened Belfast's first proper gay bar, the Chariot Rooms.

Then, in the mid-1970s, Jeff, back in Belfast, was arrested along with other gay men.

According to Jeff: 'It had all started from a complaint from a mother who had read love letters from her son's laundry. She then went to a local police officer she knew and it grew out of that. It started off as a drugs raid. The warrant was a drugs warrant but the purpose was both.'

However, the climate had already changed sufficiently to ensure that the men would not go to jail.

'They arrested twenty-odd people. They saw a conspiracy, which was in many ways accurate because we were campaigning for a law change.'

He sensed that the police who interviewed them had little experience in stitching up gay men, this being a time at which they had the more pressing concerns of routine bombings and killings.

'The guys who were interviewing me were learning on the job. They didn't know very much. Nobody was brought to court but half a dozen of us were down for prosecution until London stepped in and said no.'

The Stormont parliament had already been stood down by Westminster, in 1972, and the government there was not about to accept the embarrassment in the national media that would arise from enforcing laws in Belfast that were regarded as arcane in London.

So Jeff was spared a likely eighteen-month sentence, going by the Bangor precedent, but potentially worse too.

'In any other era we would have been committing suicide and hiding and all the rest.'

At the time of the arrests, he was already working on bringing a case to the European Commission of Human Rights to have the law against homosexuality in Northern Ireland quashed. The idea had come from Kevin Boyle, a lawyer who had had a leadership role in People's Democracy.

'I think I just bumped into him in the street and he had been involved in other cases at Strasbourg already on torture and suchlike. I don't know how he knew I was gay, because I don't think I had ever spoken to him about it. I wasn't out in those days. And then he suggested it could be done and it could be done easily.'

So Jeff, as a founder member of NIGRA , set out to raise the money to bring the case. They needed £3,000 and ran discos

at Queen's University. These were successful because there
was virtually no other social life in Belfast for young people
at a time when the city centre was gated off at night to guard
it against bombers and armed gangs on the prowl.

Seán McGouran sent donations from prison and more
regularly when he came back to Northern Ireland and worked
for a time as a binman.

But huge opposition rallied in Northern Ireland against the
decriminalisation of homosexual acts. The most prominent
campaign was led by the DUP, which raised a petition of 70,000
signatures. Rev. Ian Paisley was back on the street urging his
followers to 'Save Ulster from Sodomy'. The Catholic Church
also opposed reform and no political party had the imagination
or courage to align itself with the campaign.

There was qualified support from the General Synod of
the Church of Ireland, which argued that homosexuality,
though morally wrong, should not be something for the law
to deal with. And the general mood at the time saw this as a
distraction from the real business of the Troubles and the
constitutional question.

In the European Court, Jeff was able to cite his own arrest
and the confiscation by the police of his diary to illustrate
the urgency of a change in the law. The British government
argued for retaining the law on the grounds that Northern
Ireland was more conservative and religious and had stricter
laws governing heterosexual conduct too. The court was not
impressed and took the view that the norm in European
countries was that homosexual relationships should not be
regarded as criminal. This was in 1978.

The campaign against legalisation continued but in 1982 the Homosexual Offences Act was passed and allowed homosexual relations between consenting men over the age of twenty-one.

Up to this time, Seán McGouran and others in NIGRA had been travelling every year to London to join the Pride parade. Then someone suggested they should have their own parade in Belfast. According to Seán, one of the disincentives for going to London was that they took abuse there from 'English lefties' for not supporting the Provisional IRA. Seán's own war was long over. He had stayed with the Official IRA after the split that had produced the Provisionals.

Seán organised a parade with P. A. MagLochlainn, an ebullient member of the SDLP and a campaigner for gay rights. P. A. had been a catholic school teacher in Dungiven in County Derry, at the foot of the Sperrins, and for a mountain man had the unlikely hobby of sailing.

Some years earlier, his yacht had been overturned off the coast of Cork and he had spent twelve hours in the water before being rescued. In those twelve hours he had realised the value of his life and resolved to come out as gay, give up teaching and move to Belfast, where he could live more openly the life he wanted.

He and Seán planned a parade route of almost two miles, from Donegall Street to Botanic Gardens.

Seán told me: 'People keep saying what a small number it was but I was on the first Gay Pride parade in London in 1971 and there was less than a thousand people at it and when you consider that the catchment area was the whole of England and Wales that's not a good number. We had one hundred and seventeen. I counted them. In fact, I may not have counted myself. There may have been one hundred and eighteen there.'

He said it was an 'awful long walk'. So long that most of them got on to the bus that accompanied them for the journey back, leaving Seán to carry the banner.

This being the first gay parade through Belfast, it attracted some attention.

'There were some kids standing at the bottom of Castle Street who knew they ought to be doing something about us. The kids suddenly realised that there was one hundred and seventeen people, and having a ruck with people who outnumber you ten to one isn't the way things are done in rowdy land. So it went off quite peacefully.'

Seán said that from the beginning the Pride parade was meant to be a protest.

'We were telling people, "Look, this is a celebration but don't forget it is a civil-rights march. You can do the two things at the same time. You can demand things with a smile on your face." That was in the handout we gave people.'

The growing tip of LGBT activism now is the concern for the rights of the transgendered. But this divides the gay community. For his part Seán McGouran is happy to see transgendered people at Pride; he told me that the issues may be different but it makes no sense to turn away people who inflate your numbers.

'Very few women want to become men. Who could blame them? It's mostly stacked towards men who want to become women. And the other thing is of course, you are not going to become a woman. You are not going to acquire a womb.'

That is a radical opinion now and those who air it on social media can expect to be attacked.

Nora Calder, a lesbian and daughter of Eileen Calder, campaigns on Twitter against the acceptance of men as women. And she gets a lot of abuse for the position she takes as a trans-exclusionary radical feminist, or TERF. Her argument is founded partly on a consciousness of 'male violence'. Men rape women; women don't rape men. So, for example, letting a man into a woman's prison on the grounds that he identifies as female is just putting women in danger.

One challenge to her on Twitter says:

> If you don't get why people feel and behave the way they do about a thing that's not in your experience it's not part of your journey. Stay in your lane.
> It's like a man commenting on period cramps or tampons vs pads.

The case she made in response is:

> A male bodied person entering a female changing room, prison, hospital ward, shortlist, all female awards, sports, shelters, safe spaces – absolutely impacts me.
> Male violence is real, perhaps you ought to read up on that and you'd understand the risks.

But she endures a huge barrage of abuse for taking that position.

There were several drag queens marching with Belfast Pride in 2018. They were the most colourful participants. One of them was Electra La Cnt, or, when he is not in character,

Deaglan Agnew. He had walked in an earlier Pride parade wearing a tiara that had been dipped in HIV-positive blood. In 2018 he wore a gown with images on it of the 1968 Stonewall campaigners.

Deaglan accepts the pronoun 'he' as applied to himself but routinely uses 'they' as a singular pronoun to avoid being precise about the gender of another. He is a big man with no eyebrows – when I met him – charming and camp.

He comes from a west-Belfast republican family but told me that he was a unionist himself before Brexit.

'My standard is if you are a nice person you could laugh me into bed. That's about it. I don't really care how you present. I was a gay man but now I am just queer.'

And he is a little suspicious of the merely gay, fearing that when they succeed in their campaign for same-sex marriage they will lose interest in street protest and leave the trans people and queers without support.

Deaglan went to St Mary's Grammar School. My old classmate Caoimhín de Búrca was his Irish teacher and Deaglan spoke well of him, though he said the school failed to notice or care that he was being bullied.

St Mary's is a Christian Brothers school; Caoimhín had left the order but worked there as a lay teacher and was eventually made principal when the order had almost died out.

Deaglan said, 'He was a great guy. I took my Irish GCSE in a year so we had a GCSE class for a year where there was nothing to do. So they gave Caoimhín de Búrca to us and he would come in and throw Irish questions at us. That is how I remember him. He was always very supportive.'

I asked him if the school supported him as a boy who was gay.

'No, no nothing like that.'

But, in his final year, he and another boy won a schools debating competition at Stormont; yet when they went into school the next day, the successes of the Gaelic Athletic Association teams were announced but no mention was made of the debate. Deaglan and his friend complained to Mr de Búrca, who was by this time the school principal, and he made sure that the debate was included in the announcements after that.

'Because for us, sitting there as two gay guys who were using their voices and using that sort of thing that we had been bullied for, our intelligence and our ability to form sentences and argue and debate and have fun about it, and be eloquent and not be afraid of eloquence as a young boy, he was supportive of that.'

Deaglan caused a political row at Stormont ten years later, a week before the 2018 Belfast Pride. He had been invited to speak at an event called Alternative Queer Ulster. This had been organised by the Green Party and access to the Stormont building had been approved by Paula Bradley of the DUP. She, however, felt that her willingness to help had been thrown back in her face when Deaglan as Electra la Cnt finished his speech with 'Up the fucking queers!'

It was a rousing speech, arguing that queers are past asking for acceptance from society.

He told me, 'My argument is: don't engage with the people who are unwilling to listen. You need to stop doing that because it gets us nowhere. If you are unwilling to educate yourself about the modern world, then I am on a train that is heading too fast for you. If we ask for acceptance we dilute our own queerness, because people are forming wonderful different relationships in this modern world.'

I only found out about Deaglan because he had used the word 'fucking'. I got a call from the Stephen Nolan show on Radio Ulster. I am often a guest on it. On this occasion I was on with Malachai O'Hara of the Green Party and the right-wing evangelical christian Jim Wells of the DUP.

I hadn't heard Deaglan's Stormont speech at this stage and could only comment on the clip played on the programme, which included the beeped-out word 'fucking'.

Jim Wells said that when I heard all of it I would be truly shocked.

What I thought, in fact, when I did hear it, was that this was the best piece of oratory I had heard since Bernadette Devlin and Eamonn McCann, the top platform performers of the civil-rights movement. There was Deaglan, swanking in his gown, flashing his big eyelashes and guldering, 'I am queer and I fucking love it.'

He was tearing into the media and the DUP and arguing that asking for acceptance from them was equivalent to acknowledging that you present a problem – and you don't; they do.

He loves dressing in drag.

'When I am dressed up I call it a higher state of self. Everything is heightened. You are pulled and tucked and tweaked and everything is on up. Your body is completely different. The way you walk is different. But it is a heightened sense of self. You are conscious of the fact that you are reacting. You have to react to everything around you, because if you don't you are not doing your job. If somebody says hello to you, you have to reply, keep up the energy.'

This used to be called transvestism, but that category seems diluted now within the whole transgender movement.

I asked him which toilet he uses when he is in drag.

'There is no going to the toilet. I have very large pads that are built into underwear and then there's about four or five pairs of tights over the top of that. There's no going to the toilet for twenty hours on Pride Day. You've just got to suck it up. Train your bladder.'

Easier perhaps at his age.

'But your feet are in agony. I could barely walk after Pride.'

I am actually an honorary member of the Belfast Butterfly Club, a support network for trans people and their families. This happened through my journalism. I reported in 1998 that a group of Belfast transvestites had been ordered to leave the restaurant in a Belfast hotel. The same hotel was to be used for a conference on equality issues. The organisers of the conference then threatened to withdraw from the hotel unless the transvestites were given an apology and assured of future welcomes there.

So the transvestites rewarded me by taking me out to dinner and presenting me with a Barbie doll with a butterfly tattoo on her stomach.

Electra La Cnt, in these more accepting times, reads to children in libraries.

'So lovely. So nice. So moving when parents come up to you and tell you that they are determined that their kids are growing up in a diverse culture. And you literally take their hand and say, "You are so good; keep going the way you are going."'

So it still comes as a surprise to him that he is accepted, at least in some places.

'I need to check myself in some company. Are my hands too floppy? Is my voice too high-pitched. I know that in my day-to-day job there will be some hard lads in. Some guys in the Kennedy Centre are rough. And you do question yourself for doing that, but it is just for an easier life. My eyebrows are off at the moment because I am working so much and I ran out of glue and people look at me and they think, *There is something not right here.*

'So you always get that. You are walking into a room and you just need to evaluate whether or not I am going to be me or not. You do find at times that you need to tone down parts of your personality. Days like that are fewer the more defiant I become. But it's born from years ... I joke that I was bullied in nursery school, but I actually was. That's how far back the otherness goes, and you are always thinking, *I do not belong here; these people do not like me.* That eats away at you.'

He does not agree with the position taken by Nora Calder, that you can't be a lesbian if you were born with a penis.

'They [the TERFs] upset me because they define their womanhood by not having a penis. That for me is not what a woman is. So for you to turn around and say to someone, "You are not a woman because you have a penis"; that puts the penis at the central focal point.

'What is between your legs is not what a woman is.

'What they are saying is: "You do not understand the struggle that women have been through. You do not understand what it is like to go into a room and have four potential men rapists in front of you." True. But transwomen have their own struggles. They have their own issues.'

They also say that transwomen don't understand menstruation; that they don't have a womb and never will.

'I think attacking each other in that respect is not going to advance any movement. We need to know who our allies are and find out how far we have to go.'

Deaglan is not inspired by the campaign for same-sex marriage. Northern Ireland in 2018 still had not legislated for it. But how radical is a demand for marriage rights anyway? Go back to 1968–69 and the radical idea about marriage then was that we could dispense with it, that it implied a form of bondage. This was the time when people were starting to form stable relationships, set up homes and have children without seeking the endorsement of the Church or the state but relying exclusively on their love for each other. And that was seen as a revolutionary thing to do. It probably was facilitated by contraception becoming available to single people, so that they could try out live-in sexual relationships without having children or merging their bank accounts.

Fifty years on, there is something a little paradoxical about the radicals in the field of sexuality wanting to have marriage rights that heterosexuals were discarding back then.

Seán McGouran, as a gay man, is surprised that a campaign

for same-sex marriage is now the cause being championed by Pride.

'It's a bit like gays in the military. Yes, but I am not particularly enthusiastic about it. When we started, apart from being gay we were all mad lefties. We didn't believe in bloody bourgeois marriage. But if someone puts a demand under my nose and asks me to sign it, I will sign it.'

For Deaglan it is not important either. It is something for 'cis-gendered gay people'. And the danger is that when they get their marriage rights they think that the war is over, while for him the rights of trans people remain to be fought for.

'I am not saying that we shouldn't have equal marriage – I believe that we should – but I am not campaigning for it. The job is not yet done in terms of real social change and people knowing what we are fighting for, which is why, at times, I find a campaign for equal marriage frustrating because that's not the end. That is step twenty in a thousand million steps that we still need to take. So great, let's put our efforts behind that, but don't take the foot off the gas when that happens.'

We talked about the speech John O'Doherty of the Rainbow Project gave at a rights rally in Belfast in June 2018, in which he had lumped several rights together as his concern, including the right to an Irish Language Act.

O'Doherty had said, 'On behalf of Love Equality, I would like to send our solidarity to campaigners for reproductive rights, for language rights and for the rights of victims and survivors of the Troubles and of institutional abuse. Your struggle is our struggle. Our struggle is your struggle. Our rights are not in competition. We say: rights for all!'

Deaglan said, 'Where do trans rights fall into that?'

He said he wants to be sure that the campaign continues for the 'trannies and queers after the gays have got what they want'.

'Pride should be a protest. Are we celebrating what we don't have, or are we protesting for what we want? As far as I am concerned there should be no celebration here. I am very proud of who I am but from the second we set off until we finished we were shouting "Up the Queers!" the entire way because as far as I am concerned we need to get our voice out there and that simple little hashtag has rallied people.'

*

There were five of us in a Belfast restaurant. I was there with my wife. She actually wore a man's suit that night, thinking that this was a tribute to the TVs, but they didn't seem to notice. P. A. MagLochlainn was there. This night he was with his partner, who hardly spoke the whole time.

Linda Marshall was the hostess. She was not a glamorous transvestite seeking to be tantalising or alluring. Her upper arms were thick and strong, her chin larger than the average woman's.

And it was plain from her demeanour and attire that her transvestism, as it was then called, had nothing to do with sexuality. I hope she won't think me unkind if I say that she looked more like a housewife than a model, as if she was devising her image with greater reference to her mother or her neighbours when she was young than to celebrities.

We had a little ceremony after dinner and that was when Linda presented me with a Barbie doll with a butterfly tattoo and declared me an honorary member of the Butterfly Club. I felt proud.

There was another TV with her. I met this person on the street a few weeks later, in men's clothes, and he affected not to know me.

I was fascinated by the transvestites because I thought there could be nothing more mortifying than to be seen in a public place dressed as a woman while everyone about you saw you as a man.

P. A. told me about someone back home in Dungiven who would come to farmers' markets with the frills of a blouse visible under his coat. This told me that the transvestites were more comfortable dressed as women than as men, even though they were likely to be stared at, mocked and abused. So it wasn't a frivolous inclination.

Looking back now, it appears that Linda Marshall was much less radical than Electra, Deaglan Agnew. She wasn't out to shock anybody but she was a deft political operator in that she organised the Belfast Butterfly Club – the BBC – and formed relationships with other groups like NIGRA and the Belfast Humanists. I had first met her at a humanist dinner and on occasions after this presentation she asked me for help in applying for funding and once in chairing a one-day conference on transgender rights in Belfast.

That was instructive, for among the transvestites and transgendered attendees I met a diverse range of people, including churchgoing christians. They were not united by any ideological urge other than to be accepted as being of the gender they declared.

So, after meeting Deaglan, this raging and rampant activist, I looked Linda up again and found that she was now living away from Belfast and had stopped cross-dressing but still regarded herself, even in male clothes, as 60 per cent female.

She told me there has been a change in the culture around transvestism and that few now use the word; and that there has been an increase in the number transitioning though there is 'still a Health Service culture designed to dissuade people rather than genuinely support them'.

She said, 'Those who don't transition are either content to be part-time in the opposite gender or are constrained by the practical difficulties of living successfully in a completely different role where they are not accepted by a large section of society. Not everyone can pass without detection in the opposite gender; indeed those who can are the exceptions. Clearly the driving force behind those who seek to transition is also considerably stronger than with those who have accepted their lot.'

When the Butterfly Club sought closer relationships with the gay community in Belfast there was one NIGRA member who was hostile and argued that their concerns had nothing to do with sexual orientation.

And Linda agreed with this point – indeed, she asserted it emphatically.

'It is generally accepted by the medical people who work in this field that there is absolutely no connection between sexual orientation and gender identity. Otherwise all male homosexuals would want to be women and all lesbians would want to be men; whereas the reality is that only a tiny minority in both cases would even consider this.'

So, the transvestites were mostly heterosexual men, sexually attracted to women. They wanted to express themselves as female but not to the extent of forming sexual relations with men.

So are transgender people who participate in Pride getting something wrong?

She said she thinks they understand the issues well enough but are seeking 'strength in numbers'. There is a Trans Pride movement emerging, but it will inevitably be smaller since there are fewer of them.

According to Linda, 'They are welcomed by LGB because the numbers as a result will be greater. This is not unreasonable from both points of view. However, the separate Trans Pride events organised this summer recognised the fact that we have different issues.'

I note that Linda doesn't use the full popular acronym of LGBTQI+ and there is a logic to that. The LGB part – lesbian, gay and bisexual – is about sexual orientation. The latter part – transsexual, queer and intersex – is about gender. And if these are distinct and unrelated, should they really be bundled together into one umbrella category?

So trans campaigners make a clear distinction between themselves and gays who are just as cis-gendered as any boring old heterosexual like me.

A Fair Cop

They are the cops, the peelers, the rozzers, the fuzz, the pigs, the filth, les flics. What bound protest movements of the past and abroad was their shared contempt for the police, expressed in the derisive nicknames they gave them. For all the hate-filled words spat out at the uniformed front-line of the state's authority, only one affectionate term comes to mind: the Bobbies.

And even in recent years in Belfast there have been protests in which the police were attacked, petrol bombed or shot at or had paving slabs dropped on them. Yet, common to all the protests I attended in the city fifty years after the civil-rights agitation, whether for abortion rights or against Israel, was the civility of the police, their tactical detachment and even their amicability.

One of the major irritants in starting the Troubles fifty years ago was their crass management of protest. And one of the major reforms through the peace process was the creation of a new policing culture governed by their responsibility to defend human rights. I saw the beginnings of change within policing up close, as a trainer – work that I had not sought and was wary of taking on.

The first time I was asked to speak to trainee police officers was a little bit awkward. The IRA had called a halt to its 1994 'cessation' and bombed Canary Wharf in London. This was 1996. The students that I was being asked to meet had been recruited during that cessation, at a time when many thought that the IRA had ended its campaign for good. So they were young people in their twenties, mostly, who had had reasonable expectations that they would never be shot at, would never have to look under their cars for bombs in the morning, would never perhaps even have to don flameproof clothing or carry a shield against petrol bombs.

The Troubles were over.

They were, however, to be trained by police officers who had lived and worked through times when they would have to be constantly alert to the danger of ambush, whether from a bomber or a kid on the doorstep with a pistol when they were putting the cat out.

My tack until then had been not to think too much about the police. My main dealing with them was through the press office, and some of them were grumpy men who assumed I was only ever going to criticise them, was never going to understand them, and was therefore not worth going to much trouble for.

When a mediation charity asked me to go into the training centre at Garnerville outside Belfast I wished it hadn't, because I knew I could not reasonably say no.

My excuse for refusing might have been that I would be putting myself at risk, not of being abused by the police but of being caught up in an attack on them. The IRA had killed people for working for the police, so I would enter the category of 'legitimate target'. On the other hand, I knew that the IRA was highly disinclined to kill journalists. And I was also disinclined to refuse to do something just because the IRA disapproved.

Another get-out might have been that I would alienate friends and contacts. If they saw that I had become friendly with the police they might be more guarded in their dealings with me.

But the real reason for my hesitation was that there was more comfort in being estranged from the police. When so many people hated them and feared them I would make myself an exception among friends and family if I acquired sympathy for them. Better not to take the risk that I might like them and begin to think like them.

I also wondered what use I could be. The attraction may have been that I was a catholic. I had grown up in the catholic community and could speak out of some experience. But that's not how I described myself by then. I was highly critical in some of my writings of the IRA and other nationalist movements. That would have suggested the possibility that I was being invited as a 'safe catholic', one who could be expected not to go full-on with my criticism of the police.

But, while I wanted to be critical of the IRA, I did not want my stance to be used as cover by other bodies and forces in Northern Ireland; I did not want to risk being appropriated as an ally.

There was the danger, too, that if I spoke to the police as a 'catholic' then others in the catholic community would see me as presuming to represent them when it was already obvious through my media work that I was an unlikely delegate for working-class communities with grievances against the state.

But I believed in talking to everyone, or thought I did. I even had a slightly superstitious notion that I should go where openings arose, that life might have plans for me.

The first event I participated in was staged in a bar in the RUC training centre at Garnerville. This was an old converted school, much like the one I had gone to myself, built in the sixties with lots of glass and panels. A polite young woman in jeans and jumper welcomed me at the door. She was clearly physically fit – as you'd expect in a police trainee. She had been delegated to receive me and to put me at ease, yet I could see that this courtesy was learned and rehearsed, a part of the job. But then, what courtesy isn't learned?

She led me to the bar and introduced me to several officers. Some of them were obvious peelers. I'd have spotted them as such out of uniform from the haircut, the bearing, the manners and the confidence and, what seemed to me, a patriarchal presumption of being right.

And the other guest of the night was a catholic priest who had accepted a drink – I was driving – and was enjoying the company.

A man from the mediation charity led us to seats before an audience of trainees dressed in casual clothing. He chaired the session and invited us to speak from our experience of the police.

I wanted to assure them that I wasn't there to attack them, so I spoke first of growing up on the Riverdale estate in the

1950s, where some of my neighbours were policemen who cycled to work in the morning. But I also told a story about a time, at the start of the Troubles, when I had been detained by police officers in north Belfast and taken to a station in the back of a Land Rover, flanked by armed cops in uniform. I had been with friends looking for a party. We might have looked suspicious, driving slowly up narrow streets, looking at houses. A mixed patrol of soldiers and constables stopped us, made us get out of the car and searched us. Then a soldier got into the car and ordered my friend to drive it to a police station. I was taken in the Land Rover, seated between uniformed and armed men. One of the cops behaved oddly. Perhaps he hoped to have some fun with me. He started poking me surreptitiously in my side, about waist level, probably with a finger. I could only assume that he wanted a reaction from me. At first I just thought he wanted my attention, perhaps to whisper some reassurance. But I turned to look up into his face and he was grinning. He poked me again. I was squeezed up against him because there was so little room and he was just, bizarrely, jabbing at my side with his finger.

This worried me.

I said clearly and out loud, 'I don't know why you are poking me, but I wish you would stop.'

And he looked around embarrassed at the others, who clearly were not in on this. Their looks told him to stop.

I told the trainees that I assumed that the guy poking me had hoped that I would push back at him or react physically in some other way, and give him an excuse to strike me with his baton or beat me up. I had little doubt that another frightened young man in my position, or myself with a few drinks taken, might have obliged him.

But, I said, that taught me an important lesson: that some RUC men were thugs who would relish the opportunity to beat me up if I gave them the slightest cover, but also that they weren't all like that.

The priest talked about his great respect for the RUC and said he hoped that he could be of service. He said he knew that some people thought priests were not their friends, but that he had the same interest in the welfare of the community as they had.

There was an interval after our presentation. The trainees in their jumpers and jeans didn't move much from their seats. One came forward and offered to get me a drink from the bar. I suspected he had been delegated to do that.

I asked the man from the mediation charity how he thought it was going.

He said, 'I think they take you for a soft Provo' – meaning an IRA sympathiser. Which amazed me. If these people were so far from knowing the difference between a supporter of armed republicanism and an ordinary member of the catholic community who mostly votes for the SDLP, then there was work to be done.

In the second half of the evening, trainees individually read out questions and we answered them as best we could. Later some of them would tell me that the questions were written by the staff and that all were on their best behaviour because the staff were there monitoring them. So they were being tested on how well they retained composure in the face of criticism. This was more an exercise in manners than an education in politics and social awareness. But manners are important for a cop.

I became a regular at these sessions in the training centre and I learned a lot about the police. I also met the other people who came in to join the panel.

After a few weeks the mediation charity withdrew from the training over reservations I wasn't clear about, though I had my own – the obviously scripted questions, the monitoring of behaviour, the sense that the trainees were not allowed to relax and be candid with us.

Then the police took over the project fully. An officer invited the panel regulars to dinner in the centre and over fine food and wine in crystal glasses he explained that we could bill him for a fixed fee. His own sense was that the fee was low so there would be no quibble about the added expenses, which he encouraged us to claim.

There was a presbyterian minister among us who declined this apparent invitation to fiddle a little.

At these events I met a member of the UVF. He had been a long-term prisoner. The IRA wouldn't participate but the brother of a leading member of Sinn Féin came. One night he and the UVF man showed each other photographs of the foreign trips they had made talking about the peace process, in South Africa and Nicaragua. And I was soon more at ease with being there, though bemused by the way they worked.

One day they asked me if I would take it further and work with the probationer trainees. These were police officers who had been out on the job for a year and a half and were brought back for top-up training to finish them off. I was happy with that.

This was the time of the Drumcree protests in Portadown. The Orange Order had refused to accept rerouting of a routine parade along the mainly catholic Garvaghy Road. Their protests had built up into huge standoffs and had ended with the police clearing the way for the parade to go through or holding their ground against it. The pass-out class at the training centre, under the supervision of the camp commandant, took part in those operations. The first job as police officers out in the real world for the polite young trainees I had been meeting would be to draw batons against whichever side the police chose to oppose that year, the Orangemen and their supporters or the protesters.

A senior officer called Ken arranged for me to be picked up off the train at Portadown and driven to Gough Barracks in Armagh for my first training session with the probationers. I equipped myself with purchases from the Sinn Féin shop on the Falls Road, a copy of the Proclamation of the Irish Republic and a cassette tape of rebel songs.

The Garnerville training centre was in a relatively safe area but we were more exposed in Armagh, within reach of the South Armagh IRA, who were much tougher, deferred mostly to their own leadership alone and were known to be sceptical of the peace process. A new cessation had not yet been agreed so there were attacks and would be more. A mortar bomb had been prepared for launching near the station and abandoned.

In his office I asked Ken which direction a mortar would be most likely to come from.

'Through that wall behind you,' he said.

'And how much protection would that wall provide?'

'It's about as much use as paper,' he said.

He led me down to my class and introduced me to about a dozen police officers in uniform, ten men and two women, none of them looking enthusiastic or at all interested.

I had designed a lecture explaining the differences within the catholic community between those who supported the IRA and those who didn't; those who wanted a united Ireland right now and those whose main concern was that the aspiration to have a united Ireland be respected and would then be happy for it to be put off indefinitely; between physical-force republicans and constitutional nationalists.

It did not go well.

The probationers sat in a semicircle in front of me, and they looked uncomfortable in their tight uniforms and wary of me. I realised later that they thought that most of what I was saying was obvious and trivial. I had had my petty victory by playing the Wolfe Tones to a captive audience in Gough Barracks but I doubt that I had taught them anything or challenged their thinking. Only one person was getting anything out of this and that was me.

I had been asked to speak to them about ways in which they might be aware of prejudice when dealing with catholics; what stereotypes might get in their way. They had already had some discussion on this, though I am not sure it had done much good.

Ken had discussed the Drumcree trouble with me, and the intentions of the protesters. He said it worried him that one of the community spokespeople was a Jesuit priest.

'Aren't they known for being a bit devious?'

I said I thought that an educated priest was more likely to be a restraining influence than a disruptive one.

I said to the trainees, 'Imagine a situation in which you are visiting a catholic home to bring news that a child had been killed in a road accident. If one of you is catholic, is it better to let the catholic one do the talking?'

I got a resentful response. 'It is our job to treat all people equally.'

And I thought that was right. My suggestion that catholic officers should be pushed forward to deal with catholics in trying situations was a bad one. But then I struggled to work out what useful ideas I was really going to give these people.

The cop who drove me back to the railway station in Portadown that afternoon was older and more experienced than the trainees. He had been in ordinary uniform in the station, and was in casual civilian clothes as he drove, but was much more interested in counter-terrorism than he was in routine policing – even excited by it. I knew journalists like this as well, who relished the vocabulary of weaponry and tactics.

At that time the IRA threat near the border included the use of a long-range sniper rifle. This man told me that the IRA had three of them. He had little details like that, which a journalist could make use of to affect an impression of deep insight.

After two sessions at Gough Barracks the police moved the classes to Maydown outside Derry. A security assessment had decided that we were not safe in Armagh. Maydown was a large complex and the main building where we did the training was bombproof. The doors were heavy and spring-loaded. A sign warned of the danger of hurting yourself opening them.

The classrooms were long, like the upstairs of a bus, with small windows. I began to think that if I could not teach these people very much then I could at least entertain them. I also realised that if they sat sullenly there and I did all the talking I would be exhausted after the two-hour session. So I would make them talk.

But I also learned from the police officers that they were sceptical about their own organisation.

Their routine nickname for the chief constable was 'Chief Con', though they respected the Chief Con of that period, Ronnie Flanagan. They thought the organisation was unwieldy with procedure. One told me a story that Gough Barracks had recently been provided with new cupboards for each office. These were found to have faulty locks.

'Instead of sending out a man with a screwdriver to go round and do them all in one day, they sent a truck to bring all the cupboards back to the workshop and repair them there. That tells you what the RUC is like,' he said.

And I learned in time also that the community-awareness programme, or CAP, of which I was a part, was commonly referred to by them as the CRAP. There was constant complaining about 'political correctness gone mad'. The trainees believed that this training was not a serious effort to raise their consciousness but a device for getting the force off the hook of the charge that it was sectarian. If any of these men or women was later faced with a complaint about sectarian behaviour, the RUC could simply say that it had met its responsibility to train officers to be above prejudice and then disown them, thereby mitigating the expense of a compensation claim.

While I was slow to work out ways in which I could be of value to the police trainees – and many groups passed through, getting little from me – they taught me about themselves.

They were all very fit. The staff in the office took breaks for exercise and might be fragrant from the shower.

I picked up gossip occasionally but little real intelligence. Once at a desk I saw a wee piece of fluted dowelling rod tapered a little at one end and with a loop through the other. One of the other trainers told me that it was the safety peg for an under-car bomb. An IRA bomber would secure a device with a mercury tilt switch under a car then pull the peg out. Without the peg, the mercury might tilt and connect the terminals and complete a circuit and detonate the explosion.

So a little peg like this one, if found lying close to a car, was a sign that there was a mercury-tilt switch bomb nearby – that is, if the bomber had been careless enough to just throw it away. And a suspect found in a search to have such an innocent-looking peg in a pocket was well worth detaining.

I learned that the police thought of themselves as the third community in Northern Ireland. Since the trouble over Orange parades, many had had to move out of protestant areas for their own safety. Many had stories of siblings and other relations accusing them of betraying their community.

Fewer than one in ten of them were catholic, but that meant that there would be, on average, one catholic in the group I was dealing with at any time. Sometimes there were two. They would often reveal themselves and say they were comfortable in the RUC; that sometimes there was banter but you had to be big enough to take that.

The most common point made was 'We never talk about religion.'

I would ask why not – in a normal society people are free to talk about everything.

This wasn't a normal society. Their way of getting round the problem of religion was not to mention it. But the predominant protestant culture in the police was not as coy of expressing itself as the catholic one was.

Once, sitting at a desk waiting for my class to start, I found a leaflet about the activities of an evangelical prayer group, so leaving religion out of it was not a custom universally applied.

I learned about how the police believed that they were becoming more professional.

One man explained that in the past, a policeman who stopped a drunk driver and found that he was another policeman would wave him on. 'We were losing more men that way than to the IRA.'

He said that the modern RUC of the 1990s would not tolerate drunk driving.

There were divisions of opinion still about how they would deal with the trauma of violence. There was a policewoman there who had been a trainee fifteen years earlier in Enniskillen when the training centre was bombed. She told me how the Chief Con at the time, Jack Hermon, had visited them that night and congratulated them on the work of the clear-up. He had given her a little patronising chuck under the chin with his fist to remind her what tough people they all were.

But as she spoke to me, telling me this story, she stroked her arms and shoulders nervously and it appeared to me that she was still wiping the dust off her clothes.

I wondered how many others were still traumatised.

A senior officer said, 'You can't be prescriptive about these things. Some can go home after an ambush, drink a bottle of whiskey and never let it bother them again. Others need therapy, but don't dismiss the whiskey bottle.'

I went to Maydown every fortnight in training time for three years and became a familiar face to the staff, including the guards at the gate, but I never saw a group of trainees more than once. I didn't have time to develop a good relationship with any of them. Any mistakes I made would be corrected with future groups, never put right with the groups I made them with. I have sat in that room, I believe, with every single member of the RUC who joined eighteen months before I started until eighteen months before I finished my work there.

I have since met some of them out in the street.

I knew better how to get on with them and get through to them at the end than I did at the beginning.

I would learn how to spot a pecking order within a group, and there always was one. Once a conversation had got going, I would see that one or two members of the group were deferred to by the others. Some would be shy of speaking and would look to another first for reassurance that it was OK to air an opinion. Some would wait to know another's opinion before declaring themselves. My strategy when dealing with a group's de facto leader was to look him directly in the eye when speaking. I felt that if I made plain that I was not nervous of him, the others would be easier to manage. Only once was the top person in the group – the one who received most deference – a woman.

The men were outrageously sexist. There were rarely more than two women in the group and the men would often speak over them in a way that they would not speak over other men. Some of the women dealt with the sexism by adopting the brash humour of the men. They sought to be 'one of the boys'. Indeed, I'm sure some of them enjoyed being one of the boys. One told me that she had grown up with three older brothers and nothing about men surprised her.

There were big changes being anticipated in the RUC at this time. The secretary of state Mo Mowlam had said that there would be police reform, though the negotiations to the Good Friday Agreement ultimately backed away from the challenge and passed it on to a commission chaired by the former governor of Hong Kong Chris Patten.

I believed that the 'Royal' in the title Royal Ulster Constabulary would be scrapped. Senior officers were appalled by this suggestion and said there was no need: 'What about the Royal Victoria Hospital? There are no complaints about that.'

I said the name change would lose the word 'Ulster' since it annoyed people by ignoring the fact that three other Irish counties belonged to the province of Ulster. They said, 'What about Radio Ulster and Ulster Television?'

The organisation was preparing itself for change and at the same time hoping that change would not be as radical as such a name change. Discussing this with the trainees one day I suggested they might become the Northern Ireland Police

Service. One of the women said, 'If you think I am going out on the street with a badge on my chest that reads "NIPS", you have another think coming.'

I shifted away from trying to persuade the trainees that I had valuable insights into the catholic community that they would benefit from hearing. They were all brighter and more thoughtful people than I had taken them for. Well, nearly all. Some were apparently hired for their physical strength, because you need people like that in the front line during a riot.

I brought my own doubts about the RUC to them.

I had been researching the joyriding culture in Belfast around that time, and I had spoken to many of the young lads who stole and raced cars. This was a surprising culture to have grown out of the area in which I had lived and gone to school. It was nihilistic and it was illiterate. It was also rooted to a high degree in republican families and I was developing a theory that it was largely the kickback of kids whose fathers were in the IRA.

Many of the car thieves told me that they had been beaten up by RUC men arresting them. They also said that they had been offered tradeoffs once caught. If they would plead guilty to stealing a lot of cars they had never been in, they would be treated more gently, get a lighter sentence.

I would ask the trainees if they believed that sort of thing happened, and some would say they did.

I told them the stories of joyriders who were absolved of prosecution if they agreed to become paid informants, often for little money. What would happen was that a boy or young man who had been caught in a stolen car would be questioned by a Crime Branch detective and, at the point at which he was to be charged, another officer, from Special Branch, would enter the room, take the prisoner away and no charge would be levelled.

Did the trainees think that happened? Did they think it was right?

It felt like a breakthrough when one of them said, 'It isn't right.' But he then went on to say, 'Our primary responsibility is to protect lives, and I can live with this if I can believe that Special Branch is saving lives by gathering intelligence in this way.'

But what about Pat Finucane?

Pat Finucane was a solicitor with brothers in the IRA. He was disliked by the police because the IRA used him as a defence solicitor for its members. This complicated the turning of IRA prisoners. Special Branch would hold a man, work on him through blackmail and other pressures to get him to become an informant, and then the first person from the outside that he would speak to would be Pat Finucane. The RUC feared it was losing possible agents at that point in the process.

One night, Finucane had answered his front door to a caller and was shot dead. Numerous investigations in later years pointed to the killers having been directed to Finucane by Special Branch.

So what did the trainees think of that? I said, 'What if Special Branch conspires in murder? Is that OK?'

And the young man who had responded to my question about joyriders being beaten up or used as informers said, 'I have difficulty with that.'

One of the few friends I spoke to about my work with the police was Denis Bradley. Often I would visit him after training sessions. Denis had been a priest and during the 1970s had developed a friendship with a senior officer in Derry, Frank Lagan. He and Lagan had brought members of the IRA and the British security services together to negotiate a ceasefire in 1975, with Lagan going so far as to provide safe passage for men who were wanted.

I had first met Denis in the BBC canteen when I was working on religious-affairs programmes. Later I became a frequent visitor at his home, stayed nights there and helped out for a few days once when his wife, Mary Wilson, was ill. They were catholic believers and psychologically astute people who worked in addiction counselling.

Frank Lagan was a catholic too. Ironically, he was also the officer who broke the window of republican offices on the Falls Road in 1964 to remove a tricolour, which sparked a riot.

Denis told me, 'He and I became fairly … well, "close" is a strange word because Lagan was a very tall, austere human being, not the kind of guy you would have a close emotional contact with, but I was very trusting of him and he was trusting of me. He partially educated me as to what the difficulties were and what the possibilities were and where the hurdles were. He had suggested, way back in the early seventies, that he would use Magee College in Derry as a training centre for police and almost run two different police services in Derry under him. In other words, that catholics would join and they would have a police force and they would be united at the top but they would police different areas. That was just a recognition of how far out catholics were. He realised that you had to gradually take them in and he also realised the depth of mistrust.'

But Lagan did not persuade him, or even try to persuade him, that the RUC was a wholly moral and principled force.

Denis said, 'I also was aware through him of the difficulty with Special Branch because he was informing me quite often of how difficult it was. He used me on a number of occasions to get things stopped because Special Branch would have let it go ahead and people would have ended up dead.'

That remains the strongest allegation against the police response to the paramilitaries: that they colluded with killers at least as far as turning a blind eye to killings or covering for them afterwards when they were running them as agents.

I got stories from the probationers about their own police work.

One of them had taken umbrage with Mo Mowlam when she met them to assess their attitude to change and asked, 'Do you want to go back to the days of shoot to kill?' They were appalled. They did not believe that the RUC had murdered people.

They had stories about Martin McGuinness, whom they called Art Garfunkel because of his hair. They did not like him and said he could give them an unnerving steely stare when they detained him. Once, police stopped his car and he phoned Mo Mowlam on the spot and complained to her in front of them. On another occasion, police were at his son's school giving children advice on road safety and McGuinness stormed in to remove his child from the dark influence of the RUC.

Once one of the trainees made a pejorative remark about Tony Blair. I asked then why he had joined in singing 'Happy Birthday' to him on a visit to the training centre at Garnerville.

'Under orders,' he said.

This period when I worked for the RUC overlapped with the key years of the peace process, during which the IRA preconditions for talks were met and their cessation renewed, Sinn Féin entered the talks, the talks arrived at the Good Friday Agreement and defecting members of the IRA bombed Omagh.

The IRA had demanded that the talks be limited to a timeframe, that decommissioning of their weapons did not need to start before the talks. To reinforce the message that they were otherwise willing to continue with their campaign, they shot and killed two constables, Robinson and Grahame, in Lurgan in June 1997. I was in the town for hours after the ambush. I did not see the bodies on the side street near the station, but I stood with the media pack in a position opposite the station, observing life go on and filing news reports to the *Scotsman* newspaper.

Many people came to the station and laid flowers in tribute to the dead men. More just walked past doing their business, shuffling children to hurry up and not get distracted – perhaps not knowing what had happened; often, it seemed to me, not caring.

I went up to the array of flowers and read the cards with them and jotted the messages down. A gruff policeman came out of the station and demanded to know what I was doing and why. I didn't mind him being angry and suspicious; two of his colleagues were lying dead under white sheets round the corner, having been shot in their heads by – most likely – a man from this community.

Next day I went to Maydown to teach and I expected to find the mood darkened by the reminder that they still faced the danger of murder. The mood was no different from usual. When I started by offering the class my commiserations they were perplexed until I explained. Then they made light of it.

Sometimes they shared their black humour with me. One told of helping in the clear-up after a bomb in which many people had been killed, some torn into pieces. A colleague had turned to him in the business of assembling body parts and said, 'Do you want a hand?' – then tossed one over to him.

I had a sense that the attitude of the trainees in the later stages was different from that of those I had met at the beginning. I heard less of the grumpiness about political correctness and human rights. I made this observation to one of the other trainers.

He said, 'They know what's good for them. They know that they have to fit in to get on, and this is going to be the way of the future. They can't change it. If they really don't like it, they can leave.'

This was before the Patten reforms, which transformed the RUC into the PSNI.

But I got a great insight into how policing culture in another country was behind us on political correctness and sexual-harassment concerns and how officers there were still sceptical of these being serious problems.

The Garnerville commandant invited me to dinner in a French restaurant to meet two senior women officers from South

Africa. He explained to them the details of a contemporary sexual-harassment case in which the complainant had been awarded compensation. One of the women laughed and said, 'What's that you're saying? You get felt up *and* you get paid?'

Much talk of the RUC dismisses them as thick-headed bigots who had needed to be got rid of or re-educated, but they were far better people than that presumption allows for and they had anticipated and worked towards reform years in advance of Patten.

I told the trainees often that the shortage of women in the RUC was as big a problem as the shortage of catholics. I said they were all men affirming each other, and that in a lot of the cases where I could imagine having to deal with the police I would rather talk to a woman than to a man.

'That's sexist, Malachi.'

In the old ways, being a policewoman was virtually a different job. Women officers had not been allowed to carry guns. Before that, they had been required to resign when they got married. The traditional understanding had been that women were more sensitive and could better handle a distraught relative of someone killed in a road accident, for instance. Now, the argument was that they were doing the same job as the men and that the men should be sensitive too, as and when required.

There were still some areas in which women specifically were needed; for example, interviewing rape victims. And one of the trainers at Maydown spoke to me about the Care Unit and the work developed for managing rape and abuse offences. He believed that the RUC was good in that area.

But some of the men didn't understand the fuss about sexual harassment.

'One of the lads used to tease new women in the station. He used to chase them down the hall with his truncheon between his legs. It was all a laugh, but now he is out of a job because one of the women complained about him.'

The man who told me this story thought that was completely unfair.

A woman trainee said, 'You have to let off steam occasionally, don't you? Everybody understands that.'

One day I asked a group why they had joined the police.

The response was so illuminating I wished I had asked it on my first day. They nearly all gave the same answer. They wanted to be of value in their community. I had expected them to say they wanted to fight the IRA or defend Ulster. Some were carrying on a family tradition but all hankered for a day when ordinary community policing would be the whole of the job.

I asked what got in the way of their enjoyment of this work. They didn't mention the threat of attack but the paperwork, the disappointment when you get into court and see your work achieve nothing.

'You know the lawyer isn't there to help you clarify the truth; he's there to trip you up.'

'Scumbags going free. That's what gets me. And paper-work.'

When I asked how they would feel about being disarmed, many said they wouldn't mind, that their guns were no use to them.

'You might have time to use it to protect a friend – but if someone fires directly at you, you are not going to be able to fire back. You won't have the time.'

They told me about a video they had been shown in training, of a loyalist attack on a catholic shopkeeper, caught on a security camera. The time between the gunmen entering the shop, shooting the man, jumping over the counter to finish him off and leaving was seven seconds.

'You can't defend yourself against that.'

Occasionally I asked them for security advice.

In one week at the start of 1998, when the political talks were on, loyalists killed a catholic every night. One of the victims was Charlie Breslin, a taxi driver who had been sitting in his car round the corner from my home. I was apprehensive. I was teaching a night class at the Workers Educational Association, so anyone could see on their programme the details of where I would be.

The trainer I called said, 'I wouldn't go, if I were you. Not worth it.'

But I reasoned that the odds of them choosing me were slim and I went to my class.

Occasionally I saw my trainees in their work. This was usually around the deadlock over Orange parades in the late 1990s. One day I went down to witness a line of police holding back loyalist protesters demanding the right of a parade to pass through the lower Ormeau Road against a ban imposed by the Parades Commission. One man stood directly in front of a policeman and berated him with constant abuse: 'You're a traitor to your own kind. Some fucking Ulsterman you are.

You're nothing but scum now. You do the bidding of the IRA.
How do you face yourself? How do you look at your traitor's
face in the mirror and not feel sick?'

The accuser hardly stopped to draw breath in the several
minutes I watched him try to wear down the policeman's morale.

When I met the policeman afterwards, at the training centre,
he laughed about it. He had read my account of the incident
in an article in the *Belfast Telegraph*.

One night I went out to Portadown to report on the
preparations for a parade that the police had been ordered
to bar from the Garvaghy Road. I saw a group of Orange
bandsmen practise outside the catholic church, beating their
drums and blowing their flutes to drown out the sound of the
Mass inside and intimidate the worshippers. When the Mass
ended, they turned and filed away to make the point that
their job was done.

Down the town, off a side street, I met the Garnerville
commandant Jonathan McIvor with his pass-out class on
their first assignment after graduation. I had asked Jonathan
before whether it wouldn't be better to train some of them as
community officers rather than having them all do riot work.
His theory was that every trained officer had to have a grasp
of all aspects of the job. 'We are one force.'

And once I went to a funeral of one of them, a man who
had been shot dead in a gay bar in Belfast.

Sometimes McIvor took the trainers away for sessions in
a hotel to discuss how we might further develop our work.
He was an urbane man – he was the one who believed that
'for some' whiskey was a sufficient antidote to trauma – and

he would provide respite from the business of the day with a wine-tasting session.

I put forward the argument that police training should include something like the liberal-studies module I had had in college. This was a hard sell and they weren't going to go for it. I asked them to consider the popular stereotype of the police officer. This was that he was stupid. He was PC Plod; he had big feet and he blundered in. He was routinely depicted as one who didn't really know what was going on.

But that's not fair.

Well, there is something in it, as illustrated by the senior officer who was wary of Jesuits. I too often felt that police officers were not like the people I mixed with in my own world, that their conversations, while fascinating and full of stories about killers and prostitutes, were limited in their range. It was hard to explain why a cop should have to have read T. S. Eliot or Edna O'Brien or know the difference between Freud and Jung, or go to an art gallery and look at an abstract painting and not say something like, 'Sure I could have done that myself.' But what I most often felt about many of the trainees I had dealings with was that a widening of their education into the humanities would make them happier, better people. Don't we believe that that is what education does?

Training had lifted them out of the dull round of drab, repetitive work that limits so many people such that their only respite is television and drink. It had given them an income and a responsibility in society comparable to that of other professionals who deal with the public, who intercede in the gravest crises, but it had not made them very much more philosophical about the world or reflective about themselves. Indeed, they seemed to think that finding new ways to worry would only make life harder.

So much of policing was about following rules and orders. It wasn't a constable's job to reflect on whether a prisoner was guilty, just to escort her from the court to a prison van.

Eileen Calder of the Rape Crisis Centre said that when she was arrested for contempt of court in 1997, at precisely the time I was doing this work, the policewoman with her – perhaps one of my own trainees – wept and said, 'This is not what I joined the police to do.'

But one could see how, if she felt that way about tasks allocated to her, she might not be a fit instrument of the judicial system.

Many of my trainees had been from the families of Orangemen who were angry with them for the way they had blocked roads to them, who had always imagined that the Orange Order and the RUC were on the same side in defence of a protestant Ulster. Had the constables not been trained to leave their own feelings aside and to do their job, the state would have fallen apart.

*

After the Good Friday Agreement in 1998, a commission under Chris Patten devised a plan for human-rights-based policing. The job of the police faced with a public protest, as in 1968 or '69, would, from then on, be to facilitate that protest and defend the rights of those who were challenging the state.

He commended a rule that half of all recruits in each

intake should be catholic and he also prescribed increased recruitment of women. The specified allocation for catholics was dropped in 2011, when the proportion in the service reached 30 per cent.

Catholic involvement was difficult to achieve.

After decades of catholics staying out of policing or moving away from their families and friends when they joined, they understood logically that the peace process required them to join in.

My friend Denis Bradley joined the Policing Board knowing that some catholics were going to have to break cover and declare their support. Now he is a little contemptuous of the dilatory catholic response to the challenge to enter the service.

'The logic of it is that catholics are cowardly.'

He said that the Church should do more. 'There is a carol service in Derry every year for the police. Always in the protestant cathedral. Why isn't it in the catholic cathedral?'

But those who joined the police put themselves in danger of attack by republican dissidents, and the catholics among them are in greater danger because they are more easily got at.

When Denis took a seat on the Policing Board he had to look after his own safety. He did that by being conspicuous and outspoken when police advice was to move circumspectly and have an armed guard on his home.

'I had to walk the streets and be just normal at the same time. I was being offered guards outside that door, police officers outside that door. And I remember saying to Hugh Orde [a chief constable], "Do you want to get me killed? If I put guards outside that door I am dead, because I am then part of the establishment." My strength was: I am just Denis Bradley who walks the streets and has an opinion on these things.'

Anyone who attacked him while he was continuing to live his life as a member of a catholic community would not be excused by their own families and neighbours.

My own protection had been discretion. At the time that I was going into Maydown, the Provisional IRA was still trying to kill policemen and women. During that period they shot a policewoman outside the courthouse. She survived the bullet wound but died later of cancer.

Denis could not be secretive about his role in administering policing because it was a public appointment. And he wanted to actively set an example of catholic involvement. But he couldn't carry a gun or accept an armed escort because that would have been a declaration that he did not trust catholics, could not safely support the police.

Yet he was attacked in a bar. He had gone in with his son to watch a football match. Someone passed word out that he was there and a man came in with a baseball bat and hit him over the head with it, swiped at him again when he was on the floor.

'It wasn't a designed situation; because nobody knew until five minutes before that I was there. And the reaction, I knew, was strong enough because the next day I was having phone calls from the mothers and fathers of the people who did it. So I was winning, even though I was losing. My strength was that I wasn't walking down the street with a policeman. Now, it was a bit of a strain on my family and a bit of a strain on me at times, but it was the place to be.'

The SDLP's Mark Durkan told the BBC at the time that he regarded the assault as 'a vicious and appalling attack on a man who is simply showing public service and community leadership and who can argue his views clearly. He is a man who can take the views of others and explain and justify his actions – none of which can be said of his attackers.'

Years later, in the spring of 2019, a young writer Lyra McKee was shot dead by a New IRA gunman at a riot scene in the Creggan area of Derry. Then followed a similar public reaction, in support of the police and against the republicans who persisted with violence. Days after the killing, police said 140 local people had come forward with information which they hoped would help them identify the killer.

Lyra McKee had been part of the real revolution, young, gay and anti-sectarian. Many saw her as the first martyr of that social revolution. She was cut down by a gunman who was clinging to the possibility of a defunct revolution reshaping Ireland. For him the police were the enemy but support for that idea had already expired.

Loyal Rebels

Jamie Bryson sees himself as a champion of loyalist cultural rights. He is a short, trim and argumentative young man with an apparently bottomless appetite for contention. He was noticed by the media when he led protests in Belfast in 2012 against the decision by Belfast City Council not to fly the Union Flag from its dome every day of the year. Instead, the council would now synchronise with the custom in the rest of the UK and fly on 'designated days', eighteen of them, royal family birthdays and other anniversaries.

Jamie might have seen himself as bereft of an argument if the flag was to go up and down the pole in time with the one over Buckingham Palace. He might have considered that his right to Britishness was no more compromised by the decision than the Queen's was by the custom in London.

But he took protesters on to the streets to argue that their culture was being violated and that this was part of the steady erosion of Britishness in Northern Ireland, going back to the capitulation he saw in the 1998 Good Friday Agreement.

Nationalists, by contrast, wanted to see less of the manifest Britishness of Northern Ireland and more representations of its Irishness. A shift like that would, however, inevitably offend the British protestant who revered the monarchy and wanted to express loyalty to that imperial tradition. So we had a few weeks of street protests and several arrests mostly of young people. We saw ardent housewives and teenagers on television news expressing the hurt they felt at the insulting removal of the flag.

We also saw, through social media, a huge amount of derision aimed back at the loyalists and their 'flegs'; their working-class accents mocked. And there was a Twitter campaign to urge people to ignore the protests and to go out into the city and the bars and carry on as if peace and good order prevailed.

The protests stopped but Jamie continued to campaign on Twitter and on radio and television. The media liked him. He was young and brash and good-looking, for what that's worth. The loyalist spokespeople of the past had often been older, fatter men with moustaches; surly and humourless. Jamie could even laugh at himself. Once he rushed to Twitter to protest against Irish rugby supporters flaunting an image of a balaclava, in apparent support of the IRA:

> So during an evening of anti-British hate & abuse from Republic of Ireland supporters, they also unveil a banner of a masked terrorist. This is the country Theresa May wants to de-facto rule over N.Ireland.

On closer inspection the banner turned out to be the Munster flag. Consoling a journalist also caught out in a mistake, Jamie wrote, 'Not to worry. It could be worse. I saw a balaclava man in a Munster flag.'

And Jamie seemed to know a lot of what was going on, not just in relation to flags. He ran a blog in which he made claims about public figures that no mainstream media would dare repeat.

He gave evidence to a Stormont committee about the dealings of the National Assets Management Agency (NAMA), the 'bad bank' set up to offload properties backed by subprime mortgages after the crash of 2008. He claimed that political figures had influenced huge property sales.

And he became a regular on Stephen Nolan's shows on both radio and television, as someone who was unelected to any position but who could sound off in defence of the hurt feelings of loyalists.

After the waning of the flags protests, loyalist organisations asserted themselves anew through amplifying their bonfire tradition. They couldn't force the state to fly a flag but they could dare it to take down a massive bonfire.

In many protestant areas around Northern Ireland, children would traditionally build bonfires for burning on 11 July, the night before the big Orange Order parades. These were fiery displays of loyalist passion that often left a cloud of toxic fumes hanging over the city. In more peaceful times, in my youth, a traditional bonfire might be just a few busted sofas and some planks and crates. As the loyalist paramilitaries grew, the bonfires would sometimes be bigger and attract large crowds; they'd usually have an Irish tricolour at the top. I once escorted a BBC Radio Four crew to a bonfire in Sandy Row in Belfast. As I recall, it was about thirty feet tall, a rough pyramid of rubble and tyres, and generated huge heat. Grown men danced drunkenly round it chanting, 'Fuck the Pope', still retaining some lingering illogical sense that the Vatican was the source of all their woes.

When the paramilitaries resolved to build much bigger bonfires, Jamie was one of those who went on the media to defend these as legitimate expressions of loyalist culture – even when they were so big that they jeopardised neighbouring homes.

Journalists and radio presenters would raise the question of whether this should be stopped, but Jamie and other defenders of the bonfires would claim that this was a tradition they had a right to preserve.

When challenged to accept that these fires were dangerous, spokespeople like Jamie responded not by denying this but by arguing that the proper way to deal with the problem was to work through themselves and their community to find a resolution. They were parodying the language that had been used before by Sinn Féin when it was challenged to constrain the IRA and urge the decommissioning of weapons. By this device, the audience is never allowed to be sure whether it is hearing from the source of the problem or a mediator. At times it sounds like the language of the protection racket. 'Leave this to me; I might be able to sort something out. But, whatever you do, do nothing.'

Those defending the fires argued that the people of the areas wanted them. This seemed implausible but no one was coming out of these areas to flatly contradict him.

Things changed in 2018.

The problem for the government was that it was faced with the risk that its failure to intervene would rebound on it if property was burned or, worse, if someone died. The routine laws governing pollution and fire safety were being made to look ridiculous. That year, because of the heatwave, there was a ban on the use of hosepipes for gardening or washing cars, yet bonfires were going to require a huge amount of water to control them – and at the same time would draw fire-service resources away from actual accidental fires.

Then voices from the protestant community began to object to the fires. One such was John Kyle, a former leader of the Progressive Unionist Party (PUP) and a councillor for an east Belfast ward. He tweeted his objection to a fire being built on the Bloomfield Walkway, part of a greenway used by walkers and cyclists:

> The size of the Bloomfield Walkway bonfire is completely inappropriate for the location. It presents a real risk to life & property, breaches Fire Service guidelines, is strongly opposed by the local community & undermines the excellent work being done by other bonfire groups.

The fire at Bloomfield Walkway was a tower built with wooden pallets, eighty-three pallets high. A pallet is about seven inches thick so the tower was some fifty feet high. At the centre of the tower, invisible from the outside, were stacked dozens of rubber tyres. These would burn much longer than the wood, and would generate more heat and toxic fumes.

Jamie attacked councillors who urged that the Bloomfield Walkway fire be reduced and who threatened to seek an injunction against the owners of the land on which the fire was being built, holding them responsible. This owner was, ironically, the government's Department of Infrastructure.

When the injunction was finally applied for because appeals to reduce the size of the tower had failed, the department actually opposed it. It feared that moving against the bonfire might spark off widespread violence. In other words, the logic for letting loyalists build huge towers for fires on public land, jeopardising lives and property, was that they might make even worse trouble if they were confronted. These people were too dangerous to challenge.

The court wasn't impressed.

Jamie tweeted:

> Massive ramifications for the foolish decision by Justice Keegan. Now opens door for those targeting unionist culture (SF/Alliance/SDLP) to move against all bonfires. DFI must lodge an appeal.

He followed up with:

> All loyalists should remain calm and peaceful, even in the midst of the extreme provocation contrived by those who have whipped up & exploited the Walkway issue as part of their anti-unionist agenda. EBCI will continue to work for a positive solution.

The EBCI was the East Belfast Community Initiative, a mediation group that had offered to try to get the bonfires reduced.

In the early hours of 11 July a massive force of police entered east Belfast to secure the site of the pyre at Bloomfield Walkway and to protect masked contract workers who would dismantle the tower of pallets and tyres.

Predictably, the organisers lit the fire before the police could reach it.

I visited the site the next morning and it was still burning. The fire service had not extinguished the flames but had let the fire burn through. Police officers of the Tactical Support Group, in body armour, closed off the Walkway but obligingly showed me another route to get closer to take a picture.

It was a slightly bizarre scene.

As I prepared to take photographs, two policemen and a policewoman came over to talk to me, perfectly civilly. I wondered if they had been so bored that they were glad of the company. It gave me a chance to get a close look at what they wear when fully tooled-up, the leg shields and the shoulder pads that make them look physically more daunting.

You don't expect a cop built like a superhero to make light conversation with you, but they did. They said they had the right to stop me taking a picture but that they would not do so. But one of them walked closer to the fire to notify his colleagues that pictures would be taken and that they might want to turn their backs.

I stood on a bollard and got a good view. The heat shimmer distorted the more distant view of the great shipyard cranes. Some of the people working at the site looked like paramilitaries themselves. These were the contract workers removing the pallets and tyres, keeping their faces masked.

While we were there a bearded young man in a sweatshirt walked over to join the conversation.

'Where are you guys from? You're not local.'

One of the policemen said they were from 'all over'.

'You guys from Dungannon?' He was keen to sound them out.

'All over,' repeated the cop.

There had been disturbances in Derry during the night and the bigger story of the day, but for this move against the bonfires, would have been the six shots fired at the police there and the young rioter who had set his tracksuit alight with his own clumsily thrown petrol bomb.

The young man said, 'It's a pity you didn't put as much effort into catching a gunman in Derry as you did to take down a single bonfire that caused no harm.'

This argument had been aired on the radio a few times already that morning. Jamie had been tweeting it too. From up on my bollard I said, 'No harm? Last year fifty houses had to be boarded up and hosed down. People evacuated.'

'Nobody was evacuated,' he said.

'Well, people are not going to believe you if you say the residents here don't mind the damage to their homes and the risk of being incinerated. They just aren't.'

He didn't say anything to that.

But there had been a bad night in Derry. All week groups of young people had been chucking petrol bombs into the protestant Fountain estate. Dixie Elliott, a former IRA prisoner, said on Facebook that he had seen children pick up bullets dropped by the sniper:

Let's get real here. I drove past the Bog Inn last
night around 11:15 and saw about 100 young
people gathered, many were about 12, 13 and 14
years of age. Children not the youth of the Bogside.

Shortly afterwards someone fired shots which hit
the Derry Walls and trees. Whoever it was dropped
a bullet or bullets and we saw the photos of that or
those bullets in the hands of kids.

What would have happened if those kids hit
that bullet or bullets with a hammer or threw it or
them into a fire?

How the hell did someone manage to lose a
bullet or bullets from a weapon?

The police and contractors then moved to Cluan Place on
the Newtownards Road in Belfast, where another pyre had
been built within feet of old buildings. The Department for
Infrastructure, far from opposing the removal of a tower of
pallets there, as Jamie had urged them to, had requested that
the police dismantle it, probably because it was much closer
to private property and because a precedent had already
been set on the Walkway. The masked contractors tipped the
pyre into the road and started gathering up the pallets and
stacking them on to lorries for removal. Inside this tower too
were dozens of tyres.

This was a major operation and Jamie Bryson likened it to
the Nazis, a small echo of the past when civil-rights protesters
had chanted 'SS RUC'.

He tweeted:

> This is absolutely appalling. The PSNI are out
> of control. Who is driving this aggressive agenda
> against the unionist community?

His problem was that the police seemed to have ordinary common sense on their side. Yet by evening they had two major problems to deal with, again resonating a little with that first night the guns had come out in 1969.

In Derry, republicans opposed to the peace process were urging children to riot. The police had been drawn on to the city walls over the Bogside estate to protect the protestant Fountain area from attack by petrol bombers. The republicans had a weapon in the city and were apparently trying to entice the police into the area so that they could shoot at them again.

At the same time, in Belfast, the police issued a statement saying that they had information that loyalists of the East Belfast UVF planned to create widespread disorder.

The modern way to follow the progress of a riot is to monitor your Twitter feed. And one of the best people to follow on there when there is trouble in Belfast is Kevin Scott, a young photographer for the *Belfast Telegraph*. Kevin tweeted reports of burning cars and buses. The police meanwhile tweeted an apology for the noise of their helicopter. Never before had I noticed them being so sensitive to my need for a night's sleep.

On nights worse than this I had lain awake listening to the distant clatter of rubble, the shouting, the crackling of flames, the occasional burst of gunfire and the incessant chuck-chuck of the helicopter overhead and had little real sense of what was going on. Sometimes the noise on the breeze made it seem worse and closer than it was.

The first bangs worried me this night but they were too soft and diffuse to be gunshots. Fireworks; someone was having a fireworks party at their bonfire. You'd think when the city was in a state of anxiety people would have more sense than to add to it like that.

Loyalists lit two hundred bonfires across Northern Ireland that night, the eve of the Twelfth of July parade to celebrate the Dutch King William's victory over the English catholic King James at the Battle of the Boyne in 1690. The Fire and Rescue Service said next morning that it had responded to a 999 call every forty-eight seconds on average through the worst of the night.

Men with a pistol hijacked and burned a bus in Newtownards. Others burned several cars and, in the early evening, the George Best Belfast City Airport was closed because of a hijacked car blocking the main route from there back to the city. Had this been happening in any city in England, Scotland or Wales it would probably have been a major story on the national news. The networks broadly ignored it.

Next day, 12 July, the city was surreally silent. This was the traditional holiday period and many people just left Belfast, catholics in particular wishing to avoid the Orange parades. Winding in from the north came the thundering bands, through streets packed with cheering crowds – but away from the parade almost nobody moved. And the Orangemen, in all my life in Belfast, have never seemed inclined to view it as a negative reflection on themselves that nearly half the population of the city wished simply to be out of their way.

Frankie Callaghan, my classmate who joined the army, told me that when he was twelve years old at the Donegal Gaeltacht, he and his friends formed up their own mock-Orange band and paraded the main street of Bunbeg. There is a latent fascination with the bands that sits strangely with disdain. It is a little marvel for those who have no part in the Orange tradition that members form into lodges and march in bowler hats to assert their Britishness.

They would be unlikely to welcome a comparison between themselves and Americans who wear green floppy hats on St Patrick's Day to assert their Irishness, but nobody in Ireland wears a green floppy hat and nobody in Britain wears a bowler any more either.

These Orangemen have a high opinion of themselves in their formal lodges, committed to christian belief, yet led by bands that thunder their contempt for catholics, celebrate loyalist paramilitaries and scowl in their arrogance from the road with a knowing sense that much of the population fears and dislikes them.

This division between the lodges and the bands allows the Orangemen to bring louts on to the streets and yet to deny themselves accountable for their antics.

And they assemble at the field where the bandsmen drink and celebrate, and the lodge men gather to hear speeches and sermons and resolutions passed to affirm their loyalty to the monarchy and their resolve to stand firm against Rome, the Irish language and any pressure to enter a united Ireland.

They are strange. And what is strange is intriguing. And they are daft, anachronistic, clinging to a conception of

Britishness as quintessentially protestant, and dressed like 1950s commuters with rolled brollies.

Fifty years ago the Orangemen marched right up to near my home. They used a field at Finaghy then, on ground that the M1 motorway was later built through. Back then the parade was much bigger and the sight was awesome; the banners rising from the far side of the railway bridge, catching the full breeze at the top and then descending towards us level with the wind.

As children we would move through the groups of footsore Orangemen resting in the field and pick up their discarded lemonade bottles, and take them to the shops to get money back on them. Through the afternoon, Orangemen and bandsmen would explore the surrounding estates, including ours, often looking for a house in which they could use the toilet. My mother would cut her Orange lilies for fear they would be seen as a welcome sign.

Usually the day was peaceful.

During the worst of the Troubles, the British army erected screens to shield the Orangemen from view from streets mainly populated by catholics. In the later Troubles period, republicans raised protests against some Orange 'traditional routes' and for a time in the mid-1990s the parades were the most contentious issue in our politics. Deadlock developed into enormous widespread rioting.

Today there is little contention; the parades are smaller and the people who don't like them stay away. Many take their children out of the city so that they don't see them, for many a catholic parent has suffered confusion at how to restrain a child's enthusiasm for the marching bands and the banners. I once brought a woman and her child to see the main parade and the little girl loved it, but as we approached home afterwards to a catholic area we had to confiscate her little flag and suffer her tears.

Faced with the question of whether the Troubles could come back, one consolation is that the efforts of those who threaten us seem limited.

The UVF, having provoked a crisis by erecting unsustainable bonfires, was unable or unwilling to follow through with its revolt. It had built these huge pyres that the state had no choice but to dismantle. It had already humiliated the state in previous years, having dared it to move against the bonfires and seen it back away and even facilitate them. It hadn't grasped that the state could not continue to endure this insult to the law. Yet, when the police moved against them, all the UVF could muster was thirteen hijacked cars and a hijacked bus. This was awful, of course, but in comparison to major rioting of the past it was very small. This meant that either the loyalists could not make bigger trouble or they did not want to.

Yet all the time they were trifling with the danger that loss of life would follow from their actions. This suggests that they were neither serious about wanting to kill nor seriously careful not to. They were, therefore, amateurs, not the paramilitary army that had decades of experience but inept inheritors of the name.

And this seemed equally true of the agitators in Derry, marshalling children to throw petrol bombs at the police and at protestant houses, willing to shoot and throw small bombs, unable to kill yet taking the chance that they might. And they did a year later, at another riot. Shots fired wildly up a street felled the writer Lyra McKee.

This may not be much different from the conduct of the big campaigns that formed the Troubles. A community activist in Derry told me that in the 1980s a British secretary of state, James Prior, had sought his opinion on why Northern Ireland always drew back from the brink. We had the ingredients for civil war and never actually slipped into the chaos we feared.

One part of the explanation for this is that paramilitary groups needed to manage their recruits. There was little point in producing an escalation that would draw in thousands of people not of your organisation, have them killing and destroying but not responding to your orders or adhering to your plan. Something like that happened in August 1969, the night the guns came out. Remembered as a time when the IRA did not effectively defend its areas, it is more accurately described as a battle in which leaders on all sides lost control.

But there was another element: fluke. There were many times during the Troubles when the recklessness of these armed groups could have triggered conditions they did not want and could not thrive in. For example, we learned to assume over the decades of the Troubles that a town-centre bomb would usually not kill anyone, or at least no more than one or two people. The folly of that assumption was exposed at the end of the Troubles in August 1998, when one bomb in Omagh killed twenty-nine people. We had been lucky too often. In Dublin, in 1981, the year of the hunger strikes, an accidental fire in a dancehall, the Stardust, killed forty-eight people. In Northern Ireland, paramilitary armies setting off explosions all over the place and throwing petrol bombs at private houses and planting incendiary devices in department stores never once produced a tragedy of that scale in a single incident.

No one could have planned it that way.

The paramilitaries had got away with murder in that they had generated a scale of violence that suited them even while unable to actually calibrate it with any precision. A mad bigot throws a petrol bomb at a house and in the most appalling case kills three children, as in Ballymoney in 1998 when three Quinn children died in just such an attack. But only fate determines that the whole block doesn't go up, that the oil tank at the back doesn't catch fire and destroy the whole street. Luck of that kind prevailed throughout the period.

We discovered new averages not previously computed; that three men with sub-machine guns spraying a crowded bar and allowing themselves time to get away are likely to kill no more than six or seven people. Who knew?

But these eruptions in Derry and Belfast in the summer of 2018 seemed driven by people who knew little of how a full-on terror campaign is managed or constrained. They were like beginners. The sniper who opened fire on the police in Derry and dropped one of his bullets provided possible evidence against himself.

And the UVF burning cars to overstretch the police and fire service on the busiest night of the year might indeed have triggered calamity; but they didn't seem to have it in them to do anything with much deliberation.

The strategy of building untenable pyres could only logically have been a provocation to the state to intervene. The state, after all, has to protect lives and property, had already embarrassed itself by being so inept at this in previous years. But perhaps the people who built them were not even being logical.

While Belfast was peaceful during the main parade on 12 July, the trouble increased in Derry after a parade there. The violence felt like a faint echo of the massive rioting that followed an Apprentice Boys parade in August 1969. That rioting had extended to Belfast and culminated in the guns coming out.

Now the voices calling for a restoration of law and order were not the affronted unionists pointing to a republican conspiracy but the nationalist and republican representatives, pointing to 'dissident republicans' as 'sinister elements'.

Colum Eastwood, the leader of the SDLP, said that the instigation of the rioting was 'strategically stupid' given that violence in the past had failed. Presumably he meant that it had failed as a means of bringing about a declared goal of Irish unity. But it had succeeded in forcing the state to bend to the paramilitaries and to find a place for them in the political system.

'Mary' phoned *The Stephen Nolan Show* to make that point. She said, sarcastically, that the way to end this trouble was to give the organisers political power. That's what worked the last time. Now they draw their wages as politicians and do nothing.

One could only surmise what strategic objectives were attainable to those republican and loyalist factions who promoted the rioting. One prospect for them was that they might develop a rioting culture that would be a routine irritant and act as a reminder that the state had not settled, that the peace process had not brought peace.

The republicans using the cover of a riot to get a shot at a police officer might have been hoping that the police would come back with strength, alienate the community again and repeat the pattern of fifty years earlier.

And they may have been aware of the argument unsettling loyalists in Belfast: that the police were going easy on republican rioters while amassing huge forces against them and their bonfires. That argument suited republicans too. It made the police look bad, urged them to escalate and needled the loyalists. An IRA conspirator trying to undermine the state would have no problem with loyalists burning cars in their own areas. It all adds to the general mayhem and affirms that the peace has not succeeded.

Each period of violence in Northern Ireland starts with the expectation that it will follow the pattern of the previous one. So, in August 1969 the IRA leaders who organised the Divis Street rioting drew on their memories of the riot there in 1964. Then young men on the streets clashed with the police, and similarly almost overstretched them to the point of desperation.

But no one was killed. Indeed, one policeman caught his foot in a drain and seemed about to be overwhelmed by the mob when republicans pulled him to safety.

Those who had seen that riot might have assumed that they could replay it to the same rules, manage huge violence at the level of people throwing things at each other and ducking out of the way and going home afterwards unharmed.

The expectation of the police, many of whom had been trained during the 1950s IRA campaign to deal with armed insurgency, with more focus on the use of the rifle than on crowd control, thought that they were facing a regrouped and retrained guerrilla army and so brought weaponry on to the streets that had been designed for country roads, and for firing across fields.

With violence starting again in Derry and moving to Belfast in July 2018, many again thought for a moment that they were witnessing the return of something with which they were familiar. The past had repeated itself with people bringing their experience of past rioting to a new generation. Some had said in 1969 that it was almost as if the nineteenth century had crashed up through the cobbles and the 'Holy War' of the 1880s was repeating itself. But the more important question was: what has changed? How will it be different this time?

The Derry rioting was not of the pattern of the past, which had seen phalanxes of young people confronting lines of riot police or soldiers in battle formation. Now it looked like random little groups of twos and threes roaming the streets with petrol bombs.

A rioting mob in 1969 had to hold together, in one way more secure, like fish bundled and swirling to confuse a predator; in another they were more vulnerable to being hemmed in. The policing strategy that defeated the coherent mob had been perfected by the Metropolitan Police. Kettling. The London riots of 2011 had shown that groups could break up and reform, guided by social media. The leader no longer had to be at the front of the mob directing fire. He could be in his own living room, watching it on television and sending messages from his phone to his foot soldiers.

Then, in Belfast, on the night of 13 July 2018, someone threw bombs at the homes of senior republicans Gerry Adams and Bobby Storey. This was the last act of violence in that turbulent week.

Footage from a security camera at Adams's home showed a car pass and a passenger throw an object with a lit fuse. The police said the bomb was an 'industrial-type firework'. It bounced on the bonnet of Adams's car parked in the driveway and exploded, denting the windscreen.

So it was not a serious assassination attempt. It would have had to explode against his body to have that result and he was inside the house. It was, however, a daring act. The firework's fuse burned for only two seconds after it was thrown before exploding. That suggests that the attacker had a steady nerve and a confident throwing arm. Hesitation would have cost him a hand. Another possible inference, of course, is that he was reckless and stupid.

The immediate significance of these attacks, on Adams and Storey, was that they seemed to indicate that republican dissidents had found the confidence to attack the Provisional movement, which in the past would have struck back at them with more firepower than the dissidents themselves could muster. Paramilitary feuding has been a part of the story of the Troubles from the beginning, and the Provisionals had thrived by evolving politically but also by crushing rival pretenders to leadership of the republican cause.

Then Adams and Storey held a public meeting in the grounds of a demolished police station round the corner from Adams's home and called on their attackers to meet them face to face to discuss their problems.

Bobby Storey once accosted me because of a radio talk I had done that had referred to him and which he didn't like. He slammed me up against the wall of the Felons Club, told me I was a slug and accused me of being an MI5 agent. He is about twice my size. When you meet him on issues that displease him, he does the talking and you do the listening. The person who was cool enough to throw those grenades would have needed another level of bravado to face Bobby Storey.

What that week had shown us was that a new generation of paramilitary back-street fighters had emerged. These people were not yet deadly and had apparently been unable to sustain their commitment to rioting and mayhem beyond a few days.

It showed us also that they were backed by much more dangerous people. The Derry rioters had provided cover for a sniper attack. The east-Belfast rioting had been directed across a wide area by the UVF, according to the police. So violence can still be switched on and switched off.

What we also learned that week was that the Provisional IRA appeared not to be minded to avenge the attacks on Adams and Storey but preferred to take propaganda advantage from them, presenting themselves as peace loving and amenable to dialogue.

So the old guard who had killed over a thousand people during the Troubles were taking the chance to affirm that their own war was over. They would leave it to the state to curtail the oncoming generation. What that generation lacked, as yet, was experience and the indulgence of a much wider community, sympathetic to paramilitary aims and methods. These fighters faced the problem that the IRA had owned up to in 1962: that the people weren't interested. Seven years later, of course, they were.

*

When I met Jamie Bryson, there was the shock of recognition – and not just that feeling you get when you meet for the first time someone you have often seen on television. The surprise was that he is the same size as me. I am a small man. Usually when I shake hands with someone, the other hand is bigger. His was like my twin brother's. (And I do have a twin brother.) His hair colouring is light, like mine was once. He has the makings of a beard, though mine is grey now. Something like a genetic signal kicked in that said I should be nice to him, even protective; that we were from the same tree. We sat and talked politics for two hours and disagreed on almost everything but did not argue. Actually, that is not at all how it happened in my real family; there we argued incessantly.

Jamie, at the time we met, was twenty-eight years old; I was sixty-seven – just about old enough to be his grandfather. But he was a lot like me in ways other than the physical. He is broadly self-educated. He is a self-made journalist and commentator. He writes about politics and debates his big concerns on Stephen Nolan's shows. Nolan is criticised for using him as a frequent guest, since he is unelected and speaks for no one but himself. But the same applies to me; I've just been doing it for longer, since before Jamie was born.

We met on a loyalist housing estate in Newtownards, ten miles from Belfast. There were several Ulster flags and Union Jacks flying from lamp posts, murals celebrating loyalism and commemorating the world wars. This is not where he lives. He grew up in Donaghadee, a seaside resort, in a Church of Ireland family. His roots in loyalism are his reading. The Shankill Road was a world away. He came to political consciousness in his mid-teens, in 2005, when the passion for conflict was drained out of most people. And he sat up in bed reading the Belfast Agreement.

He opposes that Agreement but he differs from other traditional unionists who oppose it too in that he believes that the loyalist paramilitaries were right to kill and bomb for Ulster. Even sneaking regarders in unionist politics don't say that. There is a Progressive Unionist Party, which grew out of the UVF, but even its members tend to look back on the violence as something they got caught up in rather than as proletarian heroism.

Jamie sees Sinn Féin winning the battle of ideas and he wants unionism to engage more actively in it. Same-sex marriage and abortion reform have been adopted as causes by republicans, he believes, to impress naive young people who don't really feel strongly about these things, or about Irish unity, but who see them as progressive causes that they feel they should be backing.

His answer to that is to urge unionists to argue back, initially against same-sex marriage. Wherever he turns he sees plots to undermine unionism through campaigns that are ostensibly liberal but whose real agenda is the advancing of Irish nationalism.

He is running an online magazine called *Unionist Voice*. After the attack on the homes of Gerry Adams and Bobby Storey, he ran an article, unsigned, in which he speculated that the whole thing was staged by the Provisionals themselves.

When people complain that bonfires jeopardise homes in east Belfast he argues that republicans and those who have been suckered by them don't really care about those houses. And they don't really care about the routine effigies of republican and nationalist politicians on bonfires. What they are really up to is destroying the last vestiges of loyalist community.

'What the bonfire does: for the eight or nine weeks it brings together young people, it creates that social cohesion, that sense of community; and I think the opposition to the fires is an attempt to break down the cohesion that keeps the unionist community together.'

When Lyra McKee was killed in April 2019 by a New IRA gunman firing a pistol in the general direction of police lines at a riot in Derry, Jamie was one of the first to come out and express his regard for her on Twitter. Yet, he, like the gunman, takes an extreme position in the old quarrel over the Union with Britain, aligning himself with the paramilitaries of the past and their failed project. She was the same age as Jamie but represented something else, a secular liberal trend in society, away from the old division. There are still young people like Jamie, as passionate as their forebears about the old quarrel, and some like Lyra for whom the past is a curiosity, not a commitment.

Sick Society or Bad Men?

There has been a revolution in Northern Ireland but it is not the one that the media covered, or the one that the security services sought to quash or the politicians tried to manage. Fundamental change occurred between the start of the Troubles and the current period in which we hope – and, perhaps, trust – that the worst violence is behind us.

We have several competing theories about what went wrong in Northern Ireland but none of them quite explain how the society became more liberal and more secular after the ceasefires, let alone why this community ravaged itself so passionately. The violence angered a lot of people and we would expect that to have sharpened division and left us with hardened convictions. And that certainly did happen during the Troubles, with political leaders, for instance, calling for the death penalty or for the army to 'take the gloves off'. But, while the horrific experiences of danger and grief did drive some into defensive and assertive prejudiced thinking, more generally the peace found most, I believe, as good-natured as if the sorry period had never happened.

And how do we explain that?

Partly by the fact that many were hardly touched by the trouble, really; and partly, perhaps, by the relief that it was over and an enthusiasm for normality.

Competing theories about the Troubles attribute them to either a divided society or to an upsurge in terrorism. By the first view the whole of society was responsible; a failing of two communities to integrate had allowed suspicion to grow. By the other view, a few vicious people organised to overthrow the state or to oppress a minority. Some argue that the division in society was an inevitable by-product of the partition of Ireland, others that the division dates back to the Reformation and that partition was an effort to manage it, not exacerbate it, by giving each side a separate part of the country to govern.

The degree to which the wider society tolerated, indulged or even facilitated the killing is questioned. Some people wanted nothing to do with the paramilitaries – and indeed, most people voted for parties that opposed the campaigns of the republicans and loyalists. But there were times, as during the hunger strikes of 1981 or the parades protests of the mid-1990s, when the whole of society seemed so deeply divided that almost no one dissented from the position their community allegiance would have predicted.

In 1996, the most reasonable and considerate unionist would have said the solution to the parades disputes was to allow the Orangemen to march and to stay indoors if you were offended. Similarly, the most moderate and peace-loving nationalist would have said they should just go and march somewhere else. So, yes, there were times when it felt as if the whole population was divided and determined; yet at others it seemed only a few committed themselves to protesting, and fewer still to worse.

There were vicious people doing things that none could excuse, whether seeking out catholics and torturing them and carving them up with knives, as the Shankill Butchers did, or shooting dead a housewife because she was distributing census forms to augment her income, as the IRA did.

But even then people tended to be defensive against criticism of the killers when it seemed to implicate the wider community around them. To that degree, they were identifying with the paramilitaries. When protestants sneered at the IRA, I felt as if I was included in their contempt.

That is because I had a rationale for the violence that located it in the wider political context, a context of which I was critical. I didn't accept the 'few bad men' theory. I might feel that to concede a unionist criticism of the IRA was to also concede a political argument to them in favour of changing nothing.

Part of the relief at the end of the Troubles was at not having to be in that embarrassing position.

Unionists feared that the whole catholic community was secretly supportive of the IRA. Catholics believed that unionists saw them as being incapable of responsible citizenship. I remember occasions when the violence complicated relations with protestant friends.

On an October day in 1993 I heard the news that a bomb had exploded on the Shankill Road, a protestant area. It was one of those days that everyone who lived through the Troubles knew, when the very air seemed thick and oppressive. I was walking along the road and saw a protestant neighbour, a man I often stopped to chat with. Once, we had sat up through the night and drunk a bottle of tequila together. On this day, he looked away from me, angry and exasperated, having nothing to say. I didn't read that as blame, just as the impossibility of being trivial on such a day and the similar impossibility of him sharing his anger with a catholic, who would not be just as angry, who, he might fear, would make excuses.

Even friends kept secrets from each other. Some might have a brother in the RUC and never mention it; not because they feared that I would deliberately pass on information that would help the IRA target him, but just in case I did so carelessly.

Five years later, during the peace talks, there was the horrific week of killings by loyalists, one every night. This was when one of the targets was Charlie Breslin, the taxi driver whose firm was close to my home. I had often been in Charlie's car. Someone had walked up to the front of the car, while he was sitting waiting for a fare, and shot him dead for no other reason than that he was a catholic.

But what struck me most that week was how a specific threat against catholics strained my relations with a protestant colleague and friend. He was relaxed. He was busy because these killings were a story. He was getting work out of it. His mood was lighter than mine.

I said to him, 'You can go out tonight and be as safe as on any other night and I can't. I have to look around myself; you don't. If I want to go across the street for a bottle of wine, I have to consider that someone might shoot me.'

That actually happened; not the shooting but the wine. My wife asked me to get a bottle to have with dinner and I thought, *If I tell her I'm too scared to go out tonight all this will become too real; it will have come home.* So I went out and got the wine, passing within yards of where Charlie Breslin was shot.

So why did we emerge from the Troubles as better people than we had been during them? Because a stress was lifted. And that stress had been divisive. Part of it was the guilt or shame for what the worst among us had presumed to do on our behalf; part of it was just fear; part of it was exasperation that the fear itself was so often unfairly distributed.

But society after the Troubles was not just more relaxed; it was more secular and politically more liberal, and as much concerned to divide on same-sex marriage and abortion as it was on the border – and indeed on Israel.

On a Tuesday night in September – 11 September actually – about a hundred men and women were marching down Broadway from the Falls Road to the Balls on the Falls. This is a huge piece of public art with one geodesic sphere inside another. Post-Troubles public art in Northern Ireland was distinctive by its determination not to say anything about local culture or imply any allegiance. The local joke is that the big ball is Rory McIlroy's and the smaller one is Graeme McDowell's.

The people marching down the road didn't care. They were carrying Palestinian flags and they wanted to protest at Northern Ireland hosting the Israeli national team for a friendly football match.

Goodness knows what the Israelis made of this but they could be in little doubt that there were people in the city who had a message for them. That message was written in large white letters across Divis Mountain and was visible miles away: Free Palestine. And below it a huge Palestinian flag was spread out with rocks on the corners to support it. There were men up there guarding the flag.

The people coming down from the Falls to support the Palestinians were probably mostly nationalists. Some of them were former members of the IRA. I knew them. They took this cause seriously. Some had travelled to Israel and the occupied territories.

During the Troubles it would have been rash of them to march down Broadway for the roundabout there is an interface between the catholic Falls and the protestant Village area. I hardly ever went there myself, except to drive on to or off the motorway. When I was twenty-one I walked down there with a friend called Denis to see where a bomb had exploded. We knew we were in a protestant area but the concerted killing of catholics had hardly warmed up. A group of men surrounded us and demanded to know where we were from. A woman ran across from her house, still wiping her hands on a tea towel. 'Get them off the street,' she said. But then an army vehicle rounded the corner and they scattered. We walked briskly back the way we had come.

The protesters for Palestine were walking blithely into a hostile area, but presumably trusting that the police would be on hand to guard them against others and their own excesses.

True enough, at the northern side of the roundabout, dozens of police officers of the Tactical Support Groups in flameproof uniforms blocked their way and confined them to the footpath.

Diagonally opposite, on the other side of the roundabout, they could see a smaller group of loyalists waving Israeli and Ulster flags, ostensibly ready to confront them but safely hemmed in by the police, ordinary police officers this time, in uniform and hi-vis jackets.

This was the ecology of protest in Belfast. The police played the ostensible role of obstacle and that kept everyone safe. Had they not turned up that night, protest would have been impossible or violence inevitable.

Yet the pro-Palestine protesters stood face to face up close with the police. I heard one of them taunting an officer, discussing him in earshot. 'He just said we're scum. I read his lips. That's the word he used, "scum".'

For someone like me, who had covered very serious riots in Belfast, this was bizarrely light-hearted. I asked the officer who had or hadn't mouthed the word 'scum' whether he thought it was safe for me to approach the loyalists. He was civil and helpful but not cheerful. He advised me to take care crossing the road.

In the centre of the roundabout, under the Balls structure, two officers stood talking to each other. Another stood alone about ten yards from them.

I said hello. Did they think it was OK for me to go over to the loyalists?

One of them said, 'That's the boss over there but he's too important to be standing here with us minions.'

So they didn't mind me carrying on?

'Check with the others over there.'

I crossed the roundabout diagonally to the next police line, guarding – or containing – the loyalists.

'Are you press?' asked the man in charge.

I said, 'Not exactly. I'm an independent.'

'Just say yes,' he said, and let me through.

I stood around the loyalists and raised my camera. They were mostly young men and some older women. One young man in a blue jacket came forward and ordered me not to take photographs. A woman standing near him said, 'I don't mind him taking pictures.'

I thanked her. 'After all, what's the point in making a public protest if you don't want people to see you?'

'That's right,' she said. 'You're Malachi, aren't you?'

In the past, this could have been tricky.

The first rule of covering loyalist protests was to try not to look like a catholic, and trust your colleagues not to use your Irish name out loud. The press always regarded loyalists as more touchy than republicans. The IRA might blow you up in your office block or while you were out shopping but they were inclined to be civil face to face.

I occasionally appeared on television in discussions, and more frequently on radio, so there was no pretending I was a protestant.

'Fuck off, Malachi,' someone shouted. 'Go back over to your own crowd.'

One might view the dispute as a surrogate for sectarianism, displacing Orange parades or the Union with Israel versus Palestine. Or one might view it as the beginning of a maturing in politics within sectarian communities as new issues of concern are taken up. Conceivably feelings about Israel and Palestine might tempt some people to cross over to the other side in a way that past divisions had not. Of course, the 'Fuck off, Malachi' suggests that protestant identity is still a qualification for inclusion among the loyalists supporting Israel.

Northern Ireland beat Israel 3–0 that night, a result that must have pleased even some of the protesters who hadn't wanted the match to be played.

*

Are we nicer people than we used to be?

Certainly visitors to Belfast say we are and often express surprise that we so recently had a hot culture of political violence. Then again, most of us didn't. In the spectrum between the sick-society model and the few-bad-men theory, the balance tilts well away, most of the time, from any plausible suggestion that most of us wanted the killing to go on. Most of us voted for political parties that opposed it; and of the parties that openly endorsed violent campaigns only Sinn Féin grew significantly, taking the lead among nationalist parties, after the violence had stopped and it got the credit for stopping it. Others that emerged from paramilitary backgrounds, like the Ulster Democratic Party and the Progressive Unionist Party, failed to grow much at all. The Democratic Unionist Party, which was often ambiguous on violence, followed a similar trajectory to that of Sinn Féin, taking the lead position within unionism after demonstrating a willingness to enter partnership government with Sinn Féin.

So, most of us did not want the violence and most of us did reward political parties that turned away from endorsing it and towards seeking conciliation. All of which suggests that we are, underneath it all, decent people who don't want anyone shot dead on our behalf.

On the other hand, in 2017 relations between the DUP and Sinn Féin broke down, so that they could not operate a power-sharing devolved government. And despite that breakdown having left the region without ministers who might have reformed the health service and the education system, both parties increased their vote as their communities supported them in their refusal to concede to each other.

That suggests that this society is deeply sectarian, that factions will even suffer damage to public services to assert that they are right and the other side is wrong.

So, we do not have our sleep disrupted by bombs in the night and we do not wake up to the news of killings, but we still don't have a society that can knit its division together and be creative let alone minimally responsible in government.

We don't have complete peace.

In one year, 286 families were rehoused because of intimidation. There is hardly a starker figure than that to show that hatred is one of the forces shaping our society. A difference with the past is that some of those families chased from their homes are not primarily catholic or protestant in the eyes of their attackers but are black or Asian.

Yet people say we are nice, friendly and generous and we are.

Age makes this a little difficult to judge.

When I was, say, seventeen in 1968, before the Troubles started, I would walk warily round my own neighbourhood.

I was not afraid of being shot or robbed, but I was afraid of just being kicked or punched in the face, scowled at by other lads or challenged to a fight. Maybe that is how it still is for boys of seventeen.

Nobody wants to fight you when you are sixty-seven. Even the civility that surprises me in Tactical Support Group police officers, tooled up and dressed in fireproof gear, may not be what they present to teenagers.

At school, boys in my class wore Boy Scout belts, though they had never been Scouts themselves, because those belts could be whipped off at speed and swung at another's face or wrapped round the hand to create a mailed fist.

One of the strange side effects of the Troubles was that I could walk around without fear of these boys because they had an outlet for their aggression in rioting.

And conditions have changed for schoolboys now.

My generation was routinely beaten in school. Now, if you thought that someone was ordering your child to hold out a hand so that the palm or fingertips might be struck with a springy bamboo cane, you would probably be very angry indeed. I got canings like that for my bad handwriting and it didn't improve it.

And I wonder if the school punishment systems, now long banned, were the template for the punishment regimes of the paramilitaries, in which young men were not caned but shot in the legs, similarly having to turn up as ordered and be still and take it. Far more people were shot in the legs during the Troubles than were shot dead, and the perpetrators were from their own communities, often neighbours they knew by name.

So why would we be nicer now?

Life for many young men may not be as hard as it would have been during the Troubles. The suicide rates suggest that for some it is as bad as it can possibly be, unbearable. More young men kill themselves every year now than were killed during the Troubles, when the suicide rate actually declined as the violence worsened. It resumed at high levels when the violence stopped.

In 2016 nearly three hundred people killed themselves. This is two and a half times the level in the 1980s when, on average, 126 people killed themselves each year. Only in one year, 1972, did a higher number of people get killed in the Troubles than killed themselves in 2016. So arguably we have a greater crisis now than we had through most of the violence. But these deaths are silent; they are not even reported on in the media for fear that coverage will encourage others. Apparently big funerals for children who have killed themselves can make death seem attractive to friends who have never been given so much attention while alive.

No such caution inhibited reportage of bombings and shootings.

But is a high suicide rate indicative of grief and misery across the whole of society or just within a segment of it? We are back to a spectrum like the one between the sick-society model and the few-bad-men theory. Can we take the pulse of Northern Ireland through the suicide rate any more than we could have judged its health by the scale of political violence?

More, should we ask if the political explanations for past violence missed the point: if there were cultural causes of violence? If the state of Northern Ireland is to be judged, as it was through the Troubles, by the number of violent deaths, if we include self-inflicted deaths it is actually worse now than it was in the 1980s and nineties. Today people agonising about how to respond to stabbings of young men in London or mass shootings in the US profess themselves plainly bewildered. Maybe when they have worked through those problems they will find solutions that might have been more applicable in Northern Ireland in the nineties than power sharing and cross-border bodies.

Perhaps for most people things were all right, most of the time, even when they heard bomb blasts in the distance before they turned over and went to sleep.

Irish suicide figures show that between 1950 and 1970, the rate remained constant, and equally divided between men and women. Both rose from 1970 on, though with male suicide rising much higher than female.

One of the big questions agonised over in Northern Ireland today is how we deal with the past, meaning the past political violence, but the suicide figures alone tell us that there is much more grief around us than that which was caused by the killing. Add on to that the carnage on the roads and it may be that most of those sitting alone tonight pining for the sudden loss of a loved one are not thinking about the Troubles at all.

When we look at those old pictures of civil-rights parades, we are seeing a lot of people who, though young there, are already dead. Some were killed by bomb explosions or were shot; some died in car crashes and some died of cancer or heart disease and some took their own lives. Most of that would be true of any snapshot of a large crowd in any city from fifty years ago.

Those people had little idea of what the coming decades would bring, the murders and the rioting, the army raids in the night, the whining military vehicles and the gunfire; but neither had they foreseen the toll that lung cancer would take, how the ashtray would disappear from office desks and bars, how lead-free petrol would come to save us, how the fridges in our homes were oozing chemicals that would erode the ozone layer and endanger us all.

I remember my mother's first fridge. She was so pleased with it that she set a kitchen chair in the middle of the floor so that she could just sit and admire it. She celebrated with a fag, sighed with satisfaction. We could make our own ice lollies! Life was getting better. In years to come, she would even have central heating.

Had the protesters of fifty years ago really known how to make the world a better place, what might they not have been demanding?

An Teanga

The ideology pushing most vehemently for change in Northern Ireland through the years of the Troubles was republicanism. Republicans pride themselves on keeping faith with a core idea, that Ireland should be a single independent nation. They refer back to the Proclamation of the Irish Republic by Patrick Pearse on the steps of the GPO in Dublin in 1916. Pearse and his fellow revolutionaries had declared the creation of a republic that would treat 'all of the children equally'.

Yet, though a war for independence followed, the settlement achieved did not create the fulfilment of Pearse's vision but instead a partitioned island, the big bit for the catholics and the small bit for the protestants. Both would retain links to Britain. The southern part first of all, as a Free State that would later declare itself a republic. The northern (or north-eastern, to be accurate) part would have a devolved parliament.

While annually committing itself to the vision of Pearse, republicans have divided and subdivided and evolved. The largest part of the movement now is Sinn Féin, or rather the subdivision of old Sinn Féin that went with the Provisional IRA in 1970 and which was led by Gerry Adams into a peace process and a dumping of arms by the IRA in 2005 and a decommissioning of weapons that unionists accepted as the conclusion of their armed campaign.

The republicanism of Pearse had four essential ingredients: that the Irish Republic would be catholic, Gaelic and unitary and would belong to the people and treat them all equally.

Little remains of any of those four defining aspirations. Some are no longer even mentioned by modern republicans.

Gerry Adams is a catholic. Martin McGuinness, the IRA leader who became deputy first minister of Northern Ireland, was buried with full catholic rites in 2017. But no branch of the republican tradition now argues that Ireland should be a catholic country. The Sinn Féin Party takes its votes almost exclusively from catholics and former catholics but this support base no longer insists that the party should represent catholic teaching. Indeed, were it to do so, many – perhaps most – of these nominal catholics would desert it.

This is not how things were in the past.

In the 1930s, the IRA pledged itself to accepting papal encyclicals as the basis of its social policies. It had had to do that to quash a perception that it was being led by socialist republicans towards atheistic communism.

Eamon de Valera – who had fought alongside Pearse in 1916, rejected the 1921 treaty and then formed the Fianna Fáil Party and went on to be both taoiseach and president – argued that Ireland must be 'Not only catholic but Gaelic as well; not only Gaelic but catholic as well'.

He framed a constitution for the country in consultation with the Church – and that constitution recognised the 'special position' of the Catholic Church, ruled that a woman's place was in the home and banned blasphemy.

But in recent years Catholicism has lost its hold on the country, partly through the disgrace of child-abuse scandals and partly through the failure to impress sufficient people with the validity of its rules on sexual conduct and contraception. The latest in a series of referenda on constitutional change has removed the blasphemy law.

At the start of the Troubles in 1969 it did seem plain to many that sectarian violence was a remnant of the Reformation divisions in Europe. Certainly that is how Rev. Ian Paisley saw it. This was a religious war. But how do you maintain a religious war through a period of secularisation?

Many republicans also saw religion as an ingredient of their cause. In 1981, during the hunger-strike protests in the Maze Prison, wall murals in Belfast in support of the prisoners depicted them praying in their cells with the Virgin Mary appearing beside them, showering graces upon them. I suspect that was really the last confident expression of republicanism as devoutly catholic.

For unionism the religious component survived longer. Then it also seemed to be sidelined when Ian Paisley chose to give up his leadership of the Free Presbyterian Church in order to take the office of first minister and was even then ousted by his party modernists. But a few years later the party was standing against same-sex marriage and abortion-law reform when the nominally catholic leaders of Sinn Féin and the SDLP were campaigning for these reforms.

So it appears that the religious character of the division between two communities waned more among nationalists and republicans, the catholics, than it did among unionists, the protestants. Yet the political structures may disguise a much more liberal and secular attitude among unionists too.

I was invited to go and talk to members of an Apprentice Boys club in south Belfast. This is less than half a mile from my home and yet I had never been in it, never thought I would be welcome there.

I was met by a man called Nev who had a long wispy beard and decorative tattoos on both arms. We sat over a drink waiting for a meeting to end upstairs so that I could take the chair there. Nev told me that he was hoping to buy a house in the area; that he wanted to live within walking distance of this club. Indeed, several unionists who had lived in the area and moved out came back to drink there and to maintain their association with each other and the club.

And some people did look around at me with what I took for suspicion, though my own perspective might have been coloured by wariness.

The men at the other meeting were discussing charities they were contributing to. Above the chairman was a widescreen television on silent showing a football match.

When they were finished I took my place and asked for the television to be switched off.

'Oh, come on, Malachi; that's Rangers playing.'

So it was kept on, so that my audience could follow the game at the same time as listening to me.

In my talk, I wanted to set out how I believed attitudes had changed in the catholic community, how that community was growing out of being a disadvantaged minority and how the current anxiety over Brexit coloured all considerations of Northern Ireland's future.

I made the point that Brexit opened the prospect of a united Ireland in a context of demographic change. The predominantly nationalist part of the population that had voted Remain would retain the option of voting us all back into the EU by uniting Ireland, if enough people felt in the coming years that leaving had not worked out for them.

Some argued that if Ireland had any sense it would leave too.

But when the discussion moved on to how the Irish Republic had become more genial through the decline of the Catholic Church and the liberalising of social laws governing same-sex marriage and abortion, those who had sided with the DUP on Brexit said they opposed them on homosexuality and women's rights.

Suddenly these same men who seemed like hard-edged loyalists on constitutional questions were just an ordinary bunch of secular-minded social liberals. Jamie Bryson would say they had been suckered but there were more of them than there are of him.

'I don't care what gays do, so long as they don't do it in front of me.'

'I'm damned if I'm telling any woman what to do with her own body.'

So, the fact of the DUP being the largest political party in Northern Ireland may suggest that most unionists are evangelical conservative christians, but this is not actually so.

And, though the two communities in Northern Ireland are labelled according to the religious convictions of their forebears, the tension between them no longer has a significant grounding in their separate theologies.

Paisley's vision of a militant Protestantism pitched against Romish influence in Ireland is obsolete.

And on the other side, Pearse's idea of Irish republicanism as grounded firmly on Catholicism is now irrelevant. The cultural catholic traces within a nominally catholic republican community now are like the fieldwork markings still visible in the Irish countryside of old potato rills and dried-up old peat bogs. They remind us of our history but don't determine our actions today.

If religion as one of the strands of traditional republicanism has gone, that leaves Gaelic culture and the ideas of unity, popular ownership and equality.

The land of Ireland does not belong to the people of Ireland. It is all in private hands. This will not change without a socialist revolution and there appears to be no immediate prospect of such. The IRA in the 1970s committed itself to this project but quickly came to the conclusion that it might fight on for a united Ireland but that after that the people as a whole should freely decide if they wanted socialism.

Republicans still argue that Ireland should be united but have agreed within the terms of the Good Friday Agreement that this can be achieved only through the consent of majorities in both parts of Ireland. That doesn't mean that the issue is dormant. They urge a border poll, as provided for in the Agreement, but do little to convert unionists to the idea.

The principle of equality is advanced strongly by Sinn Féin today in ways that Pearse could not have conceived of.

He would have endorsed their claim that the Irish language should have equal status with English but he would have found wholly bizarre in his time their argument that there should be equal same-sex marriage rights.

So, traditional commitments to unity, Catholicism and ownership of the land have been compromised on. This leaves just one strand of the four-stranded thread that republicanism was woven out of, and that is Gaelic language and culture.

In the spring of 2018, negotiations between Sinn Féin and the DUP to repair a collapsed power-sharing government at Stormont foundered on how an Irish Language Act might be framed. Sinn Féin insisted that it be a stand-alone act. The DUP came close to finding a compromise that would have set the Irish Language Act within a complex of three Acts, one for the Ulster Scots dialect and a culture Act that would have embraced the other two.

Close to the apparent point of agreement, the DUP leadership decided that it could not sell the deal to its base and so the Assembly was not restored.

One of the strongest advocates of an Irish Language Act is Linda Ervine, who is not from a republican tradition. So the Gaelicisation of Ireland is no longer a cause republicans can have ownership of. Yet this is the concern they have decided to block all political progress over.

Linda is the daughter of Terry Bruton, who was a member of the NICRA executive, and the wife of Brian Ervine, who was the leader of the PUP after the death of his more famous brother David – a former UVF bomber and long-term loyalist prisoner.

Linda's family were communists and she had had a difficult relationship with the loyalist community in east Belfast where she lived.

Once she poured out her heart to a loyalist leader in a club about how her family was virtually ostracised by protestant neighbours. He had expressed his sympathy and support for her until he realised what her family connections were, then drew back from her and said, 'I won't be helping you.'

Linda in adult life became religious and joined a church. She also returned to education and got a university degree and became a teacher. It was through teaching that she met Brian Ervine. Brian took her on her first-ever visit to Donegal. She talks now of having 'fallen in love' with the Irish language. She told me, 'You don't say you *speak* Irish; you say you *have* it – "*Tá Gaelige agam.*" And I wanted to have it. I wish I had known twenty years ago that I could just go and learn this.'

At the beginning of her interest she struggled with the kind of inhibition that governs the attitude to Irish of many in the DUP. 'There is a wee hump you have to get over, a feeling that this is a catholic thing. One of my students actually asked if he was betraying something by learning it.

'But there is something about the language that is so attractive. Is it, as somebody once said to me, that without knowing it, it is in us because it is all around us and is the language of our ancestry and place names? Something naturally draws us to it. I can't answer that but I know for me there just was this overwhelming desire to get this language.'

She now runs Irish-language classes in east Belfast with the support of her church. And she is working against quiet resistance from people who feel that she is an embarrassment to loyalism.

'We got a bit of stick on Facebook. I remember one guy – he's a local paramilitary, UVF I think. When I looked up his Facebook page he had used my brother-in-law's picture; it was quite ironic. And he had a bit of a rant and at the bottom of it he put, "We are a separate people," meaning protestants. He's actually the uncle of my cousin's grandson and his mother is a catholic.'

The PUP supported Linda and allowed her to speak on her work at their annual conference, but some people in education and in the churches were more wary than these inheritors of the legacy of gunmen were.

'I developed this PowerPoint on protestants and the Irish language and just wanted to get it out; and I approached schools and churches and a lot of them said, "This is great; we are very sympathetic – but no." They were scared of their own congregations. Which is very sad.'

Linda Ervine is a gentle and lightly built woman who has made a personal journey from a difficult childhood and wayward teens, through a long period of marriage and child-rearing to find her own bearings in life against powerful resistance.

People scoffed at her when she wanted to study for GCSEs.

She told me, 'I grew up in a world in which you got out of the way of the men, and what was your role in life but to marry one of these men and have children? And these men could do whatever they wanted; they could be violent and drink and your place was to put up with that; that's what your working-class background told you. And you looked round you and nobody seemed to be any different.'

She hesitated to work towards a university place but eventually took an English degree.

Now she has set up Turas, an organisation for the teaching and promotion of Irish and is a regular campaigner on Irish-language concerns in the media.

And, while political parties within unionism urged her to hold back on campaigning for an Irish Language Act, she was incensed by the derision displayed towards Irish by some in the DUP. One of the MLAs, Gregory Campbell, had entertained the party conference with his mockery of Irish.

'What I saw there in the audience was these ones laughing and clapping and a few got up and walked out. And I thought, *This is just unacceptable.* And this is what's wrong in this country, an attitude not just to Irish language but to Irish identity and the fact that people don't know all these things.'

But she is similarly wary of being seen as an archetypal protestant housewife who has stepped out of her community to distinguish herself from it.

'Even though I came from a very political family, for the first time in my life I started to see what was going on. I felt quite incensed by it and I started to speak out and Brian was kind of, "Be careful, be careful; you're trying to do this work with the unionist community. You have to keep yourself."

'But I also started to feel: I am being presented as this kind of loyalist. I am not a loyalist. I don't even come from a unionist family. This is not who I am. We were communist. People are putting this on me; this is not who I am.'

Linda organised a discussion on the civil-rights movement at the Skainos Centre in east Belfast.

'What struck me was that the rights my father was looking for in the 1960s were British rights. We have the same situation here now only it is different rights. It is equal marriage, rights for women and it is language rights. One of the lines that struck me was: "British rights for British people." Well, these *are* British rights for British people. So how far have we really moved when British people are still asking for the same rights as other people in other parts of the British isles?'

She made the case that unionists should favour an Irish Language Act because it is the British way to respect minority languages and give them their place. This was of course the civil-rights argument fifty years ago: that if the state says we are British then we should have the same rights as people in the rest of Britain. But, as happened back then, resistance to the claim and the prolonging of the dispute shapes it into something purely factional.

Republicans may feel that preservation of the language is part of their purpose but they cannot be accused of appropriating the language to their political agenda because the language is bigger than any one ideology could grasp. It is alive.

Unionists see it as the property and concern of nationalists. But Linda would argue that giving Irish a statutory position would end the tradition of it being used emblematically on behalf of one community to distinguish itself from the other.

'We want an Irish Language Act because we want it to be taken out of the political realm. We want it to stop being a political football, which it obviously is, and we feel that if you bring in legislation that is what will happen. You have the language commissioner, which is a neutral post, so the very thing that the unionist community are getting worked up about – the idea that this belongs to Sinn Féin – an Irish Language Act will stop that. It's a solution but people don't realise that.

'And when I talk to people and they tell me the things they don't like about an ILA – that there is going to be compulsory education, it's going to cost billions, you're going to have to have Irish to go to your doctor's – none of it is true. They don't have an issue with the things that are being asked for; they have an issue with the things they *think* are being asked for.'

I learned Irish at school from the Christian Brothers, who saw it as intrinsic to basic nationalist chauvinism. There is more to the Irish culture than that now. My wife and I went to a book launch in Cultúrlann, an Irish-language centre, to hear the poetry of Cathal Ó Searchaigh, some of it homoerotic love poetry likening the country roads to the legs of a lover and the land to a beautiful body. The Brothers would have gagged at the thought. Another of Cathal's poems was a tribute to a Palestinian boy burned to death in an attack by Israeli settlers.

So the language is being used creatively to express sexuality and politics.

A woman I spoke to in Cultúrlann told me that what she loved about the Irish-language community in Belfast was that people did not correct your grammar as you spoke.

'How many people have been put off speaking Irish by pompous perfectionists? It's not like that here. People are just so glad to hear you try that they encourage you.'

Even members of the DUP seemed for a time to be softening their resistance to an Irish Language Act. The problem, as a party adviser explained to me, is that unionists feel the need to win a round against Sinn Féin and won't let the party concede. Unreasonably or not, their support base fears that they will always lose when they are negotiating with republicans.

If republicans get a straight win on the Irish language, he said, then they will come back later with another demand to further reinforce Irish identity. At some point we have to say no. According to Linda, though, 'If you think like that you won't legislate for anything.'

Irish-language activists, including republicans, have in the past seen the need to prevent the language being politicised, made the property of one community and weaponised against the unionists.

My old school friend Caoimhín de Búrca told me a story that illustrates how that caution was once exercised.

'I've always been terribly interested in the Irish language and I would value it greatly for what it is, but when politicians start meddling in it then it becomes a bloody political football. That is what happened here.'

He said that a former Northern Ireland minister, during the long period of Direct Rule from Westminster, considered dropping Irish from the school curriculum. Caoimhín involved himself in a campaign to prevent this happening and was to be part of a delegation to meet the secretary of state, Tom King, to urge against it. As it happened, the catholic primate Cardinal Tomás Ó Fiaich stepped in to use his influence and the idea was dropped.

But it is what happened before that that is illuminating.

'I remember at the time there were one or two guys who were prominent in Sinn Féin and when I was asked if I would go up in a delegation and meet the minister, I said, "Yes I would, but who's going?" And I said, "If they go" – the Sinn Féin members – "it's over. It will just turn into a political bloody thing." And I actually spoke to one of them and they said, "Right, we'll not go."'

So Sinn Féin, which blocked the return of the NI Executive, the entire running of Stormont, to enforce a demand for an Irish Language Act, had previously tried to help the language by staying out of the quarrel.

They had seen the sense then of holding back so that Irish wouldn't become just one of those things that unionists and nationalists fight over.

It's God's Fault

The first response in much of the world media, after the guns came out in 1969, was to see the problem as a war between religions. They saw that catholics and protestants had clashed on the streets and therefore saw a sectarian riot; just as they would have seen a race riot if this had been whites fighting blacks or blacks fighting Asians. This seemed to be a legacy of the wars after the Reformation, and the historic lineage was there. But it was superficial to assume that catholics were fighting for the authority of the Pope against the authority of the monarchy; though who can say that some old chauvinists weren't thinking in those terms?

People still say to me, when I travel, 'I can't understand why people fight over religion.'

And I am inclined to reply that they don't. The people who go to church are not the people who manned the barricades, imported arms and bombed the towns and cities. Except that some of them were, and so were some of those who encouraged them or made excuses for them.

Certainly there were armed protestant gangs who sought out catholics to kill, as there were people from the catholic community who attacked protestants, but these killers were not motivated by theology. Religious roots were a label for a community but what offended about that community was its take on the Union with Britain and its inferred support for militants or the state.

Yet that association between religion and national allegiance did date back hundreds of years, so there was a logic in seeing the battle in Divis Street in 1969 as an outworking, even a continuation of an old war that the rest of Britain and Ireland had forgotten.

Rev. Ian Paisley, who was of course a huge influence over loyalist paramilitaries, did frankly express his objection to republicanism through religious belief. He was urging his followers to defend the Reformation, to spare Northern Ireland the horror of being subsumed into a catholic state that was in thrall to the Vatican.

In the same way in Israel, a largely secular state, there are still some who believe the land was given to them by God and that they are doing His work by fighting for it.

Republicans say that they are not a religious movement, even if most of their members are from the same religious tradition, but that they are committed primarily to uniting Ireland as a single nation. The modern republican movement did not start out as liberal. Seán McGouran says he did not join the Provisionals after the split from the IRA in 1970 – represented politically since by Sinn Féin – because they were 'Holy Joes'.

A story often cited to illustrate the moral obsession of the Provisionals was their initial refusal to use condoms in incendiary devices. They had been shown a detonation mechanism that relied on acid burning slowly through rubber. The anomaly was that the Catholic Church banned condoms as contraceptive devices but had no theological objection to their being used in other ways. It did, however, have strong teachings against murder and the destruction of other people's property. That teaching did not impress the IRA.

The republican movement at that time perhaps saw the assertion of its religious convictions as a counter to the presumption of others that people who bombed civilian targets were morally wanting. When I worked with a BBC religious-affairs programme in the 1980s, I phoned Martin McGuinness, one of the most senior members of the IRA, to ask him how the violence was reconciled with catholic theology. He argued that the Second Vatican Council endorsed freedom of conscience and that the IRA man who killed a policeman on a Wednesday and read *Playboy* on a Thursday might go to confession on Saturday and unburden himself of the sin of reading *Playboy* while feeling under no onus to mention the killing because, by his own conscience, it was not a sin to kill policemen.

However, theologians participating in the same programme dismissed this reading of catholic teaching.

Some paramilitaries gave up their violent ways after turning religious, finding God, as some of them did in prison, and seeing a clear incompatibility between killing and praying. And yet, while it seems wrong to suggest that republican militants were driven by religious faith, practically all of them were raised as catholics, educated in catholic schools and, when killed, given catholic funerals.

Republicans often recited the rosary at commemorations for their dead. Memorial plaques on house fronts on the Falls Road in Belfast and in Derry often include a prayer to Naomh Mhuire, Banríon na hÉireann, Holy Mary, Queen of Ireland. Republicans may deny that they were driven by religious belief or by contempt for the theologies of others, even that they are not essentially catholic, but to an outside observer, their Catholicism is obvious and ubiquitous.

My rejection of the simplistic theory that the Troubles were driven by religion seems common sense to many, yet they lightly forget sometimes that religion was in the mix.

The graffiti on the walls declared 'Fuck the Pope' and 'Fuck the Queen'. You could argue that this was written by people who knew little about papacy or monarchy and wanted only to needle the other side; that if relations were stable and friendly between two communities they would not pick on each other's shibboleths; that the war was not over the cultural and religious divisions but that these were given significance when the two sides were at odds with each other; that they sneer at each other's religion as they sneer at their football teams. It is the contempt that is telling, not the content of it.

Clearly the churches and religious leaders frequently condemned the violence and urged people not to get drawn into it.

Pope John Paul II came to Ireland in 1979 and begged the killers – on bended knee – to stop. They paid no heed to him; which might have come as a surprise to some protestant churchmen who thought he was a dictator running the lives of docile and impressionable catholics.

One, Rev. Martin Smyth, had said at the start of the IRA campaign that if the Bishop of Rome put his house in order the killing would stop. He genuinely believed that the Pope was behind the IRA, urging it on with the hope of bringing Northern Ireland into a catholic state, the Irish Republic, thereby expanding the papal empire.

*

Republicans killed all kinds of people but claimed to be most interested in killing soldiers and police officers and loyalist paramilitaries. They would say that those killed by bombings were not killed deliberately; they often gave warnings in advance of bombs. They have often insisted that the murders of protestant police officers were not sectarian (most police officers being protestant), as killing border farmers was not sectarian; those targets were chosen because they were part-time soldiers. As for the wife who was killed alongside the farmer soldier, it's hard to see how she was a legitimate target.

The main reason given by loyalist paramilitaries who killed catholics was not contempt for their religious beliefs or fear of Rome but retaliation against the IRA. The sneering at their religion, they suggest, would not have been taken as far as actual murder but for the IRA campaign.

Republicans point out that loyalist violence came first, with two killings in the mid-1960s. They argue that loyalists would have been attacking catholics whatever the IRA did, though when the IRA ended its campaign the loyalists ended theirs.

And in the 1960s, those loyalists who killed catholics believed that the IRA was training for another uprising – and it is true that the IRA was armed and recruiting and training at that time.

But if we suppose that religion was a powerful motivator for violence we might also accept that it discouraged some from joining paramilitary organisations and taking part in the routines of murder and destruction.

The christian teaching in both traditions is that violence is wrong, that one must 'turn the other cheek'. Of course, few seriously adhere to the pacifism of Jesus or are even expected to. But they are enjoined to 'love' their neighbour; and the definition of 'neighbour' is wide in the Gospels – wide enough to include a Samaritan and therefore, by extension, a protestant or a catholic.

Religious influence did not reach people only through Church but through education and family too, and through organisations like the Legion of Mary, the Sodality, the Boys' Brigade and the Scouts and the Orange Order. If such a broad range of influences did not restrain people from hatred and sectarianism, then they failed horribly in their purposes.

Yet we have also seen that as religion declined in influence over people the violence also declined. That does not mean that there is a direct relationship between religious conviction and violence but it may be evidence that Church teachings are not adequate to the moral challenges of the time. If there is no connection between religion and the decline of violence then that reflects very badly on religion; it suggests that the biggest movement preaching peace and love failed completely. If there is any connection at all, at a time of religious decline, it suggests something more appalling for the churches, that they were an actual irritant.

Priests and pastors, as I saw them – and as a religious-affairs journalist I saw a lot of them – were shallow thinkers, pallid orators and detached from the society they worked in. Drawing on Jesus as an exemplar didn't seem to work for the twentieth century. The preachers were easily indicted of being out of touch with their own messages of love and forgiveness.

And one could see in that period that the churches were not opposed to war. The protestant churches were routinely decked with regimental flags and monuments in honour of 'the fallen', those who had made 'the ultimate sacrifice'. Clearly they did not object to all war.

Lesley Carroll, who was later ordained a presbyterian minister in Belfast, recalled that the church she went to as a child in New Mills near Coalisland in County Tyrone was proud to have a Victoria Cross memorial. 'And not every church in Northern Ireland has that, so that history was connected to the village.'

The congregation there included police officers and soldiers and, she said, people who probably had family connections to the UVF.

A story from her teenage years well illustrates how religion insulated people from sectarian realities rather than encouraged them to confront them. According to Lesley, 'There was a kind of split between Church and world. So I remember for example one of the really shaping memories of my life was when Gertie and Jim Devlin were shot.'

Gertrude and James Devlin were driving home with their daughter one spring evening in May 1974 when a soldier stood out in front of their car and ordered them to stop. This looked like a routine search, common enough in those days. James stepped out of the car. Gunmen then fired on them. James fell beside the car. Gertrude died in her seat. Their daughter was wounded but survived.

Lesley continued, 'They were significant members of the SDLP, ordinary nationalists, not interested in violence at all. Gertie worked in Coalisland library with my aunt, so I knew her well; Jim not so well. And they were shot by the UVF simply because they were members of the SDLP and catholics.

'And that was never mentioned in church. Never mentioned.

'So the religious culture was such that we were very pious. We prayed about a lot of things and talked about religion all the time but no mention of that. I could never get my head around why there wasn't mention of our neighbours in that way. And it may have been that there were UVF families connected to the congregation, who knows?'

A theological distinction between Catholicism and evangelical Protestantism may be relevant to this. Catholics pray for the souls of the dead to help them get into Heaven. Evangelicals don't do this and even take offence when others do pray for protestants who have died. This is because their faith tells them that they are either saved or not saved, by grace, and that the prayers of others play no part in this.

Still, there would have been no heresy in praying for the family of the dead, for the wounded daughter, that she might have peace and comfort. That would have been the normal thing to do had the dead couple been protestants.

Lesley says that the culture she grew up in encouraged her to keep catholics at a distance. She couldn't go to the funeral of the Devlins. 'We couldn't go over the door of a catholic church. That would have been to give credence to this corrupt faith, papism, you know?'

This was, she maintained, about preserving their spiritual integrity. She and the people around her believed that they had a true religious conviction that had to be protected against dilution. They were on guard not just against Catholicism but also the modern world. It was hard to maintain that distance when you had gregarious catholic neighbours, though.

'Our next-door neighbours were two catholic sisters and their brothers were all priests, in Africa and all sorts of places. And when the brothers came home, they used to come round to visit, so I will never forget, and my father will never forget, the first time one of these priests was coming up the driveway. There was a kind of, "Oh my goodness; look who's coming up the path!" Panic in the house.'

But the Carrolls were polite neighbours and would not turn him away, even though the priest's visit was an embarrassment and a challenge to their evangelical reserve.

'We became the best of friends but you wouldn't have had that mix normally. That was something alien. That was the nature of that community. And we were not a minority among protestants. The purity of Christianity had to be protected. On a religious level, you wouldn't have allowed anything into your thoughts or into the arena of your experience that might have corrupted that purity; and Catholicism would have done that. And, by extension, catholics would have done that.'

But if religion was divisive in one way it was also at times a powerful counter to violent impulses.

The soldier who had led the UVF killers to the Devlin home that night in May 1974 later went to an evangelical service in Dungannon and found God and repented. The judge said of him, 'It's a pity he did not become a Christian before May 7, 1974.'[8]

Lesley Carroll was aware of the civil-rights campaign as a small child. She can remember Bernadette Devlin and other civil-rights leaders being mentioned in conversation in her home. The first march from Dungannon to Coalisland passed her front door and she wondered why her own family didn't join in.

And there were contradictions in her family's attitude to catholics.

One of the leaders of the civil-rights campaign then was Austin Currie, who later helped found the SDLP.

'On the one hand, my mother would have said, "Those Currie boys are very handsome." And then the next thing they would have been in the civil rights [movement] and there would have been a suspicion of that. So there were very ambiguous feelings.

'And there were all sorts of social implications and political implications because we weren't talking to people who were different from us very much. We weren't understanding where they were coming from. We weren't articulating where we were coming from. It was a very closed-off world.'

It was also, during the 1970s and after, a dangerous world. She cannot remember the number of times that their front door was blown off its hinges by bomb-blast attacks on the army; a nearby culvert was a favourite spot for booby traps.

She told me she lived through her schooldays in a state of 'hyper-vigilance'. There was another panic when the local catholic school invited the pupils in her school to attend a play. The pupils from the two schools did not mix with each other.

'So suddenly everything is on hyper-alert. What was the play? O'Casey's *Juno and the Paycock*. Talk about a tense atmosphere. It was a nightmare. I remember my heart being in my throat for the whole thing. But it was fine. There was some kind of sense of: would it all kick off when the ending comes? Of course not.'

Councillor John Kyle also told me a story of his cultural separation from catholics as a youth.

He had first heard of the civil-rights movement as a sixth former in Grosvenor High School when a trainee teacher called Ann took the class. Ann was a member of People's Democracy and had taken part in some of the protest marches; she told the boys stories of the clashes with the police and explained the demands the marchers were making. But when John went home to his father, who was, he says, a moderate man, he heard the counter-argument that this civil-rights movement was not what it pretended to be. It was a challenge to the state, motivated by people who would bring it down.

So he wasn't going to accept Ann's version without challenge.

'And of course, being in the late teens we loved a bit of an argument, so we argued about it but I have to say she was very engaging and very persuasive – we probably all fancied her; she was pretty and that definitely made her more interesting.

'I suppose we had mixed feelings. On one hand: gosh, that's really unjust; how could this possibly be in our country, which we think is great, where you can trust the police, where everything works as it ought to work, where people are safe ... And [on the other hand] you've got these folks who, OK, they've got a bit of justified anger – but they are destabilising the country.'

Today John Kyle is a councillor for the PUP, which evolved from the UVF. John would not have knifed me if he had met me on a dark street in, say, 1973, but some of his party colleagues would have done. He is a family doctor, a christian believer and an utterly genial and decent, soft-spoken man. He joined the PUP because he saw them maturing towards exclusively peaceful, socially aware politics and he wanted to be part of that, though he had not been part of their paramilitary history. John invited me to meet him in his council office in Belfast City Hall.

There he gave another account of why protestants distanced themselves from catholics and from the civil-rights movement. He said part of it was that they were afraid that they would be outclassed by the eloquence of the other side. One of the routine jibes from unionists at nationalist and catholic spokespeople is that they are 'Jesuitical', that is, too clever in their reasoning.

'The stereotypical perception is that catholics tend to be more artistic, more dramatic, more Latin in their temperament, whereas prods are more forensic, more rational, more measured, are less inclined to being dramatic in the way that they conduct their relationships.'

I wondered if this argumentative streak in catholics was fostered in their bigger families, where children had to shout to be heard.

'A minority in our school would do English for A level. I mean, why would you do English for A level when you could do maths and physics and chemistry? I think there may have been differences in the culture in terms of what was valued.'

He told me he sees that difference as having played through the whole political history of the last fifty years with unionism rarely if ever throwing up a good orator.

'We tended to think that the unionist politicians got completely out-debated by the nationalists. They really were not good at answering the nationalist argument. You didn't have to be particularly able to become an elected representative for the Ulster Unionist Party, so it didn't attract the most able people.'

John Kyle did not see the violence from 1968 on as political at all really. For him, religion offered explanations that politics could not. He joined a charismatic renewal group with catholics who agreed that the violence was satanic and that the answer to it was prayer.

'We saw the IRA as being agents of Satan. This was evil, motivated and driven by demonic powers. That included the loyalists. It was from the pits of Hell.

'And we saw our friendship and our appreciation of our catholic brothers and sisters as being the counter-narrative to what was happening politically. This was God's riposte to this hateful political narrative. And I actually still believe that. I believe that God was active in allowing catholics and protestants to find a sense of brotherhood and kinship and appreciation that was in stark contrast to the entrenched political animosities that were played out every night on TV.'

However, this analysis didn't provide for the possibility that a political solution might be found so the gains of the peace process came as a big surprise to him.

'I thought the solution had to be a spiritual one, when people's hearts were changed.'

John holds still to the idea that faith is a stronger counter to human badness than mere political dealing but that institutional religion has been a hindrance to many of the changes which most of us think make life better.

As society institutionalised more liberal attitudes towards women, to sex and sexuality, the churches were getting in the way, or trying to. The secularising tendency wasn't just a movement away from regular church attendance. It had its own values, which included feminism, gay liberation, the reduced significance and size of the family.

Lesley Carroll did not diligently preserve her resolve as a child to keep her distance from ideas and influences that would broaden her mind. She did decide at seventeen that she wanted to be a presbyterian minister and applied to Union Theological College, part of Queen's University in Belfast. But, struck by what she now calls 'dissonances', like her church's failure to acknowledge the murder of the Devlins and the discovery that her catholic neighbours were good people, she wanted to use religion as a force for reconciliation.

First she had to take her degree. She studied philosophy, religion and sociology in an anglican college in Plymouth and found herself engaged in challenging discussions over such revolutionary ideas as that Christ's resurrection might not have been physical.

She told me, 'The faculty were nearly all fallen religious of one kind or another. One had been a baptist pastor; a couple had been priests and were married. There was an American feminist woman. They were all people of faith but who came at faith in a completely different way and certainly not in the conservative evangelical tradition that I was born in.'

She was converted to a liberal faith in Plymouth.

'At times I thought, *Flip, I'm going to lose my faith here if I go down some of these avenues*. But it was a really good experience, a broadening experience, and yet the faith thing was difficult at times but finding your way through that was a good struggle, to be honest.'

The follow-up training back in Belfast at Union Theological College was, 'a nightmare'.

'If I had allowed myself to say out loud in Union College that Christ's resurrection might not have been physical, I would have been slaughtered. I found the teaching method infantilising so I didn't engage like an adult. I just got the job done.'

*

Some say that religion was not as important as the actual fact of division. The things that communities disagreed on were not as problematic as the fact of them being separate from each other. Protestants and catholics lived on separate housing estates, sent their children to different schools, grew up apart.

Being taught by a catholic student – and a woman! – had been an exciting surprise for the young protestant John Kyle.

If the difference between communities in Northern Ireland had been something else other than religion, they would still have been inclined to be suspicious of each other because they did not know each other, though Kyle's experience of Ann the student teacher suggests that difference may inspire fascination as easily as disdain. In their suspicion of each other the two communities often lighted on differences and exaggerated their significance or used them as targets.

Indeed, in local traditions people played out the idea that actual physical differences defined protestants and catholics as much as religious belief. I don't know for sure that these were just jokes, and I suspect some people took them seriously – the idea that catholics had eyes that were closer together or 'dug with the other foot'. It was said that you could tell a protestant by which foot he used to drive a spade.

John Kyle saw immediate differences between catholics and protestants when he joined catholics in prayer groups.

'They [the catholics] didn't mind going off to the pub [after a prayer meeting] and having a pint whereas if you were a protestant evangelical you wouldn't be seen dead in a pub. Catholics would spend half their life in the pub and, for goodness' sake, you could see that they were real believers.

'Theirs was faith lived out in a different culture. We did tend to think that theologically we were more correct than they were but we were generous in overlooking their theological shortcomings because they so obviously loved God and were passionate.'

Some of that theology appalled him, but the catholics and protestants in the charismatic movement did not argue over it.

'The Virgin Mary? I thought that was completely off the wall. If they were into that they kept it to themselves. We didn't say the rosary but just got on with singing our charismatic hymns. It was fantastically happy, really positive, very affirming, very relational.'

*

Lesley Carroll told me she believes that the secularisation of Britain and Europe in the twentieth century was put on hold in Northern Ireland by the Troubles. We have been through two distinct phases since then: one in which people shook off religion with some hostility to the churches; and the phase we are now in, in which young people are expressing their curiosity about why someone like her would want to be a church minister.

'We were all great people of faith – and religion was also a cultural-identity marker; and that mattered, so we all hung in there. Then the Troubles ended and there was this avalanche of secularism, which across Europe and North America people had been dealing with for a long time.'

This period also coincided with the enthusiasm for the new atheism inspired by Dawkins and Hitchens. 'People became very anti-religion, and that also was fed by the Troubles because people blamed religion because it was a useful thing to blame and then you could ditch it.

'There would have been antagonism to people of faith. Where we are at today is a completely different place. People are interested to know why you are a person of faith. It doesn't necessarily mean they are interested in faith themselves but I find much less animosity from young people. I find, if I am out in a bar in the evening, and people hear that I am a minister, there are loads of people who want to talk to me about that.'

She said people have been deeply hurt by the Church and they want to tell her that.

She is surprised by how political culture has evolved in Northern Ireland. In 2009 she was part of a consultative group commissioned to report on how the government might resolve the inherited griefs and stresses from the Troubles period. She had no idea even then that the politics of today would focus on questions of gender and sexuality.

Her own church affronted the gay community by deciding in 2018 not to baptise the children of same-sex couples and breaking links with the Church of Scotland, which recognises same-sex marriages. She says she is disappointed that the engagement around that issue has been so damaging and hurtful for so many people.

'Theologically I struggle with the issue. I want us to find a way to be open and welcoming.'

Does that mean that she thinks that gay sex is a sin?

She avoided the question and I got the impression she doesn't think that at all but that she was exercising the canny reserve she learned as a child and deployed at Union Theological College, when letting other people know what she really thought could have got her into trouble. But I might be wrong.

She put it like this: 'We have not lived up to the image we have claimed over the last ten years – that we don't support gay practice but we love gay people. But how does a gay person hear that? That's a whole other story.

'What the Presbyterian Church has been trying to do is to live that standard, yet the decisions, and the mechanisms for taking that decision and the presentation of the decisions, have certainly not lived up to that standard of ensuring that gay people felt welcome in our Church.'

John Kyle was similarly slow to say plainly that he can commit to the whole agenda of the new liberal movement that wants same-sex marriage, legalised abortion and other reforms.

'I realise that I am in a party that supports a woman's right to choose. I would never vote for a woman's right to choose. I realise that I am limited in what I can do to argue against it but I also realise that it is such a complex issue that it is better if women debate this. I am uncomfortable about men telling women they cannot do this.'

He said, 'If my wife became pregnant and it was unintentional and there were problems and complications – or if my daughter had a child that she knew had Down's syndrome – I would not encourage her to have a termination because I feel I need to protect the unborn child. To publicly argue that is very difficult, I think, from a man's perspective.'

But it is one thing to feel a deep aversion to abortion and something different to treat the woman who seeks one as a criminal.

'And while you can be very clear on the principles you have to treat the individual case with compassion, so I have problems with criminalising or punishing women who seek an abortion. I think that is inappropriate. But I do think you need to protect the unborn child.'

He has similar difficulty assenting to the idea of same-sex marriage.

'I believe that it is not the normal, but whether it is God's will that some people should be homosexual – I'll take that up with God when I next meet him. And that is why I am very hesitant to condemn same-sex marriage. I think that same-sex civil marriage is probably a good and appropriate thing but I find it difficult to square that with the scriptural record. That's my problem. I am still trying to work that one through.'

So religion, while not the main driver of division in Northern Ireland, remains an obstacle to the reforms that many are demanding.

The Catholic Reformation

The year of revolutions, 1968, triggered such an upheaval in the Catholic Church as might even be called a reformation. Perhaps if protestants had better understood the revolution that was under way they would, at least, have been less inclined to fear the Church's influence over their catholic neighbours.

In 1968, when Pope Paul VI determined that the use of artificial contraception should be a sin, a young seminarian from Derry was in Rome. Denis Bradley had been sent there to train for the priesthood in the Irish College. It was an exciting time to be in Rome. He had seen the Second Vatican Council, which had met under Pope John XXIII to make radical changes, introducing the vernacular Mass and acknowledging the primacy of the informed conscience. Of course, an informed conscience was one that had been shaped by the Church.

Denis had had to give up his room in the college for an Irish bishop when the hierarchy from back home arrived to participate in the Council deliberations. Bishop Farren from

Derry expected him to visit him in his little bedroom and report on his progress there.

Some of the bishops skived off from the Council and went up into the roof space to idle away the days, some to recover from hangovers.

And Denis learned a lot about the way the Church worked. The Irish bishops once came together to decide whether to relax the law on abstaining from meat on Fridays. The custom in Ireland at the time was that catholics ate fish on a Friday. The bishops had been lobbied by the fishing industry to keep the rule in place and acceded to that for a few more years.

Denis told me, 'So I began to appreciate the relationship between politics, economics and religion. Those are all intertwined, and rightly so. But it was a revelation to me that it wasn't all based on saving souls. Sometimes it was based on saving industries.'

He recalled that even the seminarians in the Irish College in 1968 were caught up in the worldwide enthusiasm for student protest.

'There was a rebellion in the college and we said, "No, we will not serve." And the rector and the vice rector withdrew into their rooms for almost two years and it was left to students to run the place. That was an interesting experience; I didn't appreciate how interesting at the time. The students were in rebellion. I can't even remember the cause of it but we basically lived life for two years with no leadership, with no authority, just ourselves.'

The leaders of the protest were seminarians in a more senior class, one of whom later became a bishop. But Denis was on a delegation that met twice with the Irish Primate Cardinal Conway to air the student grievances. 'It was at the time that this was happening all over the place, and I don't know if there were international connections, but these things are in the atmosphere if they are not directly interconnected.'

But Pope Paul VI forced a choice on catholics between spiritual and pragmatic considerations.

His *Humanae vitae* encyclical that banned contraception in 1968 had been expected within the Church to rule the other way, to permit married couples to plan their families with the aid of 'unnatural methods'. Instead the Church commended that they use 'natural methods of birth control'. These included the rhythm method, for which a metronome is not actually required. The rhythm observed was the cycle of menstruation. A couple might seek to avoid conception by abstaining from sex during the fertile weeks. They might ascertain the start and end of that phase by taking the woman's temperature or – a later suggestion – testing the consistency of the vaginal secretions between the finger and thumb. What was not natural was taking a pill, or covering the penis in fine rubber to retain the semen.

Humanae vitae[9] is a horrific document. It bans not only contraception but also abortion, even for therapeutic reasons. The Pope's decision that the use of contraception was in breach of natural law presumed an extension of his own authority over us, for until then the only law he had concerned himself with was the law of God, not the law of Nature.

The encyclical makes rules that the faithful have preferred

to ignore and so the catholic world has gained through it a great fillip to independent thinking.

The catholics of Ireland, for the first time, virtually as a whole, rejected a papal diktat. That rejection was a bigger revolution than the one on the streets. It involved more people, indeed virtually every sexually active catholic adult. And it changed the character of the relationship between the people and the Church, which till then had had authority over them as direct and impressive as the authority of the state.

This was at a time when Rev. Ian Paisley was declaring that the catholic people in Northern Ireland were being manipulated towards revolt by the Pope.

Pope Paul VI said explicitly that it was better that the risk of unplanned pregnancy should continue to be a deterrent to sex than that couples should be free of it:

> Not much experience is needed to be fully aware
> of human weakness and to understand that
> human beings – and especially the young, who
> are so exposed to temptation – need incentives to
> keep the moral law, and it is an evil thing to make
> it easy for them to break that law. Another effect
> that gives cause for alarm is that a man who grows
> accustomed to the use of contraceptive methods
> may forget the reverence due to a woman,
> and, disregarding her physical and emotional
> equilibrium, reduce her to being a mere
> instrument for the satisfaction of his own desires,
> no longer considering her as his partner whom
> he should surround with care and affection.

He seemed to imagine that in the average marriage a man was best dissuaded from sex by the fear of having another child to feed than by his wife saying no.

Withdrawal before ejaculation was also forbidden:

> Similarly excluded is any action which either before, at the moment of, or after sexual intercourse, is specifically intended to prevent procreation – whether as an end or as a means.

Does this mean that if the woman takes a cramp and wants to stop, the man has to carry on rather than withdraw and thereby prevent procreation, to allow her to rub her sore leg? That's the sort of question I might have enjoyed teasing out with the Christian Brothers when I was at school.

The ban on contraception was an affront to expectations raised by the Second Vatican Council that the Church was devolving matters of conscience to the individual. The Pope might as well have tried banning central heating or the duvet, other innovations of that time.

Yet, this one new sin may have been the single greatest cause of the decline of Catholicism in Ireland and elsewhere. In Ireland there was just a gradual tailing off of the numbers going to Mass on a Sunday, people perhaps going once a month rather than abandoning the practice altogether. But the sacrament of confession has practically disappeared.

The spread of involvement in the Catholic Church is still wide, with most baptised catholics still preferring to be married or buried from a church. The depth of commitment, on the other hand, has reduced much more sharply and the indicators of that are that almost nobody joins the religious orders and very few want to be priests.

Fifty years ago the religious life was a calling; young people had a vocation. Today God is calling fewer, or fewer are hearing that call, or there never was a call and that delusion has had its day.

One of the arguments that had persuaded Pope Paul VI to rule against contraception was that permitting sex for pleasure alone, without the prospect of conception, would leave the Church bereft of a case against sodomy. That thought was put to him by the Irish philosopher Elizabeth Anscombe.

When Father Bradley went back to Derry after his ordination he had no intention of imposing this 'nonsense' on his congregation. 'I went into parishes where it was clear that women were living with domestic abuse, with alcoholism and all kinds of poverty, who were trying to be upright and rear their families and still trying to live within this catholic framework. I would have gone very quickly on the side of women.'

He was not unusual in that. According to Denis, despite the encyclical's appeals to priest and bishops to proclaim the new law, most priests ignored it unless they were trying to ingratiate themselves with the Church for the sake of promotion.

'No priests that I knew ever sermonised against contraception. My own perception was that nobody was implementing the rule either. It certainly wouldn't have been a problem to me. I just wiped it.'

But he told me that the Church was transformed by *Humanae vitae* by the very fact that most people disregarded it.

'Gay Liberation personnel in the mid
'70s who came together in Belfast
were all people who had had blighted
teenage years or non-existent teenage
years. There was a sense of anger that
we'd been denied.'

*Jeff Dudgeon, who fought for the
legalisation of homosexuality in the
European Court.*

David Sterling (second from right at banner),
head of the Northern Ireland Civil Service, marches with Pride in Belfast.

Sean McGouran, founder member of
Belfast gay Pride.

John O'Doherty of the
Rainbow Project.

Cops on bikes, managing protest more lightly than they used to in Northern Ireland.

Denis Bradley was vice chair of the Policing Board.

Jamie Bryson, a loyalist rebel.

Bloomfield Walk after the bonfire.

Pro-Palestine protesters gather at Broadway, a sectarian interface, on the night of a friendly match between Israel and Northern Ireland at Windsor Park.

Ulster Loyalists supportive of Israel rally to confront nationalist protesters supportive of Palestine.

Police officers dressed for trouble rally to contain pro-Palestine protesters.

Graffiti on the mountain.

Linda Ervine campaigns for the Irish language.

'We couldn't go then to the funeral because we didn't go to mass; we couldn't go over the door of a catholic church. That would have been to give credence to this corrupt faith, Papism, you know? We weren't able to go to the service which, you know, had a certain dissonance for me.'

Lesley Carroll, a former Presbyterian minister

John Kyle, a christian loyalist.

This old church is now a
Chinese restaurant.

Police containing an anti-Brexit
protest in Belfast.

John Barry speaks against Brexit.

'Militant republicans who are involved in armed struggle see their role as one of consolidation and keeping that torch burning until such time as there may be mass support for such actions again.'

Dee Fennell, Saoradh

Brian Kenna, chair of Saoradh, a political movement which supports the new IRA.

'À la carte Catholicism was introduced with *Humanae vitae*. And that was a healthy thing because that is where moral authority lies. It lies with the people.'

A later accelerator of disaffection with the Catholic Church was the disclosure of the scale of sexual abuse by priests and members of religious orders. The first major scandal concerned a Norbertine priest called Brendan Smyth who had been visiting families on the Falls Road in Belfast and molesting their children. The shock for many was that the order covered up for him when he was caught and transferred him to other parishes where his ways were unknown.

Two boys abused by him had been interviewed by Father Seán Brady, who was later Primate of All Ireland and made a cardinal. Brady had sworn the boys to secrecy, even from their parents. In time it became clear through reports on the horrific scale of abuse that transferring priests who raped children was standard procedure across the whole Church. The institution was more concerned to defend its reputation than to protect children. The greater tragedy was presumed to be that people would turn away from the Church and lose their prospects of salvation if they knew how many priests were paedophiles, so it was better that they didn't know.

And there were many catholics who stayed loyal to the Church despite the scandal, trusting that many of the priests were good men, untainted, but there were others who, disillusioned and dispirited, withdrew.

After one case against a priest was heard in Belfast in 1995, I was sent by the BBC to interview people coming from a weekday Mass at Clonard Monastery on the Falls Road, to record a vox pop, a sampling of opinions about the offender, Father Daniel Curran, who had been taking boys to a cottage in Ardglass, getting them drunk and molesting them.

Most of the Mass-goers that day said simply that what he had done was appalling, but they trusted that he was not typical and his behaviour would not dent their faith in the Church. A couple had a different response. They said, 'The devil tempts the good ones.'

Perversely the depravity of the sin, to them, might be evidence of the saintliness of the offender.

The Other Revolution

Belfast on a Sunday afternoon in 1968 seemed the most unlikely place to score dope, but he had already tried Dublin and failed there.

The city was insufferably bleak. All of the shops were closed. The streets were mostly deserted. The city centre had simply been vacated. It was the Sabbath and people went to church, not to work. And after church they sat at home and read the papers with the sensational stories about wife-swapping and drug dens. Northern Ireland imagined itself to be a more debauched place than it actually was. The fantasy that it was sliding into perdition thrived only in the minds of pure and decent citizens, many of whom were confident of a place in Heaven.

And if the law of God didn't keep the city free from sin then the law of the state was there in harsh support. Had the stranger been found by the police to have had as much cannabis as might be found in the roach of the joint he had smoked the night before, he could get six months in jail.

So he had to be wary, and that was part of the reason he had had no luck so far; that and the fact that there really wasn't much dope to be had in Belfast then anyway.

But suddenly, walking down Donegall Street, he happened on other hippies. The first indication was a shop window painted with sunflowers. The lights were on and there were psychedelic posters on the walls inside. And two young men with long hair and bleary eyes were looking up to marvel at the exotic creature that was looking eagerly in at them.

The two men in the shop were Colin McClelland and Arnie Knowles. They were the architects of the most vibrant part of Belfast's social scene back then. They ran the Marquee Club at the Astor. You could not call yourself cool in Belfast in 1968 if you didn't go to the Marquee. But now Colin and Arnie were about to be tested on their own cool credentials by someone who was the real thing.

According to Colin, 'This guy tapped on the window. He looked like somebody we had never seen before, long hair and a brocade jacket and white tight jeans. He was dressed oddly, not like anything we had seen in Belfast. And he came in and he had an English accent.'

The stranger said that he had come from an island on the west coast of Ireland.

John Lennon had an island there.

'He said, "I am just looking at your place here and I am assuming you are – *ahem* – socially aware?"'

The problem was that Colin and Arnie didn't have any dope, had never smoked the stuff and were stretched to think of anywhere they could get some.

'We didn't want to look like rednecks so we said, "Yes, come in and sit down and we'll make a few phone calls."

'And the only person we knew who had anything to do with dope was a DJ called Deano. And there was this scramble to find Deano.'

Cooler guys than Colin and Arnie would simply have said, 'No, we don't even have enough for ourselves. Tell John Lennon to go and fuck off.' Dry periods were well understood by people who did smoke dope, and the stranger was going through one himself, so they really had nothing to prove; but it didn't feel like that.

That these were the coolest guys in town and that they felt outclassed by the visitor tells you a lot about how tentatively Belfast was managing the sixties. The city was changing then, and the Marquee Club was a big part of that change.

As Colin McClelland remembered, 'Belfast in the mid-sixties was a drab industrial city like others in the north of England; and then suddenly for two or three years there was this explosion of flower power and pop music and clubs like the Marquee and the Pound. And in the middle of the greyness of Belfast it was a really colourful episode but then it was cut off by the advent of the Troubles.'

The Astor was where I met Jo that year, at a Sunday-night disco with DJ Louis Small. The Marquee seemed a bit out of reach to me. I had a sense that the crowd was more hedonistic than I was; that I would have seemed a bit tame and geeky in there. I don't know if that is true; I just recall that people who went to the Marquee loved it and exuded a sense of belonging there, being part of something that had already started without me, that I wouldn't have been able to live up to.

To Colin McClelland, the Marquee was part of a social revolution, the beginnings of something that was choked off, not just a more vibrant and playful Belfast but a non-sectarian Belfast.

'The accepted wisdom at the time was that protestants would dance to the south side of Royal Avenue and catholics to the north side. And people used to say to me, "You'll never make a success of opening in the Astor, because that is the catholic side of the road." But bouncers knew the faces of all the people who were coming in and they told us that they were astonished to find that after the first few months of the Marquee Club it was about fifty-fifty protestant and catholic, and this was something they had never come across. We started to become aware of this. There were friendships and relationships starting to blossom as a result of this. People were kicking over the standards and the restrictions of their parents and saying, "Religion doesn't actually matter; we're going to do it our way."'

At first, the Marquee didn't even have bouncers. Colin and a friend just stood at the door dressed in kaftan coats to signal that this was a peaceful place. The first time they had to call the police was when the crowd trying to get in was pressing so hard that there was a danger the glass doors would break.

And had John Lennon's island emissary gone there, he would have found the air filled with the familiar fragrance of cannabis smoke and felt right at home.

Colin was not part of the civil-rights movement that autumn, but told me he thinks now that if their demands had been conceded early a lot of trouble would have been avoided. But he sensed that the interest in civil rights, and even the language around the campaign, had come from the US along the same cultural channels that had brought the music and the flower power and the sense of a whole generation moving out from under a dark shadow.

All of the big concerns that transformed Northern Ireland over the last fifty years were presaged in the summer of 1969 but all our political energies were directed elsewhere. The civil-rights campaigners had not argued even for the legalisation of homosexuality and avoided all discussion of birth control, abortion and women's rights. The movement had had nothing to say about racism, mostly because there were so few people of colour in Northern Ireland; we had no one to discriminate against except each other.

The people who took up guns to confront the police and the army were not fighting for the big issues of secularisation and freedom of expression. Yet all those causes grew and all of them matter in the changed state that we live in now.

My own revolution that year was my claim for my sexual freedom as a young man of eighteen. I felt that I was every bit as much a revolutionary as my brother and friends on the protest marches when I was dancing to American music in the Astor with a protestant girl in a miniskirt.

They wanted to vote in local-government elections. Fine. I wanted to get laid. But I am more confident in defending my priorities now than I was then. And the obstacles in both cases were imposed from beyond us, decisions being taken for us by wider society.

There was no specific law against having sex before you were married but the social sanction was strong and it was reinforced by the churches; more ardently by the Catholic Church since its decision in 1968 to make the use of artificial contraception a sin. This shouldn't really have mattered to a single man like me, for sex before marriage was a sin anyway. As indeed was masturbation, or 'self-abuse'.

The chief restraint on Jo conceding to my more intimate advances was fear: fear of pregnancy but also fear of being talked about, getting a name for being a slut. I didn't mind if my neighbours found out that I had been having sex; I'd have been chuffed. But in the culture of the time she would have been regarded as having foolishly cheapened herself when she ought to have saved her purity for her husband.

We were conscious that we were part of a social revolution, though this was not an angry movement. We were insisting on living a life that our parents disapproved of. Their generation had taught us that sex before marriage was a sin. The catholic girls unfortunate enough to get pregnant outside marriage were still being shunted away to convents to have their babies in secret and to give them up for adoption. At least Jo, being a protestant, would have been spared that.

My wife, the poet Maureen Boyle, has recreated the horror of a real case in a poem, 'Weather Vane'.[10]

> Every Monday
> the nuns take me to the parlour
> to write a card telling everyone
> who needs to know that I am well
> that the sea is wild, that I am working hard,

that I miss them, when all the while
I'm sitting at an oak table
    – the smell of heavy polish in the air,

the grandmother clock ticking nearby,

dry spider plants on the windowsill
and a sad-eyed Mary hanging her head
in the corner.

So our social revolution may have seemed fatuous and hedonistic but it came with dangers and there were casualties in girls bullied into giving up their children or couples bullied into getting married. Now it is no disgrace to be a single mother. When I was a teenager an unmarried girl who got pregnant was regarded in my neighbourhood as 'fallen' or 'damaged', a disappointment to her family and, inevitably, a burden, for she was unlikely to find a husband now if the man who had landed her in that unfortunate condition would not have her.

And the child was 'illegitimate' – and I never heard anyone question the appropriateness of that word nor raised any question about it myself. It wasn't the child's fault but it would live with a taint. Coming through school I had often been asked for my birth certificate and my baptismal lines, so every teacher would have known whether I had a father.

My wife's mother was 'churched' after every birth, prayed over so that she might be made fit again to receive the sacraments. As with every revolution, not everyone was committed to the claim for sexual freedom. Many of my generation lived routine catholic lives, went through the same stages of courtship that their parents had followed, going steady, getting engaged and marrying. And many of them restrained themselves so that they might have sex for the first time with each other on the first night of their honeymoon.

Many of those I went to school with stuck to the rules.

Or tried to.

Once at the dole office, one summer in my teens, I met an old classmate, Martin Shannon. Martin's news was that he was getting married. He was seventeen. I was impressed by his sudden air of maturity, not recognising it as sorrow. And he was trying to pass off this news as a firm decision he had made himself, a good, sound idea. I went away simply perplexed, unfamiliar with what he was going through because urgent marriages in those days were shameful and not discussed.

Of course, it is possible that he had simply fallen in love with a young woman who was perfectly suited to him and that they have had a lovely marriage; but I had enough sense even then to see that as a remote likelihood.

Even the routine of getting happily married was different then. Couples would have the ceremony in church in the morning, have a wedding lunch or dinner and then drive off on their honeymoon, to be alone together in a hotel, away from their guests. And they wouldn't get a room in a respectable hotel if they were not married. A cliché in dramas about illicit sex had couples signing into hotels as Mr and Mrs Smith.

As late as the eighties I was refused a room with a partner on account of our not being married. This happened at least three times that I can remember. I suspect that this moral stand was taken more for economic reasons, forcing us to take two rooms and pay double, though there were some businesses that stuck to religious principles regardless of whether it lost them custom. Even in the 1990s in Dungiven, I was refused condoms in a pharmacy by a woman muttering testily, 'We don't sell that sort of thing here.'

So, while today the baton in the sexual revolution is being passed from the gays to the trannies and the queers, in Ireland the plain ordinary heterosexuals were still struggling to get hold of it in recent times.

*

The strongest symbol of the danger of a playful sex life in 1969 was the Manson murders, relayed to us like a warning about where our own excesses would lead us.

Sexual freedom is so taken for granted now that it is hard to imagine a society in which religious mores were reinforced by the law to keep us in check. Our guidebook to a new way of thinking about sex back then, without the coloration of religion, was Desmond Morris's *The Naked Ape.* Morris had gone from being the children's TV presenter of *Zoo Time,* in which he had taught us to love chimpanzees, to being the chief celebrant of our own animality.

We were the only ape without lavish body hair and, incidentally, we had proportionately the biggest penis. Our females had breasts that suggested buttocks for the purpose of attracting us round to the front of them. It was all amazing and liberating. Sex was what we were made for, not a gift from God to be surrendered back to Him.

Jo and I had pregnancy scares because our intimacy was almost a secret from ourselves as much as from everyone

else. It always followed the breach of a resolve not to go that
far, so there was no forward planning. I had not once worn
a condom, or 'Frenchie', in all the time I knew her. We were
timid sexual revolutionaries ourselves.

The worst crisis of that time was that after being thrown
off a caravan site in Millisle for not being married we had had
to apologise to her neighbour, whose family had owned the
caravan. But the neighbour seemed only amused.

Even in my late teens, in my first sexual experiments with
Jo, I was still conscious that I was sinning according to the rules
in which I had been raised. I didn't discard those rules in a
single decisive moment but grew progressively to revise them,
and sometimes the very relief at being free of them made my
rejection of them suspect. Was I just being selfish? Religion is
clever like that. It tells you that your own will is the problem.
Therefore, your wanting to do something can be evidence of
it being the thing you shouldn't do.

So I was opting for a life in which I was free to engage sexually
with a woman because I was a greedy, sensual, self-centred moral
failure. Allowing yourself to feel entitled to be yourself and
to follow your own nature is a respectable achievement when
you have grown up in a culture that tells you differently. My
struggle to accept that may not have earned me a portrait on
a Belfast gable or a military funeral but it was a pursuit worth
going for. And I didn't actually kill anybody. This revolution
did not bequeath heroes to us, but that's because we each
fought it individually.

The sixties were coming late to Belfast but I felt they had
arrived and I was moving rapidly through them, from 'Sugar,

Sugar' to *The Rock Machine Turns You On* in one year. That year, I went from being agog at the prospect of physical intimacy, taking Jo's bra off for the first time, to, by the end of it, indulging the mellowness of Leonard Cohen's 'So Long, Marianne', though I had yet to smoke my first joint.

I saw the growing violence as out of step with the age.

The youth movement was a claim to peace by the first people to reach adulthood after the Second World War. Peace was their theme, and it looks awfully trite and fatuous now, the apolitical aspiration of John Lennon's 'Give Peace a Chance', as if war was an indulgence and never a necessity. But some who had seemed to be in step with the worldwide civil-rights activism of the previous year were now about to break with the rhythm of the time and opt for violence. Enough of my neighbours wanted to give war a chance to make it happen.

I should have been at Woodstock or at the Isle of Wight Festival, where people had that same sense that they were changing the world. Back then, watching *Top of the Pops* on a Thursday night had seemed like a revolutionary act, the very cheek of it amplified by the experience of your father coming home to tell you to turn that bloody racket off.

Because the fathers of that generation were the problem. They were men who had lived through the war and thought those of us who hadn't were superficial and lacked all seriousness. That's what the hippies were rebelling against, a previous generation that was shaped by war, that didn't understand fun other than as something that contrasted with horror. And what did we know of that?

America was having its bellyful of war again in Vietnam and the country was about to go berserk in rejection of it. Britain had opted to stay out, had just pulled out of Aden after a succession of colonial withdrawals.

So what was different about us?

There was the national question. Were we another British territory that had waited too long to be let go of? Not by the view of most of the people who lived here, who identified as British. But we had a growing minority that identified as Irish. Even they were not as restive as they might have been expected to be, for material conditions were better in the North than in the Irish Republic. We might feel that we ultimately belonged as part of that unitary Irish nation, but we had strong incentives to defer on that: the welfare benefits and employment prospects in the North, the more liberal social regime. Contraception was illegal in the Republic; the Catholic Church cast a shadow over much of life there.

But there were some for whom a united Ireland was more important than anything else, who would never realise majority support for that but would feel entitled to go to war for it anyway.

The young among them did not have the aversion to war that their peers in the youth movements had, and their parents had generally not had the experience of war that the parents of the peaceniks had had either. Bad as the Belfast Blitz had been, it had lasted only a couple of nights. We had not had conscription here.

We had not known war the way England and France had.

We had not had our bellyful of it. So we retained the appetite for it.

The week the guns came out was the week of the Woodstock festival. Number 1 in the UK that week was 'In the Year 2525' by Zager and Evans. It is a perversely upbeat dance song for a forecast of human decline and extinction driven by automation and the squandering of the Earth's resources. That is what was wrong with the mood of those times; the most serious of messages, the bleakest dystopian vision, was just a song and a beat. It didn't require as much commitment as rioting did. Fighting in the street seemed more conscientious by contrast.

But it would be too easy to assume that we got gunfire because that expressed the will of the people. It didn't. Protest and activism continued around the same concerns that mattered elsewhere – chiefly women's rights, sexual freedoms, the rejection of the hold of religion – and we ended up with a society that was changed more by those forces than by the energies of killers and saboteurs pursuing the wrong revolution.

My sampling of the sixties social revolution was hesitant and, by London standards, paltry. One drawback was that Belfast was limited in its provision of excitement – or I was limited in my understanding of where to access it. The ceilis of my early teens were more sociable than the disco. One didn't really just dance with a girl but with a group, moving hand to hand from one partner to another. There was no 'smooching'. I discovered later that at discos you might spend a whole dance just holding a girl close and walking her backwards round the floor.

There was no drinking or smoking in the ceili halls. One boy caused outrage once by holding up a clenched-fist salute with a black leather glove on during the Irish national anthem at the end of the night. I'm not entirely sure why, but some of the boys there wanted to beat him up for doing this.

I had simply thought it unlikely to impress anybody.

He was mimicking Tommie Smith and John Carlos, who had raised their fists to honour the Black Panthers at the Mexico Olympics in October 1968 after receiving their medals. Presumably, even at this start of the revolutionary year, just weeks after the first clash with the police at a civil-rights march, the gloved fist was regarded as too appalling and not remotely a plausible intimation of what was to come.

There had been more of a scene in Belfast for a time in the early sixties, when Van Morrison led Them and recorded 'Gloria'. Maybe the fault was in me, slow to get out there to meet people, but then I had virtually no money because I was still at school.

Jo had a job and an income.

I had a birthday three months after we met and she surprised me by buying me an electric-indigo-coloured shirt with button-down lapels on a high collar and a matching kipper tie. Every other item of clothing I had had been bought for me by my mother. These weren't all disgracefully out of sync with the times. I had beige hipster bell-bottom trousers and a pink cheesecloth shirt, though, which had probably alerted Jo to the need to do something about my sense of style.

'Blue', she said, 'because you have blue eyes.'

As the trouble grew and extended, some noticed that the greatest force in Belfast drawing young protestants and catholics together was the disco scene. A priest, Father Tony Marcellus, managed a couple of bands. Colin McClelland had seen in the Marquee Club how disco brought protestants and catholics together, but the club declined after moving out of the Astor. The NILP MP Paddy Devlin joined Marcellus and McClelland with a plan to organise a huge outdoor concert, Pop for Peace.

Looking back, it seems to have been a daft idea, far too unpolitical for a hard-headed class warrior like Paddy Devlin. But they believed that something real had happened in Belfast. Protestant and catholic youth had found each other through music and the growing violence was going to pull them apart.

And John and Yoko had made music part of a peace movement. There was a chance they might come.

Colin recalled, 'I think somebody said we [were] already aware of the social changes in Belfast among young people; so maybe if we could get all the young people together and demonstrate that it is possible for catholics and protestants to assemble for a rock concert, it would be a demonstration that we don't want any part in the sectarian conflict. But we were unaware of the much bigger, darker forces that were behind all this. To think that a pop concert could cure it was naive but it was very well intentioned. I'm not sorry we did it.'

I thought it was a trite idea. Going to a pop concert wouldn't change the drift towards violence. But then, I wasn't envisaging what was coming. Few if any were. And had I known, I would have thought any desperate measure to distract young people from sectarianism was worth trying. Maybe my sense of the fatuousness of the gesture, looking back, is coloured by the knowledge of what followed. If the problem was just that the police were getting too heavy with civil-rights protests and sectarian factions were hardening their suspicion of each other, then a big pop concert in which protestants and catholics danced together, didn't fight and didn't need heavy policing would have been a grand statement appropriate to the circumstances.

Colin McClelland was by this time a freelance pop journalist for two papers I would soon be writing for myself, *Cityweek* and the *Sunday News*. He had high hopes of bringing 10,000 people to the concert at Minnowburn, by the River Lagan, near Shaw's Bridge. This was open countryside hardly five miles from the city centre. It was only three miles from where I lived in Riverdale.

It rained that morning. Colin suggested to Paddy Devlin that they might have to call it off. Paddy crushed that idea but they knew that some people would be looking out their windows at the rain and changing their minds about coming. What had they to lose? It was free.

But big-name bands were in town for this: the Tremeloes, Marmalade, Dave Dee, Dozy, Beaky, Mick and Tich. John and Yoko were still in Montreal. Colin was almost despondent at the prospect of having to tell these acts that they had no hope of an audience.

'I remember we were driving up to Minnowburn in the afternoon for the concert and we were astonished to see the number of people walking through the rain, so there was a commitment from an awful lot of young people.'

The world media came. NBC and CBS set up their cameras in the field and around the stage. Germany was watching too.

I wasn't impressed with the idea that I should be honoured simply to be in the presence of these famous performers. I had little experience of live concerts then and immediately thought that the songs didn't sound as good live in a chill autumn breeze as they did off the television viewed in comfort.

Colin said, 'There was quite a battery of cameras and still photographers and TV people, but somewhere around about three-quarters of the way through they all started to leave. And we couldn't figure out why. I think Unity Flats was the first flashpoint and they had obviously heard, though I don't know how when this was before mobile phones.'

A junior Orange Parade going up towards the Shankill Road past the ironically named Unity Flats had clashed with catholic youths. Then mobs came down from the Shankill Road to attack the flats in the first nakedly sectarian riot of a fortnight that would end with gun battles on the streets and the army coming in to restore order.

In one sense this vindicated the timeliness of Pop for Peace but also its inadequacy. If the organisers hadn't grasped before then how bad things could get, they would soon know that the fundamental division in Belfast had the potential for violence that would not be quelled with good intentions.

'The word spread quickly that there was a bigger story happening. So then we tuned in to the six o'clock news to see the big coverage of Pop for Peace. The main story was the riot at Unity Flats.'

Pop for Peace was a footnote.

Colin said, 'I think it was a good thing to do but we were naive. I think we all believed it would have some effect; that it would be a demonstration of unity between the young people of Belfast but we were really pissing into the wind, you know.

'At that stage it looked as if it was civil unrest, there would be some street fighting and stone throwing but it would all peter out. No one had any idea it would take thirty years.'

I can't say that the pattern of my life as disjointed and mischievous was set by the experience of seeing my home city collapse into disorder and madness. There were other influences that distracted me from the course that a sane and stable life would have followed. For one thing – and we forget this – my generation was worried about the Bomb. We lived with an understanding that a four-minute warning might be all we would get before the sky turned to fire and all life ended.

And I was who I was, a boy who in any other city would have followed his impulses rather than behaved and slotted into education and career because I wanted to be free. But what I wanted to be free from and free of was local and particular: the shadow of a tight religious and disciplinarian culture; one of those postwar fathers who didn't know how to be wrong.

My classmate Frankie Callaghan rebelled and joined the army and spent the 1980s on the Eastern Front waiting for the Russians to come over.

Even Caoimhín de Búrca rebelled in a way, after training to be a Christian Brother then realising that he was expected to live his life among older, duller men.

Poor Tony Henderson's rebellion was joining the IRA. So was Joe McDonnell's.

I might have left Belfast anyway but with less urgency, less horror at the sight of a city coming apart. There were others who stayed, who saw political purpose in the violence. I saw madness in it.

And it wasn't just the bombs. In a way, it wasn't *even* the bombs – for it takes application and nerve to make and plant a bomb, and very few people did that. It was the rage and the exhilaration.

Even before the shooting started – a week or two before it – I was walking up the Falls Road after a protest, with hundreds of other people. The buses were off. A rumour went through the crowd that two policemen had been attacked by some in the crowd and beaten up. I don't know if this happened or not. An ambulance came down the road towards us, slowed down to nudge through us. I thought we were a formless crowd. The ambulance driver probably saw us as a mob. Then, behind me, someone shouted and threw a large stone at the ambulance, smashing the windscreen.

A few years later I saw perhaps the most violent scene I have ever been near. I was in Delhi. An old man was pushing his bicycle with a load on it. He was on the footpath and the bicycle on the road. He had his head down, bent with the effort, or just distracted. He bumped into a young man going the other way. It was a simple accident. But the young man responded by head-butting the old man. The old man, terrified, let go of his bicycle and clasped the young man's head and pushed fingers into his ears. The young man was bouncing towards him, head-butting him over and over again, and the old man, clinging on, drew blood from the young man's ears. They were damaging each other badly. But what happened next brought me back to the mad moment in which a deranged idiot threw a stone at an ambulance.

A crowd had gathered. People were suddenly frantic with a need to respond to this horror of two men killing each other. They argued among themselves about what to do. In the middle of the crowd was a young man in a green jacket, a hefty, fit man, dressed like a professional among these labourers. I saw him turn and punch a man beside him hard in the face. I have no idea why he did it. Maybe he had always wanted to do that to someone and had never had the chance. And then others were fighting and it was as if an electric charge had gone through that crowd and changed all of them into killers.

And I got away from there, afraid that someone might for no reason at all attack me, but also afraid that the charge that had gone through them would reach me and drive me mad too.

And, for all that people argued with me in later years that the violence in Belfast was political and inevitable, I always believed that part of it was simply madness, a pleasure taken in anarchy and destruction.

Yet, I ask myself, if that energy can destroy the social fabric in seconds, what holds it together and maintains it despite that?

Belfast did not plunge into civil war. It reached the limit of its wrath in 1972, three years after the battle in Divis Street, and something like a habit of civilisation dampened it down in the succeeding years.

Now one of the divisions is over how that period is to be remembered.

The Past Catching Up

Sinn Féin routinely commemorates the IRA campaign as a noble and decent and necessary defence of the people and a struggle for equality and freedom.

Who gained equality through the Abercorn Bar bomb? Ask them that and they will accuse you of being fixated on criticising them and ignoring the other atrocities they could list, like Bloody Sunday and the Ballymurphy massacre. But still they don't explain how putting a bomb in a pub or a bus station improved life for anyone.

The loyalist paramilitaries sent men out to trawl the dark for random catholics to torture, sometimes with knives. They deploy the symbols of First World War Remembrance to honour their dead, lest we forget that they were good men doing what they had to in difficult times, to keep Ulster free and British.

The common factor in both is the cloying sentimentality, a refusal to see the ugliness and illogical nature of what they did and defend.

Former Sinn Féin publicity officer Danny Morrison gave a stark recital of the republican attribution of blame at a seminar on the civil-rights movement in St Mary's Teacher Training College, as part of the West Belfast Festival in August 2018.

He said, 'So the first bombs to be planted were planted by loyalists.

'On the fourteenth and fifteenth of August 1969, I took part in a civil-rights march in Divis Street. The RUC and the loyalists and the B-Specials came down on to the Falls Road. The reason why that protest took place was because the RUC were going to be sent to Derry.

'The Battle of the Bogside had taken place after an Apprentice Boys march. The RUC was exhausted. They were going to recruit forces from Belfast.

'The reason why the kids in the Bogside refused to let the RUC back in was because six weeks earlier, during a civil-rights march, the RUC broke into the Bogside and beat to death Sammy Devenny. It was one of the biggest funerals in the Bogside.

'So the first civilian to be killed was killed by the RUC. The first child to be killed, nine-year-old Patrick Rooney, was shot dead by the RUC, and when a police officer came across from London the RUC refused to take part in the inquiry, which is why he said, "I have met with a conspiracy of silence."

'The first soldier to be killed, Hugh McCabe, a catholic, home on leave, defending Divis Flats on the fifteenth of August is shot dead.

'The first journalist to be killed – a Polish journalist shot dead during the curfew [1970]. And during the curfew, when the British army surrounded the Falls Road and gassed ten thousand people and shot dead five people and refused people to be buried, to go to Mass, they were coming in to raid for arms that had been there solely to defend the Falls Road.

'The state started the violence and my community and myself and others reacted.'

That the IRA's 'reaction' killed far more people than died by any other force was, apparently, beside the point.

The audience seemed content that this was a fair summary of how the Troubles had started but then Brid Rodgers, a former SDLP minister in the Stormont Executive, got an even bigger applause for her riposte.

'Fifty-three per cent of the people killed in the awful atrocities of the last thirty years were catholics. And most of those were killed by the IRA, not by the British state, not by the loyalist paramilitaries. So I just want to know how the IRA defended the catholic people. And as far as the Falls Road is concerned, they have been through hell and back, from the British army, from them going in to raid the Falls, and from their own community, and the idea that the IRA were set up to defend the catholic people – maybe they thought they were going to defend them, but the reality is the opposite; they did not defend anyone. And again the response of meeting violence with violence – how did it all end up? It ended up with nothing.'

This was at a discussion on the question of whether the civil-rights movement had been a 'lost opportunity'.

Thousands of people died and their relations and descendants don't accept the justice or necessity of their loss. Many of

them see the conflict continuing as an argument about who
was right and who was wrong and simply opt to stay out of it.
I know people who had a brother or a father shot dead who
have never appeared in the media to make any comment.
They have been seen in public once, at a funeral, perhaps as
a child, walking behind a coffin, accompanied by hundreds,
perhaps thousands of mourners, for tragic killings drew huge
community sympathy and media interest, but they have then
stayed out of the argument.

Others have campaigned for justice.

What rankles for some is that the legal definition of a victim
now covers everyone who died or was injured in the Troubles.
The bomber, who died by his own bomb, is legally entitled to
be regarded as a victim, as much as the others who died with
him in the blast.

From the start of the peace process, the state has taken an
ambiguous position on the nature of the Troubles. The formal
documents, like the Good Friday Agreement, acknowledge
that the 'conflict' was a product of bad history. This can be
read as assuming that no one was really to blame.

Yet killers went to jail and have criminal records.

There is a sense too that those who got caught are not the
ones most responsible but that political figures like the late
Martin McGuinness, who directed the killing, escaped justice.
McGuinness went to his grave as a hero of the peace then was
honoured on his headstone as a soldier of the IRA.

And what of the senior police officers and soldiers who
directed spies and even enabled or covered up ambushes,
like the senior Parachute Regiment officers who facilitated

the lies to the first inquiry into Bloody Sunday that absolved the soldiers, their responsibilty plain when the Savile Report, thirty-eight years later, prompted an apology from Prime Minister David Cameron, who was only eight years old at the time of the killings.

Denis Bradley with Archbishop Robin Eames led a Consultative Group on the Past, investigating means of setting the past to rest. Lesley Carroll was also a member. They issued a report in 2009 commending a time-limited investigation into the causes of the violence and measures for reconciliation between the communities.

There had already been a Historical Enquiries Team set up by the police to review cases of Troubles killings to offer information to families. It was not primarily a criminal-investigation body seeking to secure convictions.

One of the detectives explained to me that the information families wanted was sometimes very basic, not 'Who shot my son and why?' but 'Had he had his lunch that day?' He said a mother had asked only that and he had been able to assure her that the boy did not die with an empty stomach.

The Eames-Bradley plan had envisaged a commitment at the heart of the Northern Ireland Executive to reconciling the two communities, focusing on the past for the sake of seeing more clearly how to fix the future. There would be a day of remembering, 21 June, at which the first ministers would recommit themselves every year to reconciliation and peacemaking.

The plan floundered almost immediately because it had accepted the statutory definition of a victim and recommended a payment of £12,000 to the nearest living relative of each of the dead. That would have meant giving money to perhaps the parents, siblings or children of people who had been responsible for their own deaths while killing or trying to kill others.

I don't know who would have got the £12,000 for Tony Henderson, my classmate who had died in an IRA training camp, but nobody did anyway because the plan was never implemented. It was simply followed a couple of years later with yet another proposal for resolving the clash of histories and laying the basis for reconciliation.

The Stormont House Agreement, which followed intensive talks after a breakdown in relations between the main political parties, envisages a Historical Investigations Unit, an independent commission on information retrieval, an oral-history archive and an implementation and reconciliation group.

The political parties have shown little enthusiasm for reconciliation or putting the past to rest. Sinn Féin still organises commemorations for people who are regarded by unionists as mass murderers, like Thomas Begley, the man who carried a bomb into Frizell's fish shop on the Shankill Road and blew himself up killing nine other people. Unionists campaign for soldiers who murdered people here to be absolved prosecution and have blocked funding for inquests in cases that put the army or police under suspicion.

Denis Bradley told me it is impossible to ignore the past. 'We are dealing with the past every day through inquiries, tribunals and inquests.'

As we spoke, a man who had been shot in the face by a paratrooper on Bloody Sunday had just been awarded compensation of nearly £200,000. Michael Quinn had had his cheekbone shattered by a bullet when he was seventeen. Denis thought more claims would follow, and then some who had never realised that payouts like this might be available to them would come forward with claims. Without a process to resolve the past as far as possible and then close it down there would be no end to the hearings and the expense.

Currently we are sifting through the past using the criminal-justice system. The police follow the evidence wherever it leads, or say they do. This annoys loyalists, who claim that they are suffering disproportionate attention, though that is perhaps because they were less competent at covering their traces.

In 2014 the police arrested Sinn Féin's then president, Gerry Adams, potentially jeopardising the peace process. Leaving the law to take its course could have unsettling results.

History is contested. Parties do not want to take the blame for the carnage and destruction but victims want the responsibility fairly apportioned. They do not accept the simplification that the Troubles were not the doing of those who pulled the triggers and set the charges.

Denis explained, 'Your substitute is either a complete amnesty, close it down. The difficulty with that is you are almost breaking the law by doing that and there is no political ability to do that. Neither government will say that and none of the political parties will say that. So you don't really have that option.

'So if that is not really as available to you as you think it is when you examine the situation, then you have to look for an alternative.

'And we looked at all those things and one of the things we said was that society has a right to get rid of this stuff. But you have to also listen to the people who want justice or want something else. So we did that and we handed it to the government. And our big mistake, looking back, is that we handed it to *one* government. We should never have done it without the two governments being involved, because nothing really changes here unless the two governments are involved, in agreement with each other.'

He says now that he regrets proceeding with the consultation without Irish government support.

'We couldn't get the Irish involved. I tried very hard. Actually, I should have walked away and said, "If you're not getting involved, I'm not getting involved." I think that was a mistake on my part.

'And, of course, when it came to it, the British ran away. We gave them a report and they were perplexed: "Do we do this or do we not?" Because look at the reaction out there. And of course the reaction out there was the same as you would have got to the Good Friday Agreement or to the Anglo-Irish Agreement. It wasn't any different. It's still the same fight. Still the same emotions involved. So you either do it or you don't do it. And you did it with policing, you did it with decommissioning, with two governments on board, and you held out. But they didn't do it on the past so we are left open to this situation where we are now about to do it, supposedly, under the Stormont House Agreement.'

He said he believes now that the Stormont House Agreement is in danger of creating 'a monster of governance'.

'But it can be done over five years, and then you say to the victims, "That's what we can do; we can't do any more."'

Implied in the repeated efforts to sort out the past is another problem, the prospect of the Troubles coming back. The challenge is not simply to give justice to the bereaved but to remake a society that cannot be so easily torn apart again.

Four former secretaries of state for Northern Ireland wrote to the contemporary holder of that office, Karen Bradley MP, in October 2018 to urge her not to waste resources on the search for unattainable outcomes.

The letter was signed by Peter Hain, Paul Murphy, John Reid and Tom King.

> We understand why many victims and others attach great importance to the prosecution, conviction and sentencing of those responsible for the appalling loss they have suffered. Their views clearly deserve the utmost respect [...] But experience suggests that it would be a mistake to expect that judicial outcome in any but a tiny percentage of the crimes that have not already been dealt with.
>
> Most of the cases were not easy to investigate immediately after they were committed and the passage of time – up to 50 years – has only made the chances of a successful outcome much less likely.

Victims Commissioner Judith Thompson saw the flaw in the argument.

She said that, while victims understood the difficulties in getting prosecutions, they wanted to know the truth about what happened to them and their loved ones.

'This call is for all harm by all people to be shoved under the carpet and forgotten about. That is not what victims and survivors are asking for.'

The suggestion from the former secretaries of state seeks to deny the victims the very thing they most want, but it faces a cold reality that prosecutions will be few.

Sinn Féin, during the talks that led to the consultation process following the Stormont House Agreement, criticised the British government for saying that there could not be full disclosure of security-force activities because the lives of agents would have to be protected.

Republicans had themselves benefited from a huge concession on evidence about the IRA's operations over decades.

The government had already agreed that if the IRA gave up the bodies of the disappeared no forensic evidence would be taken from them, and that all weapons, many of which had been used in murders, could be 'decommissioned' beyond the reach of investigators. So the peace process had already diminished the prospect of justice for most of the victims.

Robin Eames and Denis Bradley had said in their report that their guiding principle was that 'The past should be dealt with in a manner which enables society to become more defined by its desire for true and lasting reconciliation, rather than by division and mistrust, seeking to promote a shared and reconciled future for all.'

What possible hope is there of that?

The simple understanding at the heart of this aspiration is that Northern Ireland's problem is the division between two communities, the protestant unionists and the catholic nationalists, and that the solution is to bring these communities closer together in compromise and in some shared understanding of their past and of the forces that pit them against each other.

But that is not the solution that is foreseen within the core movements in these communities.

Back in 1969, politicians who wanted peace argued that the division in society was between moderates and extremists. The word 'moderate' was used in the nineteenth century too. Daniel O'Connell, the leader of the movement to repeal the Act of Union, whose statue now stands in O'Connell Street in Dublin, declared his contempt for it. The assumption behind this idea is that most people in Northern Ireland are decent and civilised neighbours who wish no harm on each other and that each community has a coterie of intemperate, potentially violent people who are averse to compromise and need to see sense.

Yet the experience of the past fifty years is that the centre of concern in each community shifted between the presumed moderates and the presumed extremists. At times of high trauma – like during the hunger strikes of 1981 or the parades protests of 1996 – communities were virtually coherent within themselves on the positions they took.

And the peace process itself appears to have merged the moderates and extremists in both communities. The republican extremists, the IRA, have ended their rampage and handed the initiative to their political representatives in Sinn Féin. Sinn Féin preserves the legacy of the republicans as one of noble struggle, and their vote has grown to make them the majority party in the nationalist community, something they had been unable to achieve during the Troubles themselves.

Something similar has happened in the unionist community. In 2007, Ian Paisley, who had inflamed passions during the Troubles, led the DUP into partnership with Sinn Féin in the Northern Ireland Assembly as the majority unionist party.

When this happened, it was common to hear people in Belfast remark that the solution had proven, after violent decades, to be bewilderingly simple. The cynical view was that both parties had shown that all they had ever really wanted was power and that when that had come within reach they had been ready to settle terms.

Ten years later we saw that it had not been so easy after all, and it did not work. Putting parties with such fundamentally different visions into partnership – it now seemed obvious – was never going to work.

The Eames-Bradley vision was that the communities might find deeper understanding of each other and forgive each other; but neither was going to surrender its core constitutional ambition, to create a single jurisdiction on the island of Ireland or to secure the Union with Britain.

And there were now forces in play that had not been significant in their influence fifty years ago.

When Ian Paisley had thundered about the defence of protestant Ulster and the protestant people, he was living in a time in which protestants formed a majority in Northern Ireland.

This fact was fundamental.

The nationalists/catholics had complained of discrimination against them as a minority, their identity and culture excluded from power in a system in which the majority would always be on top. The Unionist Party had governed Northern Ireland continuously for fifty years.

But now, with the centenary of Northern Ireland approaching, its future in the UK, as secured by its entrenched majority, is in doubt.

The Irish border had been drawn to create a little state in the North, which would have a protestant/unionist majority, but now most schoolchildren are catholic and most pensioners are protestant so the catholic majority is almost with us. That does not mean, as Paisley feared, that catholics will inevitably vote for a united Ireland in a border poll provided for in the Good Friday Agreement.

But it does mean two other things.

Protestant Ulster is finished and the Union now depends on the support of a section of the catholic community. If Paisley came back today to rally his people in defence of Ulster against the hordes from Rome he would not be dangerous, merely ridiculous.

So a unionist politician who appeals to the Orange tradition or the evangelical culture to secure votes may be alienating others. Those 'moderate' catholics are unlikely to vote for the DUP but they can most likely be relied on to vote against a united Ireland in a referendum.

This pulls the DUP in two directions: towards its traditional protestant base for support for the party in elections, while needing to embrace or at least placate catholics, to make the Union comfortable and safe for them, so that they won't throw the switch that destroys it and pitches them into a united Ireland.

Of course, the rest of Ireland might not want us, which would come as a severe shock to nationalists and force them to make their home here with the unionists.

Yet, unionists in a united Ireland might find that they had more power there than in the UK, where only an occasional grasp of the balance of power gives them clout at Westminster, while they might hold that balance by their numbers in virtual perpetuity in an all-Ireland state.

For now, unionists are condemned to living with an uncertainty that only Irish unity can bring to an end. They will always be vulnerable to circumstances in which a catholic community, alienated from them as before by the traumas of August 1969, the hunger strikes and Drumcree, might cohere against them.

And republicans work to an aspiration that has no finality to it but success. Theirs is an open-ended project that no one else can close down for them, unless perhaps the Irish Republic makes plain that it doesn't want a united Ireland after all.

But even then the prospect would remain that the Republic could be persuaded in time to change its mind. No plausible similar change of mind, after unification, would restore six north-eastern counties of Ireland to the UK.

There will be a border poll but the precedent of a badly managed Brexit referendum tells us that we must not walk blindly towards it. The Good Friday Agreement says that a simple 50 per cent plus one vote will be enough. But how could we allow ourselves to be as reckless with our future as David Cameron was when he put a simple yes/no question on EU membership to the people of the UK on the same basis?

In Northern Ireland one immediate danger of Brexit was that the invalidation of the regional Remain vote on the basis that it could only be considered as part of a whole-UK vote would produce just the coherence among nationalists that previous shocks had done.

For they didn't have to leave the EU. They could vote themselves back in through a border poll.

During the long negotiations, the Irish question featured mostly as a worry about how border checks would provide targets for dissident republicans but I always felt that the great threat to the Union was the insult to nationalists contained in the reminder that England decides.

*

When people express their fears of the return of the Troubles they imagine that they would come back in the form they had before. Security correspondents commenting on dissident republicans assure us that these smaller groups do not have the resources or skills to mount a sustained campaign like that of the Provisional IRA. This assumes that they want to. It assumes even that the Provisionals, if they came back, might be able to repeat what they did before. This isn't necessarily true.

Their own campaign evolved over the years, often in response to changes in technology that became available.

For example, in the early 1970s the Provisionals produced some skilled snipers who could kill soldiers from hideaways and escape. The army developed a means of locating instantly the direction from which a bullet came and sniping passed out of the general tactics until the late 1990s, when the IRA acquired long-range sniping rifles that they used only in open countryside.

They also improved their own bomb-making technology because they were losing members blowing themselves up. Half of all IRA losses in the early years were 'own goals'.

And in the eighties they redirected much of their energies into their own communities, with vigilante groups hunting down and 'kneecapping' or killing joyriders and drug dealers.

It isn't possible to say how a new IRA campaign would be mounted or how it would evolve in a few years. We now live in an international culture in which terrorism is crushed much more harshly than it was in their time.

The United States would hardly be likely to object now if the British used helicopter gunships against IRA bases, though this would have been inconceivable in the 1980s.

And a new movement would be challenged to consider whether it could use suicide bombers, a key tactic not only of Islamists but also of the Tamil Tigers. And there are practical reasons why it is desirable for your bombers to be disposable. If they die they can't then be followed back to headquarters with ubiquitous CCTV cameras or traced by their mobile phones.

A new IRA campaign in a new technological environment would have to find new ways of inflicting damage.

And while it might work through hacking and other online trickery, this would lack the advertising potential of the loud blast in the night, the recruitment opportunities of the mass riot, the platforming of acts of heroism available in a gun battle.

A year of protest had led up to the night the guns came out. The year leading up to the fiftieth anniversary of that night saw just as much protest on the streets of Belfast and Derry. The issues this time were different: demands for abortion-law reform and the legalisation of same-sex marriage; support for the Palestinians and opposition to Brexit; defence of the right to life, or bonfires and of flags.

People gathered also to protest against killings by the paramilitaries, of Ian Ogle in East Belfast by loyalists; of Lyra McKee in Derry by the New IRA. There was a new resentment against the armed groups in both communities.

Another difference was that in most of these protests the police were not viewed as part of the problem. People did, however, see their difficulties as founded on the fundamental division in Northern Ireland. Frankly, the gay community and the campaigners for abortion-law reform saw their problem as being the unionists, driven by the same evangelical theology that had opposed civil rights as the stratagem of Rome.

Some things are different now and some fundamental irritants are still there.

And some of the protest movements might have had cause to brush up against the police and attempt to counter the restraints they imposed on them, but they didn't.

And some still see the police as a challenge to them that must be confronted. That is the view of Jamie Bryson and the loyalists. It is also the view of dissident or purist republicans who have not accepted the peace process and want to fight on.

Brexit

Three o'clock on a Saturday afternoon in October, as with the protest that kicked off the Troubles fifty years earlier, they gathered with their placards and their demands, monitored closely by the police.

This time the focus of their ire was Brexit and its likely impact on Northern Ireland.

Like the original civil-rights demands, it had a similarly unhappy potential to enflame the divide between communities, British and Irish, protestant and catholic. Here everything ultimately comes to be about that.

Just as many unionists had rejected the civil-rights demands as insincere and devious, a cover for a republican plot, so many were saying fifty years later that Irish concerns about the status of the border after Brexit were false too, a device for advancing the cause of a united Ireland. This is the big problem with a divided society: every issue is presumed to be sectarian at heart. And every issue ends up being appropriated by one side and opposed by the other.

The European Union was proposing that, in order to keep open the border between Northern Ireland and the Republic, customs and regulatory checks should be made between the two islands. Or Britain and Ireland would align their regulations on trading standards.

People were using different vocabulary, as always. Theresa May talked of the border between 'Northern Ireland and Ireland'. The EU talked of 'the Irish border'. Republicans preferred to call it 'the British border in Ireland'.

This was not to be a march. A platform had been erected in front of the City Hall. Speakers would address the crowd from there. The police were determined to keep traffic flowing in front of the platform rather than disrupt the beautiful new Glider bus service.

This had a dampening effect.

There were about two thousand people there. There wasn't room for more. There was nowhere for them to stand but on the footpath in front of the City Hall and the corners across from it. There had been between 350 and 400 people at the October '68 civil-rights march that turned into a riot, so this was about eight times bigger.

But there would be no riot this time.

It would have been easy to get one going, by working the same tensions that ignited chaos in Derry. No one was going to confront the police, though. And by the harsh law of journalistic interest this would therefore not be a global story. Regardless of the morality, the legality, the civility or the risk, there was only one way to be sure of getting into the evening news and that was to block the road.

No one was going to do it.

The case was being made in the media debates around the negotiations that Brexit could bring back the Troubles. A small demonstration of that would have been timely but there was no McCann there to advance against the police and throw placards at them as Young Socialists had done in Derry.

At this sensitive time in the negotiations between Theresa May and the EU, when many in Northern Ireland would have liked their majority support for Remain to be heard, they would voice it in the soft and civilised tones of decent citizens who care about the economy and the peace.

They were appalled that since then the DUP, led by Arlene Foster, had entered a Confidence and Supply Agreement to keep the Conservatives in power, their numbers having fallen short of a majority after a recklessly called General Election in June 2017. And they didn't like the idea that DUP voice was being heard as the voice of Northern Ireland.

The DUP wanted Brexit. The party took a huge donation to advance the campaign. But it certainly did not want customs and regulatory checks between the two islands, a 'border down the Irish sea'.

That's where we were at, with a few other added complications.

As in 1968, all parties except the Unionists joined the protest. The Ulster Unionists were having their annual conference anyway, and there was little hope of determined support from many of them for special consideration for Northern Ireland. It seemed that if Great Britain was about to be struck by an asteroid shower, the Unionists would want some of the rubble to fall on us too, to keep us equal.

And there was no government in Northern Ireland in which the plans being discussed for us over our heads could be debated and a coherent statement of interest could be made.

At this stage we had not had a parliament sitting in Stormont for nearly two years.

Sinn Féin had walked out in protest against not being treated as a full partner in the Executive. That is how they interpreted Arlene Foster's refusal to accept the advice of Martin McGuinness that she should step aside while a subsidised renewable heating scheme that had run over budget was investigated.

Then, in negotiations after another election, to repair relations with the DUP, with whom they shared power, Sinn Féin settled on the single issue of an Irish Language Act. Some in Sinn Féin say this was an effort to make it easier for the DUP to concede. To the DUP it looked like a tripwire so they held out against it.

In the week of the protest against Brexit in Belfast the secretary of state legislated to allow civil servants to take administrative decisions without ministerial approval, there being no ministers in office.

The oratory from the platform was of a high order. As before, the political talent had gone to the smaller parties. People with wit and imagination preferred not to have power at all rather than present themselves to the world as spokespeople for sectarian factions. That hadn't changed in fifty years.

John Barry of the Green Party was terrific.

Claire Hanna of the SDLP said, 'Brexit isn't just an economic issue, but jobs and opportunity underpin our peace and prosperity … Brexit threatens our shared rights and protections, for the environment, workers, and threatens our ability to address all the issues that don't stop at borders. Brexit threatens the thousands of EU nationals who have come here to work and make it their home, and who as Belfast South MLA I am proud to represent.

'But probably worst of all, Brexit rips through the complex relationships and delicate equilibrium that allows this place and us its people to co-exist and imagine a shared future.'

The sad part of that last line was the word 'imagine'. We could 'imagine a shared future', a coming together of separate communities in common interest. It was still a long way off.

Naomi Long of the Alliance Party ended to rapturous applause with a simple statement: 'The DUP doesn't speak for me.'

Theresa May had conceded a 'backstop', an agreement that, in the event of the UK and EU failing to reach a trade deal that would keep the Irish border open, the UK – or perhaps just Northern Ireland – would remain aligned to the EU, operating the same tariffs and regulations. At this stage in the negotiations she was caught between the DUP threatening to bring her down if she didn't scrap that idea and the EU, which was reminding her that she had already committed herself to it.

Businessman Gerry Carlile took the stage and said, 'I find it incredible that the DUP, a party that regards itself as a party of business, will push for economic ruin rather than countenance a backstop arrangement because they think it somehow undermines the Union.'

John Barry stood up in cycling shorts and a yellow hi-vis jacket. He held up a roll of toilet paper and said, 'Theresa May doesn't give a Brek-shit what happens to Northern Ireland in terms of remain.'

He said, 'I do not think that everyone who voted for Brexit is racist and xenophobic but I think that every racist and xenophobe voted for Brexit.'

*

This need to be European was not there fifty years ago. After the referendum on Brexit it suddenly seemed fundamental.

In the 1960s, Ireland was not really interested in Europe. There was an exception in relation to Catholicism. The head of our Church was in Rome but authority was being delegated back to the bishops after the Second Vatican Council and Mass was now being said in English or in Irish, not Latin.

Denis Bradley had had his training to the priesthood in Rome.

Frankie Callaghan was sent to Germany by the army to help monitor communications across the Iron Curtain.

But unless you were a priest or a soldier you were hardly likely to even go to Europe for a holiday.

As part of the UK, Northern Ireland had been rebuffed in applications by President De Gaulle of France. I had never been to the continental mainland and few of my friends had. You had to be well off to take a holiday in Spain then and when you did you had to be careful, for the country was governed by a fascist. We had stories in our own papers about how dangerous Spain was. Women had been arrested for crossing the road from the beach to the hotel in a bikini. Greece was ruled by a military junta then too. We knew those countries through war films, though some of us were beginning to discover Sartre, de Beauvoir and Camus.

Much of Europe was as exotic as Asia; and, while France and Germany were nearer, ill feeling after the Second World War played on the minds of some of my neighbours.

A boy I went on Legion duty with had a summer job with an engineering firm that made a point of not disclosing to clients that some of the parts they installed for them came from Germany.

'Some would refuse to take it if it was German.'

Still, I saw plenty of Volkswagen cars around then. I did hear its ubiquity cited as evidence of a sneaking admiration for Hitler. In Irish-nationalist circles then he still was not viewed a wholly evil.

My favourite reading in my mid-teens was Dennis Wheatley's novels of black magic, some of them set in wartime. In one, several pages were left blank to spare the reader his full contempt for the French.

What we knew of Eastern Europe was that the catholic faith still struggled to survive there. Nearly every catholic home in Ireland had a little statue of the Child of Prague, then pronounced 'Prage'. This represented the child Jesus in a fanned-out royal cloak and with a crown on his head, his right hand raised and facing forward with two fingers up.

Several superstitions attended the Child of Prague. One was that you could spare yourself rain on your wedding day by putting the little statuette out in the yard with an upturned bucket shielding it.

But we knew no people from Prague or from Warsaw or Paris or Berlin either.

We did know that Europeans ate things we could hardly imagine eating ourselves.

Our families had extended themselves west, not east. So Christmas cards and occasional parcels of clothes came from Canada and the US, not from 'the Continent'. We called Europe 'the Continent' then, imagining it to be a place of consistent values and believing that those values were morally slacker than our own. On the Continent, there were teenage pregnancies. On the Continent, supermarkets stayed open on Sundays. On the Continent, drink was cheaper and you could buy brandy in a coffee shop at any time of the day – even on a Sunday!

Once in college a business-studies teacher told us the remarkable fact that 'on the Continent' people going to work would just pick a copy of the morning paper out of a glass case, lifting the unattended and unlocked lid, trusted to put the right coin in a slot at the side. This, we decided, would never work here. If you encouraged people to take things for free, where would it stop? The Continent's ways were dangerous; they could corrupt us. The duvet had not arrived, we were still using blankets.

The condom, before the AIDS crisis, was commonly known as the French Letter or the Frenchie, presupposing that the French, being different from us, had more need of them than we had.

But what did we know of France and Belgium and Germany, apart from the filtered memories of the war and the rare airings of Edith Piaf on the BBC? She even sang her songs in English for us, acknowledging that we were different.

Had I gone to a grammar school I might have learned French, read Maupassant in the original, but I doubt if I would ever have come to think of Europe as anything other than foreign, a place where things were done strangely.

And Ireland, into the 1960s, took pride in a conviction that it was more pure and moral than the rest of the world. You might lose your faith if you went to England, and fall into sin. In France you might even forget that you had had a faith, for the country was associated in our minds with sexual playfulness. Over there, men had mistresses and their wives didn't mind. The children drank wine with their dinner.

Working in pubs, I got to know a wine dealer who represented a company importing from France. With an idea that I should be more urbane and cosmopolitan, I would buy a bottle from him occasionally and bring it home for Sunday dinner with my parents. The bottles didn't have corks but little plastic caps. Most households then would not have had a corkscrew so the bottler had come up with a way of making wine more accessible to us.

My mother and I would sip these bitter drinks and imagine that we would, in time, acquire a taste for them and be more sophisticated then. For now, getting them down was a penance, but you couldn't tell anybody that.

Wine was only slowly coming to Belfast in 1969. We could buy Hirondelle and Asti Spumante and Mateus Rosé.

I discovered Châteauneuf-du-Pape and would make a show of ordering it when I could afford it, after I started working.

The more popular wine in Belfast at that time was Mundie's from South Africa. The street drinkers, commonly called 'winos', bought Mundie's because it was cheap.

I tried it once with a couple of lads, in the back of a car on a country road, and it was sweet and went down more easily than the rasping red wines or vinegary whites that I had been enduring.

In 1969 there were no pizzerias in Belfast. We had Italian migrants settled here and many of them had set up restaurants, but these were chippies and ice-cream shops.

I was more British than European, though I would have denied that. If I had affections abroad they were American. For a time as a child I had an American accent, gleaned from *Bronco* and *Cheyenne*.

When I was a child the terrain in which I imagined myself a man was the Wild West, where I would have a horse and a gun and a drawl and little to say. As a teenager I discovered that French films were worth suffering the subtitles for and showed more nudity. Characters agonised about who they were. The big questions concerned existence; in the Westerns the problem was always only defeating the bad guys. The hero had a good heart and a fast draw.

And while this may be the most superficial appraisal you have ever heard of why some hearts tend more to Europe than to America, it describes a reality. I discovered the Beats, of course, and knew there was American literature, but at their best and their most anguished I felt they were trying to be European; at their worst they were just cowboys, desperadoes not yet come to their senses.

It would have been inconceivable that I might one day be faced with a choice of whether I was British or European and that I might incline more to being European. I never raised the question myself; Britain raised it.

If I am honest, a big part of me is British.

I eschew that because in my divided society I identify primarily as Irish. I don't overtly distinguish myself from my neighbours by claiming not to be British, but they – some of them – distinguish themselves from me by asserting that they are British.

I was born on a European border between Derry and Donegal. Of course, we were raised on an understanding that Ireland was all one country; but it plainly had a real border and life was different on opposite sides of it, not just in the brands of chocolate available but even in a sense that the law was laxer in the Republic, the police – the Gardaí – more indulgent of the state of your car or even the state you were in driving it.

In Belfast, most of our television came from Britain and from local branches of the big stations. Radio brought more of the world into our homes. My father would listen to Gaelic football and hurling finals on Radio Éireann. My sister would sit up late listening to the Top 20 on Radio Luxembourg, sponsored by Elida.

And both the Gaelic sports and the Top 20 came to us on erratic whining and shifting signals, implying that what was of more interest was less accessible; for on the formal British channels, which delivered the news and the coy soaps, the signal was always strong and clear.

Our nearest European neighbours were the Irish Republic, Scotland, England and Wales. These all had strong cultural influences over us, though less so Wales, perhaps. Every New Year's Eve my father and mother sat up to watch Andy Stewart introduce Hogmanay. My father loved the voice of Kenneth McKellar, though he would have thought it slightly treasonous to drink Scotch whisky. Not that he'd have refused it if it was the only one you had.

My mother listened to the BBC Light Programme and Home Service through the day, *Music While You Work* and *Mrs Dale's Diary*. So her routine cultural input was English. And our neighbours supported English and Scottish football teams, sometimes following their fortunes with sectarian interest as if the English and Scottish leagues could reaffirm the normality of our native divisions. We were hardly to be thought uniquely bigoted if the strains between catholics and protestants were being worked out in Liverpool and Glasgow too, between first- and second-generation Irish immigrants. There was comfort in that.

For a working-class boy with an education the obvious way to be urbane and cultured was to be English, to moderate the accent and to enjoy a sense of being part of a great nation with a deep history and a military and monarchic tradition.

I do know some Irish people who lost their accents and chose to sound English, sometimes for the sake of a broadcasting career. And I have nephews and nieces who have grown up with native English and Scottish accents. Six million British citizens are entitled to an Irish passport. My family links extend comfortably into Scotland and England

and the Irish Republic. If the Irish did not assimilate neatly into England there would have been no Beatles, Elvis Costello, Cilla Black or Ant and Dec. The Irish seem to thrive better in broadcasting and entertainment there than the native English and have a disproportionate role, maybe because their accents have no class connotations that might alienate part of the audience.

England was too familiar to summarise. There was an Elsie Tanner on our street too. And yet something of England disdained us and we were wary of it.

It should not be easier for me to identify with France than with England. It should not logically be easier to contemplate breaking out of the United Kingdom than the European Union – and for many it isn't. A unionist from Northern Ireland would feel a fracture in the soul if the UK broke apart. Brexit is all that really tempts me to play my part in breaking it, to vote my way back into Europe through a united Ireland, perhaps more to punish Britain than to find a safe haven.

If I don't foresee that pain of a broken UK, or empathise with it, does that mean that I am failing to see plainly how British I really am? How can I not be as British as the Beatles or Cilla Black when I have watched British television all my life, read mostly British literature, paid all my taxes into the British exchequer and received welfare benefits from Britain and been treated by the British National Health Service?

How can I insist on Irishness being distinctly not British when Britain is home to more Irish people than Ireland is, and when other British people have ancestral roots far further away than Galway, in Pakistan or Somalia?

And yet the affront of Brexit feels real and immediately evokes the response, 'Bloody England!'

Why should people in Northern Ireland think of England as alien, hostile and even unintelligible on several levels when the country is just next door, speaks the same language and provides most of the print and broadcast and social media that we interact with?

The most obvious difference is the cultural diversity of England. In most English cities there are far more people of Asian and African extraction on the street than there are in Derry or Belfast, but that is not the England we harbour a gut resentment against. When Irish nationalists fulminate about England it is *white* England that they are thinking about. More, it is white *Tory* England. Most of the advances over the years in liberalising Northern Ireland and enabling the peace process were taken under Labour governments.

The real problem – for us – exposed by Brexit is this strained relationship. We feel that England has slapped us in the face, that it has made a decision for us over our heads, that a majority English vote will always trump our own will in Northern Ireland. We were asked to vote on something and given a demonstration of how our vote counted for nothing, of how the greater English population will always decide outcomes.

And it is specifically England that the Northern nationalists resent. Scotland is problematic for them in another way, as a territory into which their own native sectarian quarrel extends. It is therefore familiar.

England is divided on class, not religion or the constitution, so we don't understand it and it doesn't understand us. And that is one of the most appalling things; a sense that it is indifferent to a problem it created. That resentment does not extend to other countries in the EU because there is no particular reason why they should understand Northern Ireland any better than we understand or empathise with Schleswig-Holstein or the Sudetenland.

So the acrimony between Northern Irish nationalists and white Tory England is like the surliness of siblings who never speak plainly to each other. And, thought of that way, a break-up in the UK would be tragic for it would have skipped the possibility that the two countries would have come to understand the nature of the rift between them.

Yet, what more could England reasonably do, having given Northern Ireland the right to leave the UK as it did in the Good Friday Agreement?

We may have been on our way to an historic reconciliation but for Brexit and the declaration entailed in it that Northern Ireland's opinion is irrelevant and is always going to be irrelevant because it never has the numbers to make a difference to the outcome.

Might we be in danger of irrationally recoiling against England with as little good reason as England recoiled against Europe?

Even the BBC accepts the presumption that full Englishness is offensive in Northern Ireland. We have our regional performances for the *Last Night of the Proms* every year but efforts have been made to discourage the flying of flags, an integral part of the big London show in the Royal Albert Hall. And the local input cuts away from 'Hall' during the final rousing performances of 'Jerusalem' and 'Land of Hope and Glory'.

What this wariness of the London Proms betrays is an inability to distinguish camp parody from full-on imperialist chauvinism, or at least a lack of trust that nationalists in Northern Ireland would be capable of making that distinction. And they wouldn't, for in that finessed thinking lies danger. Best to keep it simple.

Margaret Thatcher said that Belfast was as British as Finchley and we believe we proved her wrong. But the hard part for nationalists to accept is that it is not so very different. The English language is a first language on these islands and nowhere else for thousands of miles – North America to the west and Australia to the east. So the uniformity of culture between, say, Galway and Hull is of course questionable but it is stronger than between Galway or Hull and any other city anywhere outside those islands.

I think we would find it easier to contemplate a union with Britain if Britain also had a population of only five million. But there is no fix to that.

Who Wants a War?

On a Saturday afternoon in November I drove to Dundalk, down the dual carriageway, passing the Mournes and going through the Cooley Mountains, that is, through what was known during the Troubles as 'Bandit Country'. Here the IRA was strongest. In these hills they made the big bombs that were ferried to London to blast the Baltic Exchange, Bishopsgate and Canary Wharf. These hills had army lookout posts on them serviced by helicopter.

Dundalk was nicknamed El Paso in the early Troubles. The IRA could retreat to here and operate openly too.

I parked in the Crowne Plaza Hotel and went on a nosy around the conference rooms and heard the murmurs of debate behind a door and opened it. Inside I saw the crowded hall and the Irish tricolour at the top table. The flag still showed the folds fresh from the packet it was bought in, perhaps that morning. A group of men standing at the back wall spotted me and one of them blocked my way.

'This is the private meeting of a political party,' he said.

'I'd heard there'd be an open session.'

'Come back in an hour.'

The party was Saoradh, which translates as 'Leave' – though this is not a reference to its position on Brexit. Formally Irish republicans shouldn't care how the British vote in their own referendum.

I went into the bar and whiled away my time until I heard some movement outside the conference room and went back.

The hotel staff had brought out trays of sandwiches and wraps and flasks of tea and a few people, friends of those in the conference, were waiting for the doors to open. None of them was touching the food.

I sat down and helped myself to one of the wraps, smoked cheese and rocket, and I introduced myself to a man sitting opposite. We chatted and discovered we had friends in common in Dundalk. We talked about Brexit and the likelihood of power sharing coming back and agreed that the DUP didn't know what was good for them and I had another smoked cheese and rocket wrap.

Then the door opened and the men and women of Saoradh came out for their lunch.

It was my new friend who commented on the gender imbalance. We were now among about a hundred men and five women.

This hadn't really surprised me.

I was looking for Dee Fennell. We had made contact through Facebook and he had invited me to come to the open session and record an interview with him.

Dee is taller than me and bald, probably in his thirties, and he was immediately friendly. I was on my third smoked cheese and rocket wrap and he was only just getting his first bite into a chicken sandwich but he let me take him away into a quiet corner.

This was all surprisingly genial for me. There was no prospect of Dee mistaking me for a political sympathiser. The dissident republicans he identifies with are widely regarded as, at best, a chauvinistic throwback and, at worst, bullet-headed thugs masquerading as ideologues.

Dee, of course, says he is not personally a militarist. Saoradh supports a new republican armed group established in 2012 that calls itself the IRA. It is spoken of as the 'new IRA'.

Some of the members have been with the Provisional IRA; others have come from other dissident groups that have fallen away in recent years. In January 2019 they would bomb the courthouse in Derry. They were also fond of kneecapping people.

They are called dissident republicans but really they are the purists. They say that the Provisionals are the dissidents because they are the ones who broke with a core principle that the struggle should continue until Ireland is free and that neither state on the island of Ireland is currently legitimate.

Since the Good Friday Agreement and the Provisional IRA ceasefire, dissident republicans have been very active. Their riposte to the Good Friday Agreement of 1998 was a major bombing campaign against Northern Irish county towns, Markethill, Portadown and Omagh.

The Omagh bomb of August 1998 killed twenty-nine people and unborn twins.

This provoked an enormous emotional reaction but, despite security-force successes against the dissidents in the Republic and the North, they managed to chug along interminably with a low level of violence, most of their attacks failing, their bombs being intercepted, but occasionally killing.

In March 2009 they shot dead two soldiers at Massereene Barracks in Antrim, taking the opportunity created by the gate opening for a pizza delivery.

Two days later they killed a policeman.

Often their weapons are crude pipe bombs but police seizures in recent years have included sophisticated mortars and assault rifles.

Dee himself was questioned by the police several times, including as a suspect in a murder inquiry. Michael McGibbon had been ordered by republicans to meet them in a back alley for a punishment shooting. This is still what happens in some areas: you get shot by appointment, like a child ordered to attend a headmaster's office for a caning. Some people get drunk or dose themselves with painkillers before getting shot. Someone shot Michael three times. His wife, Joanne, a nurse, held him in her arms. He died later in hospital.

Dissidents still murder people, usually alleging that they are criminals. They shoot people in the legs. They still try to kill police officers. They still plant bombs. None of this has any significant political impact but it keeps an armed campaign ticking over until such time as another opportunity for revival dawns, as happened in August 1969.

Dee Fennell told me he believes in the maxim coined by Pearse that 'England's difficulty is Ireland's opportunity'. And he anticipates that Brexit is just such a difficulty.

And, while others dismiss him and members of Saoradh as fools on the sidelines of history, he can claim to be part of the republican tradition going back a century, when others who are now revered as heroes were as reviled as he is now.

'My family has been involved in republicanism right from the War of Independence. My great-grandfather Frank Fennell was actually in the British army. He was injured in the First World War at Ypres. He came back and joined the IRA and fought in the War of Independence. He then took Collins's side after the treaty and ended up working in the Curragh on behalf of the Free State army.

'My grandfather and his brother were both active republicans from the 1930s. My grandfather's brother was interned in the North and my grandfather was active right up until the early seventies and the split. He sided with the Officials at the time of the split. His name was Jimmy Fennell.'

And Jimmy Fennell has told him stories of how, on the fiftieth anniversary of the Easter Rising, he went round the houses in Ardoyne trying to collect money to pay for bunting and flags and had doors slammed in his face. So Dee thinks being unpopular is just what republicans have always had to endure between the times when people turned to support them.

'My father and his siblings were all republican activists. My father has no convictions and they would certainly have been involved in a range of organisations, either the Official Fianna, the Provisional IRA, the INLA, the Official IRA.'

He told me he sees the movement passing through periods of alienation and disgrace and admires those who endure those periods as the true republicans.

He said, 'Militant republicans who are involved in armed struggle see their role as one of consolidation and keeping that torch burning until such time as there may be mass support for such actions again.

'It would be a matter for them to say how they do that but I think anyone that's analysing it, and if you take into consideration statements from both the PSNI and the Gardaí, what they are saying is that there is an increased sophistication and increased determination within the IRA in particular to engage militarily.'

And this is how things were in the 1960s.

The IRA in Belfast then was led by Billy McMillen and he had no more than a couple of dozen men – it was all male at that time. Women were recruited separately into a support organisation called Cumann na mBan (The Club of the Women). The IRA men had a few guns of different types and went away occasionally to training camps in the Republic to improve their shooting skills. Intelligence on these camps got back to the government in the North and fed into an anxiety that the IRA was preparing for a new uprising.

McMillen's men acted as stewards for the Easter Rising commemoration parade in 1966. I have been told that the headmaster of St Mary's school in Barrack Street, Brother Murphy, saw one of his former pupils, Gerry Adams, keeping order and commented, 'I see we have the officers.'

That period was similar to the period through which we are living now. If anything, the political climate then seemed more optimistic. The Stormont parliament was functioning well, though nationalists were in a perpetual opposition that they saw little hope of breaking out of. Relations with the south were improving. What violence there was seemed merely a gentle reminder that division in our society was not yet resolved rather than a worrying indication that it was likely to get worse.

There had been a massive riot in October 1964, when McMillen had been standing for the Falls constituency in the Westminster election. He had been canvassing with an Irish tricolour in his office window. The police smashed the window to remove the offending flag, whose display was illegal then. Rev. Ian Paisley had threatened to lead protestants into the area to remove it himself.

Republicans saw the police action as confirmation that the state would seek to crush them before it would ever allow them equality and new members joined the movement in direct response to that. One of these new recruits was Gerry Adams himself.

But no one died in that riot.

Guns were not used.

It was the first time I had heard of the petrol bomb, still known then as the Molotov cocktail, as if it was not something indigenous to Northern Ireland. It is now.

The name of Vyacheslav Molotov, the Soviet foreign minister, had been attached to the petrol bomb by the Finns in reply to his claim that bombing raids had actually been dropping bread.

Today the IRA that killed hundreds of people in bombing and shootings through the seventies, eighties and nineties still formally exists, according to a security report compiled in 2015 to inform inter-party negotiations during one of the routine deadlocks at Stormont. The same report says that the

IRA's focus is on politics rather than violence, though some members had participated that year in the murder of a former member, Kevin McGuigan. They believed that McGuigan had himself killed another former member, Jock Davison, a few weeks earlier.

The dissident IRA of today is much better armed and has far more members than the IRA of Billy McMillen that engaged the police in Belfast in 1969 and ignited decades of violence, though the level of violence produced by the dissidents is currently low.

A May 2016 report to the Northern Ireland Executive of a panel set up to advise on how paramilitary groups might be encouraged to disband said

> Almost twenty years after the Belfast/Good Friday Agreement, the greatest threat to security is the armed campaigns of what have come to be known as Dissident Republican (DR) groups. Hoax and real security alerts caused by these groups continue to force people out of their homes and disrupt traffic, business and other aspects of daily life. Attacks by DRs have also led to 12 deaths in the 6 years up to 2015. Recent analysis found that DRs were linked to bombing and shootings against 175 people in the period 2007–2015; 77% of the victims were Catholic civilians.

The loyalist paramilitaries of fifty years ago were as small as the IRA, though some of them had had arms training inside the British army. Two major loyalist groups grew up through the Troubles, the Ulster Volunteer Force and the Ulster Defence Association. Both still function with large memberships, refusing to disband. Their low-level activity rarely makes the national news so the ordinary news-aware British person has little or no idea that they exist and present a possible threat to future stability.

In the years following the eruption of August 1969, they, like the IRA, grew rapidly, anticipating sectarian civil war. Their rationale was that they might be needed to support the police and the army in their fight against the IRA. That never made much sense. The army never complained about being under-resourced in its measures against the IRA but even unionist politicians did complain that the ordinary civil law was a restraint on the state.

Over the years there were several indications that the forces of the state were content to leak information to the loyalists to help them in their targeting of republicans, but most of their targets were uninvolved catholic civilians.

Both the IRA and the loyalists also organised vigilante groups to attack criminals in their areas, notably drug dealers and joyriders. Both used the standard punishment of shooting them in the legs.

Today loyalists and the dissident republicans still commonly shoot people like this, alleging that they are fulfilling the will of their communities in seeking to reduce crime.

The trauma of August '69, when the guns came out, was able to evolve rapidly into civil war because the IRA structures were already in place, the command structures, the dormant arms dumps, the routes and connections through which arms could be purchased, the expertise of people who had participated in previous campaigns. Those structures and routes and accessible experts are intact still.

One of the reasons people turned to the IRA after the guns came out was that it already existed and had roots in the deep past and experience acquired from previous campaigns. It also had an analysis of what had created the violence. My recollection is that this was of lesser importance at first because people did not generally accept that the army coming in to protect them was an imperial force piling on their repression.

After speaking to Dee Fennell I was allowed into the hall to observe the open session of the Saoradh conference. I counted one hundred seats. They had all been full in the morning session but the whole front row was vacant now, even though more people had arrived for the afternoon events.

The main event was the speech of the new chairperson, Brian Kenna.

Brian Kenna had been a member of the Provisional IRA. He had been jailed in the mid-1980s in the Republic after a bank robbery in Wexford and he had been one of a dozen prisoners released in 1995 as an expression of faith in the peace process.

In 1999 he stood for Dublin City Council as an 'anti-drugs activist'.

And he had just come out of jail after a sixteen-month sentence for smuggling a communication from IRA prisoners to their leadership on the outside.

The form of the IRA 'comms' is well known to historians and close observers of the republican movement. These were messages written in small script on cigarette papers then wrapped in cling film. The standard means of smuggling them out was for the visitor to conceal them in a body orifice. Kenna didn't go to that trouble and was stopped by the police on leaving the prison and dropped the comm on the ground.

It contained a debriefing of three newly arrived prisoners assuring their leadership that they had not cracked under interrogation or disclosed secrets.

The judge sentencing Kenna said it was fortunate for him that the message had not contained more serious information. It was serious enough for the men it referred to: their lives depended on their debriefers believing them.

But the point about Kenna is that he has a lineage going back to the Provisional IRA. Like Dee Fennell, and like the republicans of the mid-1960s who kept the organisation intact through the bad times, he is part of a tradition; he has made this his life's mission. He may be a fool and a brute but he is not one who is ever going to doubt that he is right.

In April 2019, when the New IRA came under pressure to disband after killing the young writer Lyra McKee, Brian Kenna's response was to urge them to apologise. Which they did. They added, in a statement, that they had instructed their volunteers to take more care in future: in future attacks, that is. They are going nowhere, if they can help it, but back to war.

The Battle of the Bogside

This is how it happened the last time.

In early August 1969, less than a year after the civil-rights protest was attacked by the police, republicans in Derry were preparing for war.

In April that year, police pursuing young rioters into Derry's Bogside broke into the Devenny home and attacked everyone there.

The daughter, giving an interview on television afterwards, said that she was the only one on whom they did not use their batons. They only punched her with their fists; she showed the bruises on her back and thighs. They left her father unconscious on the floor of the living room and she prayed over him, thinking he was dead.

When Sam Devenny did die, on 17 July, three months after the beating, huge numbers turned out for his funeral. As they saw it, he had been murdered by the RUC. A resolve developed that the police would not be allowed into the Bogside again.

There appears to have been huge community support for this resolve. A Citizens Defence Committee was set up, its leading member being IRA man Seán Keenan. His deputy was Paddy Doherty, later to become a distinguished community worker who got the nickname Paddy Bogside.

Eamonn McCann in his book *War in an Irish Town* says that the Defence Committee was set up by republicans who took the senior positions before inviting other groups to get involved. They were looking ahead now to the annual parade of the Apprentice Boys around Derry's Walls, overlooking the Bogside, and campaigned to have that year's event scrapped.

A later TV documentary[11] presented by Joe Mahon traces that decision back to the death of Sam Devenny, but neither an article by reporter Mary Holland for the *Observer* nor McCann's book, much closer to the events, make any specific mention of the death as part of the motivation.

McCann says it followed from the reports from Belfast of loyalist mobs supported by police attacking Unity Flats after the junior Orange Order parade on the day of the Pop for Peace concert. That would explain why there would be specific concerns about a parade.

Doherty and Keenan met with the Apprentice Boys leaders at their hall under the walls at the north of the old city. As they walked up to it, Doherty saw new graffiti on the road: 'Give Peace a Chance'.

He told the documentary makers that the meeting was genial but that the Apprentice Boys were not going to cancel. They said, 'We'll steward our march; we suggest you steward your community.' On the way back down the road, they saw that the graffiti had been painted over. Peace would not be given a chance.

The Defence Committee organised the building of barricades in the Bogside.

Brian Walker, later an academic historian, had been one of the stewards on previous civil-rights marches. He offered his services to the Defence Committee and was told he would not be needed. He told me he believes that the Defence Committee was more concerned to prepare for war than for peace and made no concerted effort to prevent rioting on the day of the parade.

The Northern Ireland government was expecting trouble and was aware of its limited resources for coping.

Four days before the planned parade, the Northern Ireland premier James Chichester Clarke met with the home secretary James Callaghan to ask for the support of the army. He asked Callaghan if he would allow troops to be used under the direction of Stormont and Callaghan refused, 'unless you make changes to the way in which you govern the country'.

The parade set off on the Tuesday morning of 12 August in a grim expectation of trouble. Members of the order had travelled from Belfast and other towns to join in. Old footage shows the stewards trying to keep the parade moving and to prevent exchanges with catholic youths. The police were still in their peaked caps at this stage, with their inadequate riot gear propped against walls in side streets in readiness.

Young men from the Bogside stoned the police in Waterloo Place.

Defence Committee stewards formed a line in front of them to push the stone throwers back. At this stage the police let the stewards deal with the trouble. McCann's account backs Brian Walker's view that the Defence Committee made little effort to prevent violence. According to him, on the day of the march, the stewards 'made a token effort' to stop men from the Bogside stoning the police and the Apprentice Boys.

Paddy Doherty later admitted on TV that his committee had not had enough stewards to control the Bogside youths, who had been expecting a battle.

The youths then attacked the parade from William Street and some of the Apprentice Boys threw stones back at them. Brian Walker says he intervened to urge Apprentice Boys not to throw stones back but that he was ignored. This was when the police donned their helmets and took up their shields to face the Bogside youth.

The helmets the police wore were not riot helmets; they were part of the kit of the policemen who rode motor scooters. The shields were small and could not provide full body protection and many of the policemen would get leg injuries from stones that bounced at their feet. The police at this stage did not enter the Bogside area but held a line at the edge of the commercial part of the city.

Paddy Doherty in the Open Reel documentary gave some credit to the police for their management of the trouble at this stage. He said, 'To be fair to the police, they took the full rattle of the stones for about two hours and then they moved.'

He said, 'There was a tumultuous cheer in the Bogside when the police got into their vehicles and made the charge into the Bogside.'

They had taken the bait.

Mary Holland reported that the people in the Bogside were enraged by the sight of Apprentice Boys backing up the police. She says that she recognised some of them. She also says that people monitoring the police radio had told her that the first police charge into the Bogside was against orders, 'a breach of discipline'.

There is something quaint about Mary Holland's depiction of the Bogside people. She wrote in the tone of an anthropologist reporting back to the metropolis about the behaviour of an exotic tribe that lives by endearing mores and customs. Her writing is patronising and given to stereotyping in a way that a liberal thinker of today would avoid:

> One of the more charming eccentricities of rioting here is that in every small house in the Bogside there are groups of Catholics listening in to the police radio and passing on their plans to active combatants outside.

It is a long time since anyone reporting Northern Ireland thought that rioting entailed anything 'charming'.

She adds that

> when the Catholics saw the police apparently leading the Protestants in to attack them, it was as though a dam broke in the collective tribal feeling.

At every stage this 'tribe' responds as with a single mind.

The perception of many in the Bogside was that their area was now under attack by the same force that had run amok there after the Burntollet riot and that had in April broken into the Devenny home and beaten Sam Devenny and others in his house, including his daughter.

The perception of others was that this was the beginning of a revolution, a huge opportunity to break the police force and liberate an area from police control.

The rioting would be remembered as the Battle of the Bogside. There appears to have been widespread support in the area for the decision to fight the police and resist their attempts to quell the riot and make arrests. Certainly Mary Holland's journalism of the time is devoid of any criticism of those who started the fighting, let alone those who organised petrol-bomb attacks on the police after it had started.

She wrote,

> To understand the situation here it is necessary
> to realise just how tightly knit is the Catholic
> community in Derry, how confined spiritually and
> physically to the ghetto situation.

She was impressed by how

> in times of crisis the tribe reasserts its authority,
> or rather about 10 men emerge as the natural
> leaders …

She saw these men as argumentative in their dealings with each other but staunchly loyal in the face of a common challenge.

> Individually and in times of calm such leaders are
> likely to be at each other's throats. After all, this is
> Ireland.

And her reader is presumed to know what that means. Similarly,
that Open Reel documentary took the general view that the
fighting by the people in the Bogside was a legitimate and
admirable defence of the area against the police.

The police strategy of engaging in running battles with the
youth is certainly questionable.

There simply wasn't the experience or even the will on
either side to prevent escalation. The police could simply have
held their line in the city. Now they were scrambling about
the streets, being stoned and petrol bombed, firing back with
CS gas and occasional pistol shots – and this would go on for
three days, until they were bruised, hungry and exhausted.

Paddy Doherty's house became the battle headquarters for
the Citizen's Defence Committee. In the *Battle of the Bogside*
documentary, he said that he asked Keenan if they had any
money and Keenan said they had £87.

Doherty told the reporter: 'I said, "What a bloody way to start
a war."' He is obviously chuffed on screen. 'So I took the £87
and I went outside and there were two of our stewards there.
And I said, "Go and buy some petrol and …"' he hesitated,
pursed his lips as if unsure he should be so frank before going
on '… burn everything from here to the Strand Barracks. Take
out the Strand Barracks. That's the order.'

Even the documentary script seems to endorse the rioting.

'Petrol was requisitioned.' Not 'stolen'. '… and bottles
secured from the local dairy so that petrol bombs could

be manufactured in large numbers and taken to the front lines.'

The first petrol bombs were flimsy and the fuse tended to fall out but a group of women set up a production line with properly measured ingredients and tighter fuses. Journalist Nell McCafferty told Open Reel that she watched women making petrol bombs and 'I knew that the revolution had come'.

At one point she joined rioters on the roof of Rossville Flats then realised that there was only one door in and out and that if the police took the flats they would all be caught.

Bernadette Devlin was there and said later that she was on an adrenalin high, hadn't slept for three nights; that she was quite determined the police weren't coming in.

'The thing was easily stopped by withdrawing the police. You couldn't withdraw the Bogside; it was a fixed entity. Any kind of wise head in the police could have pulled the police back.'

The mayhem became an international story; that the police were trying to quell a huge riot in the Bogside.

The taoiseach, Jack Lynch, made a statement on television.

'… it is clear also that the Irish government can no longer stand by and see innocent people injured and perhaps worse. It is obvious that the RUC is no longer accepted as an impartial police force.'

Lynch ordered the Irish army to establish field hospitals on the border.

This created an expectation that the Irish forces would enter the Bogside to push back the RUC on behalf of the residents. This would have put Britain and Ireland at war with each other and was a wholly untenable prospect. Naivety and

ineptitude all around were making things worse. No Irish
leader was going to order a military invasion of the UK but
many people believed that that is what was about to happen.

Martin McGuinness told the documentary makers that he was
encouraged. 'I thought, *This is tremendous; the Irish government
are going to do something here.* I had visions of Irish soldiers
moving into Derry ... and assisting the citizens in repelling
the activities of the British state. And it became clear to us in
a very short time that that wasn't going to happen.'

Mary Holland's report says that local people approached
the Irish army in Donegal to ask for gas masks but got only
sympathy.

But republicans may have felt that they had an added
incentive to ratchet up the violence. One easily attainable goal
now was to break the RUC, overstretch them to the point where
they simply could not function. But what if they really could
bring in the Irish army? That would amount to a resumption
of the Irish war for full independence from Britain. It would
involve the UN and put the full constitutional question back
into negotiation.

Fears grew as well. There were reports that St Eugene's
cathedral was under attack. There had been some loyalist
activity in the location. Brian Walker told me he believed there
was a danger of the battle turning into a naked sectarian clash
between catholics and protestants.

The B-Specials, an all-protestant reserve force, was now on
standby to come into Derry. The government seems to have
had some reservations about letting them in, preferring to
use the British army.

The rioters wanted the army in too.

Don Anderson interviewed a group of them with masks on.

They said, 'When troops come in we'll stop fighting.'

The Stormont government notified the home secretary that it would now accept troops on British government conditions.

Graeme Shillington, the head of the RUC, had briefed Ken Bloomfield, a senior civil servant, that the police were exhausted. But things were about to get much worse outside Derry.

The Defence Committee had sent appeals to civil-rights groups around Northern Ireland to organise their own protests, to occupy the police and prevent more of them being sent to relieve the exhausted men in the Bogside.

On the second day of the Bogside riot, a group of activists met in the Wellington Park Hotel in Belfast to listen to a tape-recorded message from the Derry Citizens Defence Committee appealing for more protests.

Gerry Adams was at that meeting. By his own account in *The Politics of Irish Freedom*, 'Some of us left to make petrol bombs.' He was planning to import into Belfast the carnival of chaos in which even normally sane people had indulged in Derry and which was now ending well with the arrival of the army and the humiliation of the police. No one had been killed.

Republicans and others organised riots at police stations in Belfast and the IRA OC ordered groups from around the city to pool their weapons. He issued guns to select members of the movement. The centre of the fighting now moved to Belfast.

On 14 August the troops moved into Derry with orders not to engage with the rioters. The B-Specials, who had been waiting to go into the Bogside, were sent to Belfast. And on the third day, with peace restored to Derry, the Belfast night was alive with gunfire and nobody properly understood what was happening.

In her article, Mary Holland says,

> What is impossible to estimate is whether the trouble there came as a result of a plea from Derry or whether it would have erupted anyway.

Eamonn McCann, writing in *War and an Irish Town*,[12] had no such doubts:

> On the morning of the 14th we heard reports of fighting in Belfast, Coalisland, Dungannon, Armagh and other places; we took this as encouragement. Other people were coming to our aid.

Conclusion

Fifty years after the night the guns came out we have had another year of protest. The issues are different but some things are the same. The main obstacle to change, again, is unionism, which, informed by evangelical-christian values, bars the way to abortion-law reform and same-sex marriage.

The main unionist party, the DUP, committed itself fully to Brexit against the will of the majority of people in Northern Ireland. With less reason but equal passion the party opposes an Irish Language Act and Sinn Féin refuses to govern alongside it again until this dispute is resolved.

But there are differences in the modern pattern of protest.

The big one is that the police are responding differently and not exacerbating tensions.

The issues on which people are campaigning are more concerned with human rights than with civil rights, with the right of the individual to identify by orientation or gender or nationality. These issues are less about the relationship between the citizen and the state, as in 1969, and more about the citizen's sense of self and entitlement to relate to others.

The causes are more secular and liberal, though there are counter-causes too, which would put us into a more conservative and religious polity.

The big question is whether the tensions in this society today are capable of triggering the violence we had in the past. Certainly there are some who would like a return to murderous protest. The dissident republicans still bomb when they can. The loyalist paramilitaries still recruit and intimidate their communities. But each group seems a depleted relic of the more passionate, more strategic and better-armed groups that made life so difficult here before.

We still have a divided society that seems to want to divide wider issues between the sectarian factions. So unionists now oppose abortion, same-sex marriage and support Israel while nationalists, broadly speaking, support abortion, same-sex marriage and Palestine.

Predictably Brexit became a sectarian issue too.

And while unionists perceive that the Irish opposition to Brexit expresses a plot to advance Irish unity, the reality is that it compromises the UK for real, presenting Northern Ireland with the choice of being British or European.

Even the DUP was coming round to the view that Northern Ireland's concern for its place in the Union was more important than Brexit. That suggests the need for a reform of the UK in which constituent parts could veto decisions.

The Good Friday Agreement allows for a referendum on Irish unity when a prospect exists of it being carried. Demographic shift brings that prospect into view and Brexit provides a new incentive for unity. A united Ireland would take northeners back into the European Union and it would, incidentally, satisfactorily and perhaps irrationally punish the unionists and the English nationalists for discounting our identity concerns so lightly.

But there is major lesson for Brexiters from the period of the Troubles. Fifty years on from the civil-rights campaign and the deflection of its energies into violence, Northern Ireland is now discussing rights again and freeing itself from political and religious chauvinism, reforming itself as it might have done in the 1960s and 1970s.

We have also seen this year a new energy behind protests against the paramilitaries after the murders of Ian Ogle and Lyra McKee, the one by loyalists the other by the New IRA.

For decades, militant republican ideologues stalled all political growth and reform with their determined focus on a phantasm, the idea that Britain was an oppressor who could be ejected by force of arms. In the end, they accepted that the challenge was not to remove the British but to make peace with their neighbours – or at least most of them did.

Brexit similarly threatens to preoccupy huge political energies for decades while evading the reality that the real need is to fix Britain. If that is how British politics is to evolve – taking a side-road away from progress on an insubstantial and unrealisable notion of 'freedom' – what will be lost?

Notes

1. Purdie, B. (1990) *Politics in the Streets: The Origins of the Civil Rights Movement in Northern Ireland*, Newtownards, Blackstaff.
2. Cameron, J. (1969) *Disturbances in Northern Ireland: Report of the Commission appointed by the Governor of Northern Ireland* (Cmnd 532), Belfast, HMSO.
3. Hermon, J. (1997) *Holding the Line: an Autobiography*, Dublin, Gill & Macmillan.
4. Devlin, B. (1969) *The Price of My Soul*, London, Pan Books.
5. Adams, G. (1996) *Before the Dawn: an Autobiography*, Dingle, Brandon Books.
6. Johnston, R. H. W. (2003) *Century of Endeavour: a Biographical & Autobiographical View of the 20th Century in Ireland*, Dublin, Maunsel & Company.
7. Gilmartin, N. (2018) 'From the Frontlines of War to the Sidelines of Peace', in Burgess, T. P. (ed.) *The Contested Identities of Ulster Catholics*, Basingstoke, Palgrave Macmillan.
8. McKittrick, D., Kelters, S., Feeney, B., Thornton, C. & McVea, D. (2007) *Lost Lives: the Stories of the Men, Women and Children Who Died as a Result of the Northern Ireland Troubles*, Edinburgh, Mainstream Publishing Company.
9. Catholic Church & Paul (1968) *Encyclical of Pope Paul VI, Humanae vitae, on the regulation of birth: and Pope Paul VI's Credo of the people of God* (encyclical), Vatican City.
10. Boyle, M. (2018) 'Weather Vane', in *The Work of a Winter*, Galway, Arlen House.
11. Cunningham, V. (dir.) *Battle of the Bogside* (2004), Derry, Open Reel Productions.
12. McCann, E. (1974) *War and an Irish Town*, London, Penguin.

Acknowledgements

More people contribute to any book than can ever be accurately enumerated but for this one I am especially indebted to those who gave me their time for interviews or guidance.

My special thanks to: Angela Courtney, Anne Devlin, Barry Bruton, Bernadette Smyth, Bredagh Hughes, Brian Garrett, Brian Walker, Brid Rogers, Caoimhin de Burca, Claire Hanna, Clair Bailey, Colin McClelland, Danny Morrison, Deaglan Agnew, Dee Fennell, Denis Bradley, Dympna McGlade, Eamonn McCann, Eamonn Melaugh, Eileen Calder, Frankie Callaghan, Grainne Teggart, Jamie Bryson, Jane Ewart, Jeff Dudgeon, John Barry, John Kyle, John O'Doherty, Roger O'Doherty, Kelly Turtle, Lesley Carroll, Linda Ervine, Linda Marshall, Lynda Walker, Mairia Cahill, Mairin de Burca, Maureen Boyle, Marysa McGlinchey, Paul Arthur, Paul McAvinchey, Roy Johnston, Rudie Goldsmith, Sarah Ewart, Sean McGouran, Tina Calder, Tony Kennedy and to various unnamed members of the RUC and PSNI.

I am grateful to the Legion of Mary for giving me access to their archive.

I would also like to thank my editor Monica Hope for saving me from myself and my agent Lisa Moylett for her continuing support.

Index

A Note About the Author

Malachi O'Doherty is a writer and broadcaster based in Belfast. He is a regular contributor to the *Belfast Telegraph* and to several BBC radio programmes. He covered the Troubles and the peace process as a journalist and has written for several Irish and British newspapers and magazines, including the *Irish Times, New Statesman, Scotsman* and *Guardian.*